CW01072246

European Communication Research and Education Associatic

This series consists of books arising from the intellectual w
address themes relevant to the ECREA's interests; make a major contribution to the theory,
research, practice and/or policy literature; are European in scope; and represent a diversity of
perspectives. Book proposals are refereed.

Series Editors
Nico Carpentier
François Heinderyckx

Series Advisory Board
Denis McQuail
Robert Picard
Jan Servaes

The aims of the ECREA are

a) To provide a forum where researchers and others involved in communication and
information research can meet and exchange information and documentation about their
work. Its disciplinary focus will include media, (tele)communications and informatics
research, including relevant approaches of human and social sciences;
b) To encourage the development of research and systematic study, especially on subjects and
areas where such work is not well developed;
c) To stimulate academic and intellectual interest in media and communication research, and
to promote communication and cooperation between members of the Association;
d) To co-ordinate the circulation of information on communications research in Europe, with a
view to establishing a database of ongoing research;
e) To encourage, support and, where possible, publish the work of young researchers in
Europe;
f) To take into account the desirability of different languages and cultures in Europe;
g) To develop links with relevant national and international communication organizations and
with professional communication researchers working for commercial organizations and
regulatory institutions, both public and private;
h) To promote the interests of communication research within and among the Member States
of the Council of Europe and the European Union;
i) To collect and disseminate information concerning the professional position of communication
researchers in the European region; and
j) To develop, improve and promote communication and media education.

The Social Use of Media: Cultural and Social Scientific Perspectives on Audience Research

The Social Use of Media: Cultural and Social Scientific Perspectives on Audience Research

Edited by Helena Bilandzic, Geoffroy Patriarche & Paul J. Traudt

intellect Bristol, UK / Chicago, USA

First published in the UK in 2012 by
Intellect, The Mill, Parnall Road, Fishponds, Bristol, BS16 3JG, UK

First published in the USA in 2012 by
Intellect, The University of Chicago Press, 1427 E. 60th Street,
Chicago, IL 60637, USA

A catalogue record for this book is available from the
British Library.

Cover designer: Edwin Fox
Copy-editor: MPS Technologies
Production manager: Tim Mitchell
Typesetting: Planman Technologies

ISBN 978-1-84150-512-1
ECREA Series ISSN: 1753-0342

Printed and bound by Hobbs, UK

Contents

Introduction

Helena Bilandzic, Geoffroy Patriarche and Paul J. Traudt

E arly communication research neglected the idea that media audiences are social beings. The concept of the masses, predominant at the time, assumed that 'the members of the mass are spatially separated from one another and in that sense, at least, cannot interact with one another or exchange experience' and that 'the mass has no definite leadership and has a very loose organization if any at all' (Freidson 1953: 313). Sociologists who criticized these assumptions emphasized the role of group relationships in media selection and influence processes, pointing out 'the social nature of the experience of the members of the audience' (Freidson 1953: 316). Seminal work by Katz and Lazarsfeld (1955) demonstrated that media effects are filtered through opinion leaders and group relationships, thus calling into question the idea that audiences lack leadership and organization. The role of interpersonal communication in audience research became increasingly important, not only in terms of media effects studies but also in the examination of information diffusion in society and the negotiation of meaning given to current events (e.g. Deutschman and Danielson 1960; Hill and Bonjean 1964; Rogers and Shoemaker 1971). Agenda setting theory, for example, assumes that media coverage about current events has the power to influence topics in interpersonal communication (McLeod, Becker and Byrnes 1974). The innate fear of being socially isolated when expressing minority opinions fuels a 'spiral of silence' and therefore influences, if not directly, public opinion (Noelle-Neumann 1974). To have a topic of conversation, at work or with friends, turned out to be an important motivator for people to use media, along with other social gratifications (McQuail, Blumler and Brown 1972).

Research exploring the role of media in family life provides many examples of the social use of the media. Lull's pioneering ethnographic work delineates four areas of 'relational uses' of television – when 'audience members use television to create practical social arrangements' (Lull 1980: 202). First, television serves as *communication facilitation*: audience members obtain common ground for conversations through television topics and examples. Second, *affiliation and avoidance* describes strategies where television is used to share time with family members or, conversely, to avoid situations and interactions with them. Third, *social learning* relates how people acquire information from television but also are socialized by the televised social world and its norms and values. Finally, audience members demonstrate and establish *competence and dominance* by using television examples that underline one's perspective or role and undermine others' position.

Almost three decades after Lull's (1980) article, audience researchers have emphasized the transition 'from family television to bedroom culture' (Livingstone 2007) as a result of both the transformations of the media and communication environment and the changing conditions of family life. What is at stake in evolving domestic media uses is the family's and household's identity, culture and (power) relationships, as well as the frontiers between the private and public spheres. Similarly, research on the uses of information and communication technologies (ICTs) by young people shows that social uses are at work within peer groups: for instance, mobile phones are used to stay connected with friends, to participate in collective activities, to affirm one's group membership, to gain a status within the group, to reaffirm privileged relationships or to present oneself as a member of a (youth, ethnic or other) subculture (e.g. Caron and Caronia 2007; see also Dover in this volume).

The sociality of media audiences is not only observable at the micro-level of family and peer groups but also at the macro-level of 'imagined audiences' (Dayan 1992, 1998). Drawing on the notion of 'imagined community' (Anderson 1983; also see Dhoest in this volume), Dayan claims that the dispersion of television viewers across space (and time) does not mean that there is no shared social experience. Viewers should rather be seen as negotiating their participation in imagined audiences, which are shaped by the content of the programme as well as by public discourses about the programme or the genre in question (see also Hartmann and Dohle (2005), who suggest the notion of 'co-audiences'). 'Media events' (such as royal weddings or funerals) have been described as collective and participatory experiences, where the sociality of the audience is vigorous and widespread, combining the micro-dimension of domestic media-related conversations and the macro-dimension of public engagement in national or/and transnational communities (Dayan and Katz 1994).

Social uses are integral parts of community media in a broad sense – ranging from the community press to community electronic media, geographically defined online communities and virtual communities (Jankowski 2006). The relationships between media and community are numerous and diverse. For instance, community media and ICTs contribute to building a sense of belonging and identity, to sharing knowledge and culture, and to promoting social and political participation. Through media and ICTs, users redefine the values and norms of their community, contest existing power or gender relationships, and negotiate the boundary between the in-group and the out-group. As Mandaville puts it, about the Islamic (online) community, 'the construction of a group identity is inherently a socio*political* process, involving as it does dialogue, negotiation and debate as to "who we are" and, moreover, what it *means* to be "who we are"' (Mandaville 2001: 170, emphasis in original).

Social aspects of media use have also reached more psychologically oriented fields that look at media-evoked, intra-individual experiences, emotions and cognitions related to social aspects, but they do not actually produce any visible social activity. Examples are parasocial relationships with media characters that start to exist in the audience's mind, before transgressing into real-life contacts with the actor, if they do at all (e.g. Giles in this volume). Other examples are social motives for media use that may explain individual selections of media (e.g. to be able to talk about current affairs; see, for example, McQuail, Blumler and Brown 1972). These motives may also create a certain mindset that influences how media information is processed and learned (e.g. Bilandzic and Rössler 2004; Potter 1988), with later (imagined, actual, possible) social situations in mind.

Organization of *Social Uses of Media*

This book explores three general areas of current scholarly study of the social aspects of media use. First, the introduction of interactive and so-called social media has had repercussions for the definition of media use, reception and even our perception of media effects. It all starts with the question of how to conceptualize activity and interactivity in an age of convergent media environments and how actions in virtual and actual worlds become blurred. Take, for example, the case of interactive gaming. Here, social networking is defined by the architectural boundaries established by increasingly sophisticated, software-created virtual play environments. Friends and acquaintances who play these online games can extend these interactional rules to equally real but non-gaming social discourses when gathered together in one physical location (see, for example, Chapter 4 by Soto-Sanfiel in this book). Beyond the world of gaming, we have witnessed of late how web-based social media are used to disseminate messages of political rhetoric and action, organize 'spontaneous' mass gatherings and, in some cases, ultimately help topple long-standing governments. These kinds of issues are addressed by contributors in the first part of the book titled 'Audience Activity and Interactivity'.

Second, the recognition that media constitute social practice, which utilizes media for its own goals, has been highly influential in communication research. Scholars have addressed how media inform communication exchanges, ranging from interpersonal dyads to levels of community. Audience members use media content to reflexively negotiate personal identities, establish and maintain relationships, and display peer-group competence. Or they may employ the act of media participation to reify a sense of community, independent of content. Such aspects are further taken up by contributors in the second part of the book titled 'Media Use as Social and Cultural Practice'.

Third, media provide many opportunities for participation in cultural and political issues. Yet media also shape participation in certain – and sometimes constraining – ways. Media technologies are not transparent and include hard- and software architectures that transform the communication experience. Seminal works that focus on earlier media have long explored these features, including those from political economy, phenomenological, and culture criticism perspectives for technologies including the telegraph, telephony and electronic media (e.g. Carey 1992; Ihde 1982; McLuhan 1964). Contributors to the third part, 'Cultural, Political and Technological Participation', look at the relationships between media, audiences and participation, not only in cultural and political areas but also in technological terms as appropriating new media also means participating in their diffusion.

The chapters within the parts deal with the same topic but from different perspectives, which pointedly demonstrate today's varied facets of audience research, invite direct comparisons and encourage cross-paradigmatic dialogue. Each chapter elaborates the chosen theoretical background in detail, contextualizing the approach in a general underlying scientific field or paradigm (e.g. cultural studies, media psychology and hermeneutics) and provides a study representative of the theory and the field/paradigm as an example for the approach.

Audience Activity and Interactivity

The first part begins with a chapter by Seija Ridell who tackles the question of activity in the Web 2.0 age using an action-theoretic perspective, based on the tradition of interpretive sociology. Ridell argues that the audience, despite being proclaimed dead, is very much alive, and that the image of an audience with a fused role of 'produsers' (Bruns 2008), being simultaneously receivers and producers, sidetracks scholarship from finding more adequate and less absolutistic terms to describe audience transformations after the blurring of boundaries between production and consumption. Ridell suggests looking at structured complexes of 'modes of action' (e.g. audiencing a website or producing content), with their distinct and specific physical and mental activities. Such modes of action become connected articulations of overall projects and are unified by the overarching goal of, for example, the intention to improve a Wikipedia entry.

Tereza Pavlíčková also considers the traditional audience and its fate in contemporary media landscapes, and similarly questions the 'death' of readers, listeners and viewers after the emergence of the 'user'. She starts with Gadamer's hermeneutics as an epistemological framework to look at social uses of media. This approach conceptualizes understanding as emerging from interpretation, from a dialogue between a reader and a text, which is always contextualized in a social and historical situation. The reader has a specific horizon, comprising all knowledge, experiences, cultural and social influences, which he or she brings to the reception and use of media. This is also true for contemporary cross-media environments, where knowledge from different (media and non-media) sources merges and serves as horizons for new instances of media use.

Andy Ruddock also analyses how knowledge stocks cross media boundaries by tracing the transgression of symbolic cultural indicators from alcohol advertisements to social networking practices. Applying a critical perspective, he goes back to the origins of cultivation research – a social scientific approach to audiences – and establishes a thought-provoking connection between cultivation and cultural studies. Ruddock reconstructs how drinking-related, user-generated content by young people mimics advertisement themes and aesthetics, connecting binge drinking with sexuality and fun. He demonstrates how these practices help carry the intended commercial message further than companies are legally allowed. Motivations of users for their network activities and the actual outcome diverge drastically.

María T. Soto-Sanfiel is concerned with social relationships established in virtual communities surrounding violent gaming and how these relationships eventually leave the virtual and enter the actual world. From a uses-and-gratifications perspective, which is influential in the social scientific tradition, she traces the dynamics of motivations to play, the need for social order and connectedness between the gamers. The dynamics in a gaming community are investigated with a longitudinal design in an ethnographic, multi-method approach. Here, social, organizational and communication rules established in online gaming are carried into everyday group experiences and inform membership and social roles.

Media Use as Social and Cultural Practice

Alexander Dhoest's chapter begins the second part of the book. Within the cultural tradition of audience research, reception studies have addressed the social dimension of audiencehood in a variety of ways. One of the most prominent approaches to social use in reception studies is to theorize the audience as a group of 'interpretive communities' or what Anderson (1996: 87-emphasis in original) calls 'strategic audiences':

> The strategic audience is one bounded by a set of interpretive strategies. I belong to an academic audience *if and when* I practice the interpretive strategies of that community. […] It is the community that develops the strategies, provides the means for dissemination and instruction, and supervises particular performances of them.

Dhoest provides an extensive literature review of research on interpretive communities as well as a critical methodological reflection on the virtues and pitfalls of using 'national' and 'ethnic' interpretive communities as frameworks for empirical reception research. Drawing on case studies of ethnic majority and minority viewers in Flanders (north Belgium), Dhoest addresses one of the most important methodological challenges faced by empirical reception studies: how to account for interpretation patterns without losing sight of the fact that identities (and hence interpretive strategies) are contextual and multi-layered, as nationality and ethnicity intersect with many other positions in terms of age, generation, gender, religion, language and political affiliation.

While Dhoest's chapter is representative of the 'ethnographic turn' in the cultural tradition of audience research,[1] Caroline Dover, relying on anthropology and sociolinguistics to extensively apply the ethnographic methodology, offers quite a radical concretization of an 'everyday turn' in the field (Maigret 2008). Dover explains the underlying principles of 'media consumption ethnography' through a two-year field study in a London secondary school. The focus of this approach to audiences – or rather, as Dover would say, *beyond* audiences – is not so much the encounter between texts/ technologies and readers/users, as in so-called ethnographic reception studies, as the embedment of (and the reconstruction of) media culture in mundane conversations, in presentations of the self, in peer-status affirmation, in the definition of power relationships and in the negotiation of teaching activities.

Emphasis on media use as a social practice continues in the chapter by Philippe Meers and Daniel Biltereyst. They describe the development of film audience studies where audiences are empirically investigated from the text-oriented origins of film studies. Stimulated by other disciplines such as cultural studies, communication research and political economy, film studies have gradually adopted an interest in actual audiences, their way of actively interpreting films according to their backgrounds and using them for their own enjoyment and for meeting their gratifications – and among these feature, very prominently since the very beginning, social goals. Meers and Biltereyst provide a synthesis of film audience studies and exemplify this uprising field with a study using oral histories to reconstruct goals of cinema-goers in a historical perspective. They found that cinema-going was a social routine that supported community identity formation as well as class and social group cohesion. In contrast, actual movies, their content, their stars and prominence were of lesser importance to the routine.

Katrin Döveling and Denise Sommer connect with the long social-scientific tradition of investigating interpersonal communication about media content. The novelty of their approach is that they look at ways in which audiences process media content emotionally and then explore how they use conversations to support and accompany this process – ultimately how they socially share their emotional experiences. Döveling and Sommer introduce a German theoretical framework, the dynamic-transactional model, and use it to integrate psychological theories of emotion and approaches to interpersonal communication in one model, the 'integrative model of socio-emotional meta-appraisal' (SEMA). In an empirical study, they exemplify how dynamic concatenations of cognitions, emotions and conversational turns occur in actual reception processes.

Research that examines the intra-individual, psychological phenomena of the social use of media includes studies on parasocial relationships. David Giles provides an extensive overview of this field, which has a long-standing tradition in social scientific communication inquiry and curiously began with an article published in a psychiatric journal, and ever since has gained increasing interest within the community of communication and media psychology scholars. The basic assumption is that audiences develop cognitive and emotional reactions to media characters that, in the course of regular exposure, turn into parasocial relationships. As media characters diverge from real humans in many ways, Giles argues (and provides empirical evidence) that parasocial relationships are stronger with people who really exist (e.g. celebrities) and weaker with fictional nonhuman characters. However, fictional humans seem to stimulate more faceted relationships, as evidenced by more complex descriptions or high intimacy ratings provided by audience members.

Cultural, Political and Technological Participation

In the third part of this volume, Kim Christian Schrøder explores the relationships between media, audiences and citizenship as diversely elaborated in reception studies over four decades. He provides an overview of democratic theories of the media, going back to the seminal work of Habermas (1962) on the public sphere and emphasizing important subsequent developments coming out of the cross-fertilization between reception studies and political science. Second, Schrøder offers a methodical review of the history of reception studies from 1973 to 2010, paying attention to a range of approaches to the study of 'audience as citizens'. Schrøder refers to paradigms in the Kuhnian sense of the term (Kuhn 1962). Finally, the author presents an empirical case study illustrating the 'methodological pluralism' in contemporary reception research and exploring the changing conditions and nature of citizenship in today's mediatized world.

Lars Nyre and Brian O'Neill present a hermeneutical approach to audience participation in the media, which has been the subject of increasing research since the 1990s, when talk shows and soon after reality shows became primary television genres (see Schrøder in this book). The very notion of participation, though, has raised much conceptual debate, to a point that scholars have urged further clarifications as to what 'participating' means (Carpentier 2011). Nyre and O'Neill explore the motivations behind programme content contributed by lay-level audience members (non-professionals). Drawing from symbolic interactionism, Nyre and O'Neill approach media participation as an interpretive activity. Echoing Pavlíčková's chapter, the authors argue that hermeneutics is particularly well suited to shed light on these interactional and interpretive processes, for it intends to capture how one understands texts or actions within the context of communicative relationships, be it between the researcher and the informants (as their understanding of participation evolves during the interview) or between the researcher and the empirical material (as the former draws on the informants' discourses to understand their motivations). The authors exemplify the hermeneutical tradition through a qualitative study conducted in Norway and Ireland in 2005–2006 and focused on the reasons why media users do or do not participate in media.

While Nyre and O'Neill are interested in audience participation in media *production*, Corinna Peil and Jutta Röser focus on the *usage* side of audience participation. Peil and Röser focus on an 'ethnographically oriented approach' (the expression is one coined by the authors) called domestication research. Originating in (British) cultural studies (Silverstone, Hirsch and Morley 1992), domestication research concentrates on the integration of new media into the households' everyday life, therefore offering another variation of the 'everyday turn' in cultural studies (Maigret 2008). Corinna Peil and Jutta Röser's focus, however, is not so much domestication research in itself but rather explores its potential to address neglected issues in diffusion research. The latter is rooted in the social scientific tradition and interested in how and why innovations diffuse in society (Rogers 2003).

According to Peil and Röser, diffusion research has insufficiently addressed the role played by the (micro)appropriation of new media in their (macro)diffusion in society. The authors suggest that domestication contributes to the decline of socio-demographic differences as regards access and use, and hence to an increased 'participation' of a broader range of social groups, participation which in turn fosters the diffusion of new media in society. Peil and Röser defend their core argument using their own empirical research on the diffusion of the Internet in Germany from 1997 to 2007.

Focusing primarily on the Anglo-Saxon fan studies tradition, Mélanie Bourdaa and Seok-Kyeong Hong-Mercier also integrate insights from contemporary French sociological research on audiences, which puts into question the influential theory of cultural legitimacy. This combined approach conceives fan audiences as both 'active' and 'social' (Roscoe, Marshall and Gleeson 1995) and brings forth the notions of '(cultural) participation' and '(virtual) community', respectively (Jenkins 1992, 2002). Through a 'cyber-ethnography' of *Battlestar Galactica* fandom and East Asian TV drama fandom, Bourdaa and Hong-Mercier argue that the increasingly convergent and globalized media and communication environment is transforming the activity and the sociality of fan audiences. According to Bourdaa and Hong-Mercier, fandom opens paths towards global citizenship, as fans' participatory activities go beyond the world of the show to address broader social, cultural and political issues.

Promising Futures: Research in Social Uses of Media

In the concluding chapter, Sonia Livingstone reflects on the past, present and future of audience research. Audience research is changing, she explains, not only because of the transformations of the media and communication environment (towards networked communication, convergent media, hybridized genres, etc.) but also because of the new perspectives conveyed by other fields and disciplines suddenly interested in the study of 'audiences' and 'users' (e.g. information science, education science). The question becomes: how can audience researchers make sense of the people's changing relation to the media (and to others)? As shown by numerous chapters in this volume, the social uses of media are being shaped and transformed by increasing participatory opportunities. According to Livingstone, the future for audience research lies in the study of 'participation frameworks' (Goffman 1981) found in people's relationship to the media. She argues that the emerging 'paradigm of participation' should be acknowledged as a new, interdisciplinary perspective on audience research in the contemporary media and communication landscape.

As evidenced by this overview of the chapters compiled in this volume, a broad variety of scientific perspectives, ranging from interpretative approaches (which are often rooted in humanities and follow a hermeneutic paradigm) to quantitative approaches that follow the paradigm of natural sciences (e.g. media psychology), are pursued. We hope that this book will help further our understanding of approaches to the study of social uses of media – their diversity, their strengths and weaknesses, their shared assumptions, but also their potential incompatibilities. Rather than organizing the book along paradigmatic lines, we structured it according to the three fields outlined above and kept paradigmatically heterogeneous approaches side by side not only to accentuate their differences and their commonalities but also to ease interdisciplinary dialogues.

Ultimately, the way in which communication research conceptualizes and takes into account social aspects configures a certain model of the audience (member). This model cannot be a full representation of human capabilities (actual or desired). For theorizing and to a greater extent for empirical research, the full complexity of human reality needs to be reduced; it ultimately represents only a specific interpretation of the people under investigation (Meinberg 1988). This necessary reduction assigns certain characteristics to humans – for example, intentionality, rationality, ability to reflect or communicate one's inner states (Katz, Blumler and Gurevitch 1974), or sociality, the topic of this book. The specific model which is thus created is in a sense axiomatic, or as Blumler (1979) put it, an 'article of faith', or in Biocca's (1988) words, an 'ideological commitment'. In this sense, this edited volume is also concerned with modern configurations of audience that needed adjustment after the media landscape changed so drastically in the past decade. The goal is less to find a superior or 'truer' construct of audience but to stimulate and encourage reflection about the anthropological implications contained in audience research, being clear not only about its potential but also about its limitations (see Groeben and Erb 1991). This book is intended to inspire such reflection and vivify connections between the manifold perspectives on audience research.

Acknowledgements

This book is an initiative of the Audience and Reception Studies section of the European Communication Research and Education Association (ECREA; http://www.ecrea.eu). The volume provides a living example of how ECREA brings together researchers from different perspectives to discuss communication – or media-related issues through their respective lenses. ECREA stands for a unified association of scholars who differ quite remarkably in their general understanding as well as in their methodological approaches. By focusing on one specific topic (i.e. the social use of media), this book manifests one of ECREA's basic principles, which is to emerge as a bridge-building platform for European media and communication scholars – and beyond.

The Audience and Reception Studies section of ECREA has also initiated the COST European research project 'Transforming Audiences, Transforming Societies' (see http://www.cost.eu and http://www.cost-transforming-audiences.eu). Most of the contributors to this volume (Bilandzic, Biltereyst, Bourdaa, Dhoest, Livingstone, Meers, Nyre, O'Neill, Patriarche, Pavlíčková, Ridell and Schrøder) are active members of this ambitious project (31 member countries, 260 individual participants) running from March 2010 to

February 2014. We would like to express our gratitude to the COST framework for having provided those contributors with opportunities to discuss and disseminate their works in COST workshops and conferences.

We also would like to thank the University of Augsburg, the Facultés universitaires Saint-Louis (FUSL, Brussels) and the University of Nevada, Las Vegas for their institutional and/or financial support, without which the publication of this volume in the ECREA Book Series would not have been possible.

References

Anderson, B., 1983. *Imagined communities: Reflections on the origin and spread of nationalism.* London: Verso.

Anderson, J.A., 1996. The pragmatics of audience in research and theory. In J. Hay, L. Grossberg and E. Wartella, eds, *The audience and its landscape.* Boulder, Oxford: Westview Press. pp. 75–93.

Bilandzic, H. and Rössler, P., 2004. Life according to television. Implications of genre-specific cultivation effects: The gratification/cultivation model. *Communications. The European Journal of Communication,* 29(3), pp. 295–326.

Biocca, F.A., 1988. Opposing concepts of the audience: The active and passive hemispheres of mass communication theory. In J.A. Anderson, ed., *Communication Yearbook 11.* Newbury Park: Sage. pp. 51–80.

Blumler, J.G., 1979. The role of theory in uses and gratifications research. *Communication Research,* 6(1), pp. 9–36.

Bruns, A., 2008. *Blogs, Wikipedia, second life, and beyond.* New York: Peter Lang.

Carey, J.W., 1992. Technology and ideology: The case of the telegraph. In J.W. Carey, ed., 3rd edn, *Communication as culture: Essays on media and society.* New York: Routledge. pp. 201–230.

Caron, A.H. and Caronia, L., 2007. *Moving cultures: Mobile communication in everyday life.* Montreal: McGill-Queen's University Press.

Carpentier, N., 2011. *Media and participation: A site of ideological-democratic struggle.* Bristol, Chicago: Intellect.

Dayan, D., 1992. Les mystères de la reception. *Le Débat,* 71, pp. 146–162.

——— 1998. Le double corps du spectateur. In S. Proulx, ed., *Accusé de réception. Le téléspectateur construit par les sciences sociales.* Paris: L'Harmattan. pp. 175–189.

Dayan, D. and Katz, E., 1994. *Media events: The live broadcasting of history.* Cambridge: Harvard University Press.

Deutschman, P. and Danielson, W., 1960. Diffusion of knowledge of the major news story. *Journalism Quarterly,* 37, pp. 345–355.

Freidson, E., 1953. Communications research and the concept of the mass. *American Sociological Review,* 18(3), pp. 313–317.

Goffman, E., 1981. *Forms of talk.* Oxford: Blackwell.

Groeben, N. and Erb, E., 1991. *Reduktiv-implikative versus elaborativ-prospektive Menschenbildannahmen in psychologischen Forschungsprogrammen. Bericht aus dem Psychologischen Institut der Universität Heidelberg.* Heidelberg: Universität Heidelberg.

Habermas, J., 1962. *Strukturwandel der Öffentlichkeit.* Darmstadt & Neuwied, Germany: Hermann Luchterhand Verlag.

Hartmann, T. and Dohle, M., 2005. Publikumsvorstellungen im Rezeptionsprozess. *Publizistik*, 50, pp. 287–303.

Hill, R.J. and Bonjean, C.M., 1964. News diffusion: A test of the regularity hypothesis. *Journalism Quarterly*, 41, pp. 336–342.

Ihde, D., 1982. The technological embodiment of media. In M. Hyde, ed., *Communication philosophy and the technological age.* Tuscaloosa, AL: University of Alabama Press. pp. 54–72.

Jankowski, N.C., 2006. Creating community with media: History, theories and scientific investigations. In L.A. Lievrouw and S. Livingstone, eds, *The handbook of new media.* Updated student edition. London: Sage. pp. 55–74. (Originally published 2002.)

Jenkins, H., 1992. *Textual poachers. Television fans and participatory culture.* New York/London: Routledge.

―――― 2002. The poachers and the stormtroopers: Cultural convergence in the digital age. In P. Le Guern, ed., *Les cultes médiatiques. Culture fan et oeuvres cultes.* Rennes, France: Presses universitaires de Rennes. pp. 343–378.

Katz, E. and Lazarsfeld, P., 1955. *Personal influence. The part played by people in the flow of mass communication.* Glencoe: Free Press.

Katz, E., Blumler, J.G. and Gurevitch, M., 1974. Utilization of mass communication by the individual. In J.G. Blumler and E. Katz, eds, *The uses of mass communications: Current perspectives on gratifications research.* Beverly Hills, CA: Sage. pp. 19–32.

Kuhn, T., 1962. *The structure of scientific revolutions.* Chicago: University of Chicago Press.

Livingstone, S., 2007. From family television to bedroom culture: Young people's media at home. In E. Devereux, ed., *Media studies: Key issues and debates.* London: Sage. pp. 302–321.

Lull, J., 1980. The social uses of television. *Human Communication Research*, 6(3), pp. 197–209.

Maigret, É., 2008. L'ethnographie des publics. In H. Glevarec, É. Macé and É. Maigret, eds, *Cultural studies. Anthologie.* Paris: Armand Colin. pp. 171–175.

Mandaville, P., 2001. Reimagining Islam in diaspora. The politics of mediated community. *Gazette*, 63(2), pp. 169–186.

McLeod, J., Becker, L. and Byrnes, J.E., 1974. Another look at the agenda-setting function of the press. *Communication Research*, 1, pp. 131–167.

McLuhan, M., 1964. *Understanding media: The extensions of man.* New York: McGraw-Hill.

McQuail, D., Blumler, J.G. and Brown, J.R., 1972. The television audience: A revised perspective. In D. McQuail, ed., *Sociology of mass communication. Selected readings.* Harmondsworth: Penguin. pp. 135–166.

Meinberg, E., 1988. *Das Menschenbild in der modernen Erziehungswissenschaft.* Darmstadt: Wissenschaftliche Buchgesellschaft.

Noelle-Neumann, E., 1974. The spiral of silence: A theory of public opinion. *Journal of Communication*, 24, pp. 43–51.

Potter, W.J., 1988. Three strategies for elaborating the cultivation hypothesis. *Journalism Quarterly*, 65, pp. 930–939.

Rogers, E.M., 2003. *Diffusion of innovations*. 5th ed. New York: Free Press.

Rogers, E.M and Shoemaker, F.F., 1971. *Communication of innovations: A cross-cultural approach*. 2nd ed. New York: The Free Press.

Roscoe, J., Marshall, H. and Gleeson, K., 1995. The television audience: A reconsideration of the taken-for-granted terms 'active', 'social' and 'critical'. *European Journal of Communication*, 10(1), pp. 87–108.

Silverstone, R., Hirsch, E. and Morley, D., 1992. Information and communication technologies and the moral economy of the household. In R. Silverstone and E. Hirsch, eds, *Consuming technologies: Media and information in domestic spaces*. London, New York: Routledge. pp. 15–31.

Note

1   The use of the label *ethnographic* when referring to reception studies has been criticized because of the limited and inconsistent application of the ethnographic methodology (e.g. Maigret 2008). In this respect, Peil and Röser in this book prefer to speak about 'ethnographically oriented studies'.

PART I

Audience Activity and Interactivity

Chapter 1

Mode of Action Perspective to Engagements with Social Media: Articulating Activities on the Public Platforms of Wikipedia and YouTube

Seija Ridell

Introduction

One of the conspicuous features of the Web is that communication online does not flow, like in the traditional mass media, vertically from professional producers to the receivers ('from one to many') but horizontally and reciprocally between peers ('from one to one' or 'from many to many'). Some researchers have interpreted this to mean that there are no longer 'clear distinctions between production and reception' (Press and Livingstone 2006: 184). This, again, has led some to the conclusion that in the Web environment audiences have turned into content producers. Livingstone, for one, states that 'audiences and users of the new media are increasingly active – selective, self-directed, producers as well as receivers of texts' (2004: 75; see also 1999: 64). Ross and Nightingale speak of 'online audiences as users, producers and consumers of the media' (2003: 159). In her content analysis of blogs, Papacharissi similarly considers 'audiences as producers of media content' (2007: 21). Bowman and Willis say that with online there are 'many ways that the audience is now participating in the journalistic process' (2003: 3).

The view that digital network media have brought forth new forms of audience activity is particularly common among cultural audience studies scholars. In contrast, Internet researchers quite often seem to regard the whole notion of audience as unimportant or even superfluous when examining people's engagement with the Web. For them, several dimensions of digital media rather 'question the fundamental assumptions about the nature of an audience' (Patriarche 2007: 2). One of these dimensions is that same people (can) act as producers and consumers of online materials. While for the former this development has meant that audiences now act as producers, the latter are inclined to conclude that there are no audiences on the Web. Gillmor talks of 'the former audience', referring to people who once made up an audience but who after 'the lines will blur between producers and consumers' online will not compose one anymore (2006: xxiv, xxv). Speaking of digital games, Coleman and Dyer-Witheford state that after 'the breakdown of division between producers and consumers' there 'are no audiences, only players' (2007: 947). For Bruns, 'the audience is dead' (2008b: 254). This is because digital networking 'enables all participants to be users as much as producers of information and knowledge' (Bruns 2007).

I find equally problematic the view that audiences are simultaneously receivers and producers and the view that audience has disappeared, especially as both consider audience as an acting group- or mass-like entity. The former view endows the audience creature with additional functions to render it feasible in the new circumstances, while the latter view rejects the usefulness of audience in the digital context (without, however, rejecting the notion of audience itself as a fixed entity more generally). My proposal in the chapter is that this oppositional trap can be relaxed by redirecting attention from audience(s) as actor(s) to people's activities as audiences. I suggest that people act as an audience every time they assume the position in which they receive and interpret a cultural performance or media representation. People may do this both in relation to the mass media and to the Web, but whereas the mass media provide predominantly the position of receiver for ordinary people, the Web supplies lay people with a greater diversity of positions or roles for engagement – positions between which people can and do constantly move. One of these roles online is the role of an audience. In the following, this idea will be elaborated by employing the action-theoretical thoughts presented in Max Weber's and Alfred Schutz's interpretive sociology (see also Pietilä and Ridell 2008). I will use YouTube as my primary example and also illustrate theoretical points with references to Wikipedia. As part of the discussion the specificity of acting as an online audience will be delineated. It is necessary to begin, however, by taking a more nuanced and critical look at the view of audiences as producers.

Problems of Seeing Audiences as Producers

The talk of audiences as producers implies, first of all, that audience is something that exists independently 'over there'. And at the first glance it seems indeed indisputable that, say, the spectators of a play in a theatre form a real entity. After all we can witness theatregoers with our own eyes. But is it really an audience that we see in the auditorium? No. What we see instead are people who have come together to attend a cultural performance and who behave for the occasion in a certain culturally learned manner, following the prescriptions of this specific performance-related role (cf. Schechner 1988: 189). It is this manner of behaving and the internalized rules that structure it or, as I prefer to say, the specific mode of action that allows us to talk of the given group of people as an audience. Hence, 'audience' is a concept that is used to get hold of a particular phenomenon in social reality. Obviously, there are different ways of defining this concept.

Rather than speaking of audiences as real beings capable of acting (productively or otherwise), then, it is more to the point to say that it is real people who act. Weber rejected the view of collectives as acting bodies by stating,

[All] collectives must be treated as solely the results of the particular acts of individual persons since these alone can be treated as agents in a course of subjectively understandable action. [...] There is no such thing as a collective personality which 'acts'. (1947[1922]: 101–102)

It should be noted that individuals' activities always take place within the confines of various structural conditions. The fixity of these conditions and the recurrent, often routinized, patterns of individual acts constrain the activities into a standard mode of action, even if the activities may also mould their conditions and thereby alter their mode. The structural conditions of people's acting as mass media audiences consist, among other things, of media industry's production and distribution machinery, its ownership and legal regulation, the output of media representations, the contexts of reception as well as genre-related and other conventions of meaning-making. As regards the Web, the structural conditions may appear less obviously restrictive, but they are in no sense absent (Galloway 2004; Lessig 1999). A mode of action, then, consists of a structural dimension, on the one hand, and of the structurally framed activities, on the other. In this chapter, I will concentrate on the activity side and leave the structural conditions to the margins.

Acting as an audience – or the activity of audiencing, to use a term coined by Fiske (1994; Fiske and Dawson 1996) – differs fundamentally from performing or presenting and, in the (mass) mediated context, from the production of media content as a mode of action. Characteristic of media audiencing is the engagement with produced materials, not their creation. When people, who at a certain moment act as an audience, begin to generate content, they move from the mode of action characteristic of audiencing to the mode characteristic of producing.

The difference between audiencing and producing as activities must be plain also for those who speak of 'audiences as producers'. Why do they still use this phrase? One reason presumably is the radical distinction between producers and receivers that the machinery of the mass media has imprinted on people's minds. Another reason may be the common sense conception of audience as a real social group. These views make it easy to think that people who step out of the audience group to produce content move only temporarily out of their 'proper' place or that they remain at that place even when they do something that clearly differs from audience activity. As members of media audience, they are seen as amateurs as compared to media professionals who belong self-evidently to the category of 'proper' producers. This makes the talk of audiences as producers understandable in itself. This kind of talk, however, conflates the differences between these two as distinct modes of action and renders it difficult to examine their specificities and the specific ways they interrelate in online environments.

Remarkably enough, those who conceive of audience as irrelevant on the Web miss the fact that the audience is, as Patriarche (2007: 2) points out, far from being outdated in the era of information and communication technologies. Indeed, provided that audiencing is understood in terms of a specific mode of action that differs from other modes through which people engage with the media, the concept of audience is equally necessary in Web research more generally and in exploring the social media websites in particular, as it continues to be in the study of the mass media.

'Produsage' or Articulation?

Before proceeding further it is useful to consider whether the concept of production, for its part, is appropriate in the Web environment. Bruns, in particular, has questioned the term's habitual use in this context on the basis that 'production' – similarly to 'audience' – refers 'back to the heyday of the industrial age' (2008a: 2). For Bruns, a concept with such a connotation is unsuitable for describing people's online activities as these do not conform to the centralized industrial logic. Quite the contrary, these activities have the nature of 'collaborative and continuous building and extending of existing content in pursuit of further improvement', as he states about Wikipedia (Bruns 2008a: 2). Bruns introduces instead the neologism 'produsage', an amalgam of the terms 'production' and 'usage', and justifies it by saying that online 'people are in a hybrid position where using the site can (and often does) lead to productive engagement' (2008a: 2).

Bruns's suggestion is interesting but at the same time highly problematic. To start, precisely as in the case of 'audience', the range of meanings of production is not exclusively industrially framed. There are several forms of offline production that do not follow the industrial logic: amateur production, voluntary production and collaboratively coordinated creative production, where revisions are made constantly in pursuit of continuous improvement. A pertinent example of offline production not conforming to the industrial logic is the bee-like work where people (as users) produce collaboratively and voluntarily, improving in rotation what they use. Moreover, why should we not call production any activity that brings about something, however minor this may be?

In addition, the 'use'-based suffixes in the hybrid terms 'produser' and 'produsage' remain unspecified and therefore problematic. For Bruns, 'using the site' can 'lead to productive engagement' (2008a: 2), but it is not clear what he means with this as he does not define the term 'using'. For example, when one seeks information from Wikipedia for some off-site productive work, 'using the site' means audiencing it. But when one uses the tools offered by Wikipedia for altering, expanding or correcting the existing content, the activity of 'using the site' is connected to on-site producing. With its implication of both audiencing and producing, it would be reasonable to consider 'using' as a general umbrella term that refers to all kinds of activities related to websites. Audiencing and producing could then be conceived of as distinct subcategories under this umbrella. This solution would grant the concept of audience the place it deserves both in the Web environment and in the realm of the mass media. Moreover, it would become possible to discern more clearly the specific features of both audiencing and producing.

I employ in this chapter the concept of articulation, understood in the spirit of interpretive sociology, to tackle the problem created by the suggested blurring of boundaries between different online roles and activities. As a background for this idea, let us think of an individual actor who is striving to reach a goal. To speak in Schutz's (1967[1932]) terms, the actor has planned more or less consciously a project, the in-order-to motive of which is determined by that goal. The goal is the 'why' of the actor's effort and the source of the subjective meaning he or she attaches to the overall activity. When carrying out this project the actor often must accomplish activities representing different modes of action. These activities become articulated, that is, associated more or less loosely as subservient components or subprojects, into the span of the overall project. In other words, the actor realizes the overall project in a piecemeal fashion by articulating these activities with one another. This holds true not only for an individual actor but also for jointly pursued projects. From this perspective, it seems fruitful to talk about articulations between producing and audiencing within projects people carry out individually or jointly offline and online.

Let us take a look at Wikipedia content development, for example. I will consider these activities first as an individual process and approach them in the next section from a communal viewpoint. The overall objective and in-order-to motive of Wikipedia content development is, in Bruns's words, the 'building and extending of existing content in pursuit of further improvement' (2008a: 2). Ideal-typically, the plan of an individual project intending to contribute to this goal is composed of two subprojects. The first consists of audiencing the Wikipedia site. The objective of this activity is to check an entry or entries for potentially problematic points. In the plan the expectation is that such points will most probably be detected. Their anticipated detection functions as a because-motive for starting the second subproject, which consists of production. Its objective is to compose a revision that removes the spotted problems. In this example, audiencing is articulated as a subservient subproject into production because it serves as a way to locate problems, while producing, as the problem-erasing subproject, completes the primary project. It is of course possible that, in actual practice, no defects will be detected, and there will not emerge a because-motive for starting the productive subproject.

People visit Wikipedia in most cases presumably for some other reasons than to contribute to its content development. For example, they may consult the site to find helpful information for an off-site problem. The problem provides, then, a because-motive for planning a subproject that consists of audiencing the site for the needed help. It may happen, however, that during their acting as the site's audience people notice on it something that, in their opinion, needs to be improved. If they feel themselves competent and interested enough to do the improvements, the observation provides a because-motive for planning a side project, the in-order-to motive of which is the development of the site by producing the needed revision. In this example, audiencing which is articulated as a subservient activity into the actor's primary project functions also as a triggering instance for the side project that consists of producing. The side project, for its part, is articulated as a subservient activity into the overall content development project of Wikipedia.

What these examples demonstrate, first of all, is that audiencing a website and producing content on it are different as physical and mental activities representing distinct modes of action. Second, the examples make visible that also the objectives and in-order-to motives of these activities differ quite profoundly even when they become connected as subservient activities within one and the same project. Thus, instead of one hybrid performance, it makes sense to talk about a structured complex of articulations.

Articulating Activities Collectively

Bruns (2007) emphasizes that content production in Wikipedia proceeds through collaborative processes within communities of participants who 'engage with fellow users to discuss and coordinate these efforts'. Ideal-typically, the plan of a collaborative communal project intending to contribute to Wikipedia's content development is composed of three subprojects. The first consists, similarly to the individual example in the previous section, of audiencing the Wikipedia site's content. If somebody notices a problematic point during this activity, this observation gives rise to a because-motive for him or her for producing an announcement of the observation. This is the initial step in the second – communally oriented – subproject that consists of interaction between the participants in which they act mutually as producers of utterances and as audiences for them. The in-order-to motive here is to negotiate a solution to the problem. The acceptance of a solution functions as a because-motive for the planning of the third subproject, the production of a revision according to this solution. In this example, acting as the Wikipedia site's audience serves the interaction and is articulated with it. As part of the interaction process, the production of utterances and audiencing them are articulated with one another as turns of subservient activities. Finally, the interaction itself is articulated as a subservient activity with the production of the revision(s).

Interaction is the constituting factor of any online community. People surely have different personal objectives for interacting as a community, but they must additionally share, at least to some extent, an objective that keeps them together. In a Wikipedia community, the shared objective, the production and elaboration of the site's content, lies beyond the interaction as such but is pursued interactively. Hence, the interaction is articulated as a means into the community's project. Communal interaction of this kind can be called issue based or instrumental. In contrast, we can talk about expressive communal interaction, when the activity of interacting is the shared objective and in-order-to motive. Here the objective is not beyond the interaction itself, which is why the interaction is not only articulated as a means into the project but also constitutes its goal. The distinction between instrumental and expressive interaction is, of course, purely analytical as the pursuit of an instrumental goal may simultaneously nurture the participants' sociability.

Basically, the interaction constituting communities is oriented towards in-group consensus even though there may also emerge transient disagreements. People's acting as public represents, in this respect, a qualitatively different case. The meaning in which I use the noun 'public' here comes close to that employed in the writings of Park (1972[1904]), Blumer (1961[1946]), Mills (1995[1956]) and other theorists of collective action. Park formulated his view by stating that 'a public always develops where interests of people, whether political or economic, come into conflict and seek to reconcile themselves' (1972: 79). This idea was crystallized by Blumer as follows: the public refers 'to a group of people (a) who are confronted by an issue, (b) who are divided in their opinion of how to meet the issue and (c) who engage in discussion over the issue' (1961: 373).

I conceive of the scope of 'public' somewhat more extensively here and prefer to speak of people acting as a public when they intervene publicly in an issue that they consider, on the basis of their interests and values, to be a grievance and when they call other people's attention to it. By doing this, they may come into conflict with others who see the issue as no problem. Other people with their own interests and values may also join the debate. Each party has its own project, being driven by and championing the interests and values the party has at heart concerning the issue. The evolving interaction between the parties functions for them as a means through which they attempt to carry out their projects. The ensuing interaction is not characterized by consensus but dissension – at least until some agreement, compromise or other solution becomes possible or the dispute arrives at a dead end.

For an example of people's acting as a public, I focus my attention for a moment on the role of the mass media. An incentive to act as a public namely comes quite often from what the media tell. Amidst their audiencing project people may observe some problem that seems to require public intervention. This observation gives them a because-motive for planning an intervening project. If the problem has to do with their media audiencing project – if they learn, for example, that their favourite television programme will be terminated – a project planned for resisting this intent publicly through petitions and other means of pressure becomes articulated as a subservient subproject into their overall audiencing project. Stated more precisely, although these actors do not carry out this intervening subproject within the mode of action of media audiencing as such but within their acting as a public, the subproject is, nevertheless, carried out within their overall media audiencing project, as its objective is to prevent the structural changes in their media audiencing.

Mostly, however, the public activity that gets its impulse from media coverage concerns issues outside the media themselves. In these cases, media audiencing functions only as a triggering instance and offers the because-motive for the evolving activity which is not articulated into any media audiencing project but composes a project of its own. However, those participating in the project often act during its duration also as a media audience specifically 'in order to check the progression of "their" problem on the political agenda' (Dayan 2005: 57). This presupposes, of course, that the media pay attention to the issue. If this is the case, stepping into the role of media audience may offer the participants useful information for adjusting their activities as a public. To the extent that they act as a media audience to further their project as a public, the audiencing activity becomes articulated as a subservient element into this project.

As implied above, an activity that intervenes in some public issue often calls into arena other parties with their own interests and values, which sometimes results in more or less heated public debates. In and through this interaction, the parties attempt with various strategies to persuade other parties to accept their standpoint and to get those acting as audiences for the debates to support their cause. This sort of interaction differs from the kind that constitutes communities. However, if the parties consist of several people, the interaction within a party is very likely communal, both instrumentally, concerning the development of the party's strategy and tactics, and expressively, concerning the maintenance of its 'we' sentiment. This interaction becomes articulated as a subservient activity into the party's overall project, the objective of which is to reach in contest with other parties an outcome that is optimal from the viewpoint of the given party's interests and values.

YouTube as a Public Platform

The ideal-typical considerations are intended to provide means for grasping more sensitively the multitude of activities on diverse online platforms of which YouTube will serve as my example in the following. YouTube is included in the category of Web-based social media together with such sites as Wikipedia and Facebook (Lietsala and Sirkkunen 2008: 13–14). The characteristic seen as distinct of social media sites more generally is that they offer opportunities for peer-to-peer interaction and/or that their content is produced and shared by users, while the degree of public visibility of interactions and produced contents varies from site to site. On YouTube people can upload, view and share videos and, as the platform's slogan 'broadcast yourself' promotes, the contents are intended for a wide audience. It is possible also to take stand to other people's contributions with your own videos and text comments, and to enter in this way into interaction with other users on the site. Moreover, YouTube 'offers users a personal profile page' and 'enables "friending"' (Lange 2007b). In addition to 'ordinary' people, there are different agencies for advertising and marketing, for example, who have seized the opportunity to upload videos in the hope that the users would circulate them to each other. The activity on the site has, of course, its economic, legal and other structural preconditions.

YouTube is a public arena in the sense that anybody with sufficient net connections and skills may visit the site, view the uploaded videos and comment as well as sign himself or herself up as a user. Some researchers point out that when giving up personal information on social media websites people do not necessarily realize how extensively public this information might become (Barnes 2006). Visibility to other people is not the only criterion of publicness. At least since Arendt (1958), the notion of 'public' has been contrasted with that of 'private' in dual sense, namely by referring, besides the visibility of things, to their power to affect 'the interests of a collectivity of individuals' (Weintraub 1997: 5). In relation to YouTube, it can be said that, as regards the visibility criterion, the notion of 'public' concerns the characteristics of the site as a platform. But as regards the collectivity criterion, we are talking about the content of the video clips and, more precisely, their communicative intent. Only clips dealing with issues that bear upon the lives of many people or are otherwise of broad social significance can be called public in the sense of collectivity. Clips that do not reach beyond personal spheres of life remain private regardless of the fact that their uploading confers YouTube visibility on them.

Visibility on YouTube – or YouTube publicity, as I like to call it – is not static but variable. Video producers can regulate both how much information they reveal about themselves and to what extent they limit or open access to their videos physically by using technical means and/or mentally by manipulating the meanings of the videos (Lange 2007b). Producers who disclose relatively much information about themselves tend to be more visible in YouTube publicity than those who are more reserved in this respect. Likewise, videos that are promoted extensively, made easily accessible and/or meaningful to many people are more likely to become widely visible than are those with opposite characteristics. The visibility of the video makers and that of their products tend to go hand in hand, but there are exceptions as well. Some producers hide much of their identity but make their videos easily accessible. Some others yield much information about their identities but direct their videos only to the select few (Lange 2007b).

The exceptions are definitely interesting, but in this context it is more important to notice that YouTube publicity is cumulative in character. This is disclosed most conspicuously by the fact that some producers have risen to the status of YouTube celebrities. Their videos are commented on extensively, many users seek their friendship and their work may give patterns for novice video makers. They 'influence the discourse, goals, and activities on YouTube through their videos, comments, bulletins, and other forms of interaction' (Lange 2007a: 5). Obviously, YouTube publicity is divided into a 'mainstream publicity' composed of the top names and their followers, and a 'peripheral publicity' consisting of producers who restrict the visibility of their person or their work, or both. A similar division into centre and periphery can also be observed in the blogosphere, for example, where 'the nature of the system fosters the development of an A-list of bloggers, and controls what stories are likely to propagate through the system' (Ó Baoill 2004).

From this perspective, YouTube publicity appears quite concentrated and hierarchical. It is possible, however, to approach visibility on YouTube differently. According to some analysts, a specific feature of many social media websites is that they support the maintenance of pre-existing social networks (boyd and Ellison 2007; Lange 2007b). For boyd (2008: 126), the popularity of MySpace, for example, was deeply rooted in how the site supported sociality amongst pre-existing friend groups. On the site, such a network is supported by what Lange (2007b) calls 'a media circuit'. A circuit consists of messages – in the case of YouTube of videos and video comments – that members of a social network circulate to each other. There are innumerable social networks that have established a circuit on the YouTube site. When the site's publicity is approached from the viewpoint of these circuits, it appears much more decentralized than it does when looked at as a hierarchy of mainstream and peripheral publicity.

In addition to the visibility that the video makers and their products gain on YouTube, another criterion for the site's public nature is the extent to which the contents of video clips concern public issues instead of private or personal affairs. To shed empirical light on this would require an extensive study of its own. Lange (2007b) remarks casually that 'within a single video maker's work, some videos are personal, whereas others address issues such as environmental sustainability or racism and are intended for a larger audience'. The criteria Lange establishes for the publicness of videos – that they are promoted and/or made easily accessible and understandable – concerns the visibility of the videos and not their collectivity in the sense defined by Arendt (1958) and Weintraub (1997).

Activities on YouTube in Terms of Mode of Action

Lurking and Participating

To get hold of the diversity of users' activities and their articulations on YouTube in terms of mode of action, it is helpful to make a distinction between two umbrella categories of online (inter)action, namely lurking and participating. Lurking consists simply of surfing the site to view what there is, whereas participating refers to actual activities on it. Lange (2007a: 4) provides a five-point classification of YouTube participants, but suffice it to divide the forms of participation on YouTube into two: casual and more regular. Casual participation includes, among other things, uploading of videos that were initially not intended to be uploaded on the site, whereas more regular participation presupposes that videos are produced with the purpose to be uploaded. Regular participants engage also in video commenting and 'friending'. Under the regular participation, it is helpful to distinguish articulations of fandom as their own 'activity bundle' because of the special characteristics of fan activities.

The only YouTube-related project by lurking visitors is their acting as audiences for the site. This activity comes close to traditional mass media audiencing. For example, lurking cannot be observed. Those engaged in it are not visible on the site even if their visits leave traces. Lurkers compose part of what boyd (2007) calls 'invisible audiences'. Regular participants who do not restrict their visibility are exposed to the gaze of various invisibles, even permanently in so far as the contents they upload on the site, are filed into the system and stay accessible. For boyd (2007), two kinds of invisibles 'cause participants the greatest headaches: those who hold power over them and those who want to prey on them'. This indicates that, in their activity as online audiences, people may enter into a more intimate relationship with the Web than they do when audiencing the mass media. Lurking users can articulate their activity as YouTube audiences in different ways as a subservient activity into their offline projects.

Not only does lurking on YouTube include audiencing, but participating does as well. Among participants, however, acting as an audience is a primary project only for fans, whose manner of audiencing has been characterized as 'adoring' (Lewis 1992: 147). Yet for many fans acting as an idol's audience is only a beginning. Active fans do much more, such as participate in ongoing discussions about their idols and produce their own fan texts (Jenkins 1992). In the case of YouTube, this means that the fans of a YouTube celebrity comment on his or her work with their own videos or textual comments and participate in YouTube debates and discussions concerning the celebrity's performance or output. While lurking merely includes acting as the site's audience, fan users shift continually between the modes of action of audiencing and producing. They act as audiences not only for their idol's work but also for comments on it, and they produce not only their own comments on it but comment also on comments by others. All this producerly activity gains its objective and in-order-to motive from the fans' overall project of acting as a specific audience and becomes articulated into it as a subservient activity.

Generally, though, acting as an audience is mostly a subsidiary activity for the site's activists. More important for their projects is to produce and upload their own videos, and to comment on and discuss other participants' videos. The activities in casual participation, however, are quite restricted. These participants merely upload videos that they have shot for other purposes than to place them on YouTube. The objectives of and in-order-to motives for the uploading surely vary. People may, for example, shoot videos to document impressive or shocking occurrences that they happen to witness and think only afterwards that these representations might set tongues wagging if placed on YouTube. The particular project here, then, may be an attempt to draw attention to the given occurrence and probably also gain personal merit. But, equally well, it can be to find out how the video will be received on the site. Whatever the particular project, as an activity it is ideal-typically composed of two subprojects. The first, uploading, is articulated as a subservient act. The second is audiencing the site and also other platforms or media for possible reactions.

In the above example, the shooting of videos and their uploading on YouTube are separate projects. The situation is different if the videos are shot and/or prepared to be uploaded. I will consider this situation more closely from the dual perspective previously introduced, namely by approaching YouTube publicity as a hierarchy of mainstream and peripheral publicity, on the one hand, and as a decentralized formation dispersed into countless circuits supporting social networks, on the other. Producing and its relations to other modes of action as well as the articulation of activities more generally will take a somewhat different shape depending on the angle from which the projects on the site are approached.

YouTube Publicity and the Articulation of Activities

The mainstream publicity on YouTube consists above all of those called by Lange 'celebrities' who or at least whose works are 'quite well known both within and often outside the site' (2007a: 4–5). It is therefore reasonable to assume that the objective of the video-making projects of many of these participants has been to achieve and maintain esteem within the YouTube culture. In contrast to the previous example, here the production of videos specifically for uploading is the prime activity. Activities representing other potential modes of action are articulated as a means for advancing video making in general and for training one's production skills in particular. For example, the participants' shift from the producing mode of action temporarily into that of audiencing the site can be explained, in an ideal-typical sense, by their curiosity to see whether they could adopt ideas or draw some other benefits from the work of other video makers. If the participants seek, through acting as an audience for others' videos, solutions to problems of expression or look for general inspiration, the activity of audiencing is articulated as an advancing means into their production project.

There are reasons to suggest that the same holds true for commenting on videos. Commenting is a way to create relationships characteristic of a community, and such relationships help to acquire and maintain respect for one's productive work. Many video makers comment on others' videos 'with the strategic intent of forming social relationships with others who will support their work' (Lange 2007b). Relations are built by commenting favourably on such videos that have a point in common with one's own work and by responding encouragingly to people 'who post comments of affinity or leave thoughtful comments' (Lange 2007b). Interaction of this kind tends to create at least an expressive community and perhaps even results in an instrumental community in so far as the exchange deals, for example, with problems of expression. Be that as it may, the participation in the community interaction is articulated as a subservient activity into one's project for acquiring esteem as a video maker. The monitoring of others' reactions by audiencing this interaction serves the same function.

The itch for esteem is, of course, only one motive for making videos and uploading them. There are most certainly also producers for whom the most decisive motive for video making is self-expression. These actors do not necessarily care about popularity. Consequently, such videos tend to remain in the peripheral YouTube publicity unless an outside occurrence draws attention to them. The more original the producer's style of expression, the less she or he probably is inclined to look for patterns and ask advice from others. This kind of participants hardly join any larger community on the site, nor is their acting as the site's audience articulated as a means into their video-making projects – at least not in any imitative sense.

In addition to projects that are motivated by the participant's wish for esteem or her or his need for self-expression, it is possible that video makers aim to realize projects in which they attempt to intervene in public issues. In doing this, they begin to act as a public pursuing their objective, the intervention, through the video-producing activity. That is why video producing becomes articulated as a means into the intervening project in question. Furthermore, both the video makers' interaction as communities and their acting as the site's audience become articulated as subservient activities with producing processes in so far as the makers see that they can, through discussions and by learning from others, make their videos more effective tools for realizing the projects that they are pursuing as publics.

The articulations of activities that represent different modes of action appear in a somewhat different light when YouTube publicity is approached as an aggregate of countless circuits. These circuits are based mainly on earlier social networks. Naturally, new networks can also be created and the old ones extended through the activities on the site where everybody has a chance to (try to) form a friendship with other participants. Moreover, an active 'YouTuber' may be a member in several networks and 'make and share certain kind of videos with one set of friends, while making and sharing other types of videos with a different set of friends' (Lange 2007b). In each of the cases, the corresponding circuit consists essentially of circulating videos and video comments between the network members. In this way, they can stay in touch even over huge distances.

The activity of network members within such a circuit is determined by the satisfaction they get from their being together virtually. It is the objective for the participants to make and share videos and to post and share comments on each others' creations. The production of videos is the primary project in cases where the objective is self-expression or the attainment of esteem, but in social networking the video making is a subservient activity with the function to support the network members' primary project, which is most often their interaction as an expressive community. The activities may, however, include also acting as a public to draw attention to some social evil, for example. Moreover, the participants in the circuit naturally act as audiences for others' videos and comments. In this way, audiencing becomes articulated as a subservient activity into the primary 'sociability project' as well. In order to keep the circuit running, the participants must continually move to and fro between the modes of action of producing and audiencing.

Not only ordinary people but also various institutions use YouTube as a visibility platform. Advertising agencies, for example, upload marketing videos in the hope that participants on the site will catch interest in them and put them into circulation in their network circuits. This 'viral marketing' adapts the idea that persuasion reaches people best 'in their life context and through other people, their daily associates, those whom they trust' (Mills 1995[1956]: 92) – an idea that was invented long before there were any signs of the Internet. The participants on the site act, in the first place, as audiences for the marketing videos, but if they swallow the bait and forward the videos within their circuits, they stop for that moment acting as audiences and start acting as mediators. From these actors' points of view, the circulating of the marketing videos serves the same function of community upholding as do all the other material they circulate.

Yet the activity of the mediators is only one side of the story. Another side is the overall project of the advertisers whose in-order-to motive is to get the videos diffused as widely as possible and effect the maximum of purchasing decisions. Advertisers are eager to exploit the activities of other people by articulating them as a means into their overall project, and the exploitation takes place through delicate persuasion, by making the videos so amusing or inspiring that to circulate them is sheer pleasure. Most interesting in this case is whether the overall project of the advertisers succeeds in capturing the overall project of network participants and thereby inflects the whole network to serve commercial ends. This example shows also more generally that the activities of different agents on the YouTube site do not necessarily remain independent from each other but that one agent may be able to subordinate the activities of other participants to serve its own goals. This observation brings us near to the economic-structural problematic of the site – a problematic that deserves its own treatment.

Conclusion

The main questions considered in this enquiry stem from the fact that information and communication technologies and the Internet, in particular, have upset the traditional division between producers and receivers – a division that is still reality in the realm of the mass media. Some have reacted to this upsetting with the argument that on the Internet, and more specifically on the social media websites, it is audiences who act as content producers. Others, however, have forwarded the opposite view by arguing that the blurring of boundary lines between online producers and receivers makes the concept of audience useless as we are all now potential producers or at least 'produsers'. The objective and in-order-to motive of my own project here has been, in the first place, to argue that both views miss the point in their specific ways and, in the second place, to sketch a suggestion that goes beyond the dilemma of either extending the concept of audience too far or, alternatively, dismissing it altogether.

The view that the concept of audience has become superfluous can be countered by the simple argument that, after all, the Web is 'text-centred' (Livingstone 2004: 84) and needs to be decoded and interpreted to make any sense at all. With the rejection of 'audience' such complex processes would fall out of researchers' purviews in the online environment. However, as I have tried to show, the concept of audience as such is fruitful only if the phenomenon to which it refers is conceived of not as a group- or mass-like formation 'over there' but as a specific mode of action into which and out of which people continually move in their engagements with Web-based social media.

The view that, in the Web environment, audiences act as content producers – or that they have been replaced by produsers – conflates distinct online activities to the extent that the real differences between these activities become obscure. Even though the boundaries between producers and receivers have indeed become blurred in recent years, as activities producing and receiving (or audiencing) remain as different as ever. In fact, it is not so much activities in themselves that have changed along with digitalization and network technologies; rather the opportunities that people have in choosing and moving between different modes of action and the roles embedded in them have multiplied. Hybrid metaphors not only tend to obfuscate this development but they also serve to preclude questions about how the boundary lines, more accurately, have been transformed. This criticism hits the concept of 'produsage' as well. Bruns is perfectly right in stressing that Web environment allows 'for a relatively fluid movement [...] between different roles' (2007). A movement *between* roles, however, presupposes that the roles are analytically distinct, not fused.

In my view, the conceptual challenges raised by the blurring of boundaries between online roles and activities can be tackled fruitfully by employing the idea of articulation. The focal question then is how producing and audiencing, for example, become articulated with one another or with activities representing other modes of action within the projects that people carry out individually or jointly online and offline.

I discussed the feasibility of this idea by considering different projects that YouTube and, to a lesser degree, Wikipedia allow for users as a platform of agency. It should be noted, though, that I have dealt with possible, not actual, projects. In this sense, my analysis is conceptual-theoretical, not empirical by nature. I concentrated on what Schutz (1967[1932]: 187) calls 'course-of-action' types. All projects described above are ideal-typical constructs in the sense that the activities they consist of are selected and arranged on the basis of their objectives and in-order-to motives. I followed in my treatment Schutz's (1967[1932]: 189) view that it is 'the in-order-to motive' of a project 'on whose definition the whole typification is based'. The ideal-typical analysis has shown that activities representing different modes of action become articulated with each other in different ways within different projects that online platforms enable – a fact that escapes the analyst's gaze if the sites are approached by using essentialist or hybrid terms.

Finally, it is my contention that theoretical rigour in understanding the diversity of people's activities in the constantly evolving media environment is crucial for coming to grips with the way in which social processes work in our contemporary digital condition. Moreover, sensitive conceptualizations are needed to analyse the projects people pursue online in terms of their explicit and hidden politics.

References

Arendt, H., 1958. *The human condition*. Chicago: University of Chicago Press.

Barnes, S.B., 2006. A privacy paradox: Social networking in the United States. *First Monday*, 11(9) [online]. Available at: http://firstmonday.org/htbin/cgiwrap/bin/ojs/index.php/fm/article/view/1394/1312 [Accessed 14 September 2011].

Blumer, H., 1961. The crowd, the public, and the mass. In W. Schramm, ed., *The process and effects of mass communication*. Urbana, IL: University of Illinois Press. pp. 363–379. (Originally published 1946.)

Bowman, S. and Willis, C., 2003. *We media: How audiences are shaping the future of news and information*. Media Center at the American Press Institute. Thinking paper [pdf], Available at: http://www.hypergene.net/wemedia/download/we_media.pdf [Accessed 14 September 2011].

boyd, d., 2007. Social network sites: Public, private, or what? *Knowledge Tree*, 13 May [online], Available at: http://kt.flexiblelearning.net.au/tkt2007/edition-13/social-network-sites-public-private-or-what/ [Accessed 14 September 2011].

————— 2008. Why youth ♥ social network sites: The role of networked publics in teenage social life. In D. Buckingham, ed., *Youth, identity, and digital media*. Cambridge, MA: The MIT Press. pp. 119–142.

boyd, d. and Ellison, N.B., 2007. Social network sites: Definition, history, and scholarship. *Journal of Computer-Mediated Communication*, (13)1 [online]. Available at: http://jcmc.indiana.edu/vol13/issue1/boyd.ellison.html [Accessed 14 September 2011].

Bruns, A., 2007. The future is user-lead: The path towards widespread produsage. *Proceedings PerthDAC: Digital Arts & Culture* [online]. Available at: http://produsage.org/node/15 [Accessed 14 September 2011].

————— 2008a. From production to produsage: Interview with Axel Bruns (part one). Interviewed by Henry Jenkins for his official weblog, 9 May [online]. Available at: http://henryjenkins. org/2008/05/interview_with_axel_bruns.html [Accessed 14 September 2011].

————— 2008b. *Blogs, Wikipedia, Second Life, and beyond.* New York: Peter Lang.

Coleman, S. and Dyer-Witheford, N., 2007. Playing on the digital commons: Collectivities, capital and contestation in videogame culture. *Media, Culture & Society*, 26(6), pp. 934–953.

Dayan, D., 2005. Mothers, midwives, and abortionists: Genealogy, obstetrics, audiences and publics. In S. Livingstone, ed., *Audiences and publics: When cultural engagement matters for the public sphere.* Bristol: Intellect Books. pp. 43–76.

Fiske, J., 1994. Audiencing: Cultural practice and cultural studies. In N.K. Denzig and Y.S. Lincoln, eds, *Handbook of qualitative research.* Thousand Oaks, CA: Sage. pp. 189–198.

Fiske, J. and Dawson, R., 1996. Audiencing violence: Watching homeless men watch *Die Hard.* In J. Hay, L. Grossberg and E. Wartella, eds, *The audience and its landscape.* Boulder, CO: Westview Press. pp. 297–316.

Galloway, A.R., 2004. *Protocol. How control exists after decentralization.* Cambridge, MA: The MIT Press.

Gillmor, D., 2006. *We the media: Grassroots journalism by the people, for the people.* Sebastopol, CA: O'Reilly.

Jenkins, H., 1992. *Textual poachers: Television fans & participatory culture.* New York: Routledge.

Lange, P.G., 2007a. Commenting on comments: Investigating responses to antagonism on YouTube. In: *Society for Applied Anthropology Conference*, 31 March, Tampa, FL.

————— 2007b. Publicly private and privately public: Social networking on YouTube. *Journal of Computer-Mediated Communication*, (13)1 [online]. Available at: http://jcmc.indiana.edu/ vol13/issue1/lange.html [Accessed 22 December 2011].

Lessig, L., 1999. The law of the horse: What cyberlaw might teach. *Harvard Law Review*, 113(2), pp. 501–546.

Lewis, L.A., 1992. 'Something more than love': Fan stories on film. In L.A. Lewis, ed., *The adoring audience: Fan culture and popular media.* London: Routledge. pp. 147–159.

Lietsala, K. and Sirkkunen, E., 2008. *Social media: Introduction to the tools and processes of participatory economy.* Hypermedia Laboratory Net Series 17. Tampere: Tampere University Press.

Livingstone, S., 1999. New media, new audiences? *New Media & Society*, 1(1), pp. 59–66.

————— 2004. The challenge of changing audiences: Or, what is the audience researcher to do in the age of Internet? *European Journal of Communication*, 19(1), pp. 75–86.

Mills, C.W., 1995. The mass society. In R. Jackall, ed., *Propaganda.* Houndmills: Macmillan. pp. 74–101. (Originally published 1956.)

Ó Baoill, A., 2004. Weblogs and the public sphere. In L. Gurak et al., eds, *Into the blogosphere, rhetoric, community, and culture of weblogs* [online collection]. Available at: http://blog.lib. umn.edu/blogosphere/weblogs_and_the_public_sphere.html [Accessed 14 September 2011].

Papacharissi, Z., 2007. Audiences as media producers: Content analysis of 260 blogs. In M. Tremayne, ed., *Blogging, citizenship, and the future of media.* New York: Routledge. pp. 21–38.

Park, R.E., 1972. *The crowd and the public and other essays*. Translated from German by C. Elsner. Chicago: University of Chicago Press. (Originally published 1904.)

Patriarche, G., 2007. Audiences and users: Convergences and articulations. In: *2007 IAMCR Conference*, 23–25 July, Paris, France.

Pietilä, V. and Ridell, S., 2008. Verkkomedia toimijuuden alustana. Yleisö, yhteisö, julkiso ja YouTube. *Lähikuva*, 21(2), pp. 27–43.

Press, A. and Livingstone, S., 2006. Taking audience research into the age of new media: Old problems and new challenges. In M. White and J. Schwoch, eds,. *Questions of methods in cultural studies*. Oxford: Blackwell. pp. 72–200.

Ross, K. and Nightingale, V., 2003. *Media and audiences: New perspectives*. Maidenhead, UK: Open University Press.

Schechner, R., 1988. *Performance theory*. London, New York: Routledge Classics.

Schutz, A., 1967. *The phenomenology of the social world*. Translated from German by G. Walsh and F. Lehnert. Evanston, IL: Northwestern University Press. (Originally published 1932.)

Weber, M., 1947. *The theory of social and economic organization*. Translated from German by A. M. Henderson and T. Parsons. New York: Oxford University Press. (Originally published 1922.)

Weintraub, J., 1997. The theory and politics of the public/private distinction. In J. Weintraub and K. Kumar, eds, *Public and private in thought and practice*. Chicago: University of Chicago Press. pp. 1–42.

Chapter 2

At the Crossroads of Hermeneutic Philosophy and Reception Studies: Understanding Patterns of Cross-Media Consumption

Tereza Pavlíčková

Introduction

The social use of media – how and why media and media content are used – is the fundamental question in media and communication studies, the question of the relationship between people and media. The medium can be understood as content, a distribution channel, a technology or an institution, and perhaps even more importantly, it is inseparable from the expectations and discourse about it. The understanding of users' activity, and subsequently the power relations in the distribution and circulation of information, is also reflected in the various terms for media users. We are text readers, audio listeners, screen viewers, but facing digital media, who have we become? Do readers, listeners and viewers have to die for consumers and users to be born? The notion of consumers might yet evoke a position at the end of the linear communication process, where something is produced and delivered via the medium to be consumed. While the term 'media users' suggests activity – implying that previously, we were 'only' able to read, listen or watch – we now 'finally' use the media actively for our own purposes. We modify, add to, create and circulate certain contents ourselves. Media historians (e.g. Boddy 2004; Carey 1989; Gitelman 2006; Marvin 1988) have shown that the introduction and spread of every new medium in society has always been accompanied by the tendency to see the technology as an agent of social change, where at first the public discourse tends to attribute particular characteristics to the technology, therefore associating with it a particular use and subsequently an effect on society. Conversely, little attention was paid to the use of the media, how they are incorporated into users' everyday lives and what roles are attributed to them by users themselves.

I will argue in this chapter that media technologies do not determine their own uses; rather, the way in which media are used are anchored within, and originate from, the broader social, cultural and historical context. I will discuss how the social use of media can be understood and analysed by using Gadamer's philosophical hermeneutics, which introduces the notion of dialogue between the reader and the text as an inseparable part of their coexistence within a society and a particular historical moment. It is primarily the notion of historicity that is crucial for understanding the social use of media and the changing roles that media have in people's lives.

This chapter also describes how Gadamer's concept of understanding helps to illuminate two key issues: (1) the problem of users' activity and (2) the relationship between users and media texts with a non-linear structure. By thinking about these two connected issues, it can be argued that there are parallels between the uses of all media, as users are actively connecting all texts into their social and historical context and pre-existing knowledge. However, users' activity might be articulated differently with various media and media contents. The theoretical section concludes by discussing the relationships between producers and users, as the ability to visibly perform the use of media does not necessarily mean that the barrier between the users and producers has blended. The chapter ends by using empirical research to show that the social use of media is determined by users' pre-existing knowledge of the subject of the text, rather than by the technology. Furthermore, the research shows that media use is evolving within the context of previous uses, as particular routines and systems of references are established on the users' individual as well as on a socially shared level. In the case of user-produced content, users themselves create their own systems of criteria to assess the credibility of sources, which leads to the establishment of knowledge elites within the user base.

Understanding Is Interpretative

Gadamer's philosophical hermeneutics can be adopted as an epistemological framework to understand that every medium, its uses and the roles attributed to it by its users are situated within a certain context, which originates from previous knowledge and previous uses. Gadamer argues that 'understanding is always interpretation, and hence interpretation is the explicit form of understanding' (Gadamer 2004: 306).[1] This argument expresses his opposition to a positivist appreciation of understanding as objective knowledge that is achievable by employing the correct rules and methods. Rather, understanding is the result of a dialogue between an individual (a reader, or for that matter, a researcher) and a text, which could also be, for example, a subject or an event and thus remains primarily situated within the particular social and historical context.

Gadamer works with the terms 'prejudice' and 'tradition', which are freed of the negative connotations attributed to them by modernity. Together, they form the *horizon* that one brings into an encounter with any text or subject. *Prejudice* brought to the process of interpretation is seen as a judgement, an assumption or prior knowledge of a particular subject or a text. The prejudice originates in, and develops within, the historical, cultural and social *tradition*: the judgements and opinions to which one belongs rather than being one's individual preoccupations. Importantly, the horizon is not a fixed set of assumptions and prejudices, rather 'it is a continual and unfinished process of being formed' (Gadamer 2004: 305) through encounters with other horizons, referred to as a *fusion of horizons*.

This concept was later adopted in the field of literary theory by the Constance School of Reception Aesthetics (Iser 1974, 1978; Jauss 1982), which shifted the attention from the author's intention to the text–reader relationship and focused on the reader's role in the process of understanding. Similar questions related to understanding and the ways that knowledge is established were raised by Schütz (1972). He refers to a 'stock of knowledge at hand', describing the historicity of man where one is aware of the pre-existence of the world and is confronting life situations with knowledge already gathered that is historically and socially rooted and constructed. This idea is further developed by Berger and Luckmann (1971) who argue that reality is socially constructed as the world is intersubjective, and by the interplay between members of a particular society, its shared values and beliefs are institutionalized and further legitimized. It is a dialectical and ongoing process where a person is part of a world 'made by men, inhabited by men, and, in turn, making men' (Berger and Luckmann 1971: 211).

In literary theory the reciprocal and mutual relationships between the text and reader is referred to as a hermeneutical circle, where the user enters the process of reading (use) with certain prejudices within a horizon of understanding. The reading of each particular part of the text influences and determines the understanding of the text as a whole, which subsequently influences the understanding of a specific part of the text. The hermeneutical concept of understanding does not only apply to the actual act of reading and the reader–text relationship. The notion of a continuous dialogue being an inherent characteristic of understanding helps us to appreciate that the roles attributed to media and the social use of media are changing and evolving throughout history, and that technologies do not have an embedded nature determining their use. Gadamer's concept helps us to understand that no one can detach herself from cultural and historical circumstances in the process of understanding. Even if a reader tries to separate herself from tradition and attempts to look at a text without preconceptions, this opposition will still happen within one's tradition. As Warnke puts it, '[w]e do not achieve knowledge about the texts, works or actions with which we are concerned; we simply connect them to our own circumstances' (1987: 75).

'New' media are not completely new in the sense of that they would represent a break with other forms of media. Neither are they at any point in a fixed or final state. Nor do they come with a given use and role. These are negotiated and renegotiated within society through time and through social use across all media as well as non-media. New forms of media, as Marvin (1988: 4) argues, can also lead to negotiation over existing power roles within society, 'who is inside and outside, who may speak, who may not, and who has authority and may be believed'. Therefore, every new medium or new media technology is incorporated into the continuous process of social negotiations over the norms and standards of use and consumption as well as production and circulation, as all media are complex systems of social, technological, textual and economic practices. Gitelman offers an interesting model, arguing that there should be a distinction between a medium as a technology and its *associated protocols*. These are 'a vast clutter of normative rules and default conditions, which gather and adhere like a nebulous array around a technological nucleus' (Gitelman 2006: 7). These protocols of use result from public debate around each technology, from its uptake by early adopters to later acceptance by the general public. Gitelman's protocols are far from static, even though they represent standards and norms. They do change and, as she points out, the technologies are changeable as well. The old meets the new, and that is where users bring the horizon of the present into the process of use and reading in their encounter with the (new) technology or text.

The use of any medium is therefore negotiated within and derived from the use of other media with which one is familiar. Bolter and Grusin's (1999) theory of remediation argues that there are mutual relationships between different media where each has the need to accommodate the characteristics of the previous as well as of the latter, while establishing characteristics that distinguish it from the rest of all media. Bolter and Grusin acknowledge the continuity and historicity of media and recognize the coexistence and mutual relationships between old and new, arguing that 'what is new about new media is therefore also old and familiar: that they promise the new by remediating what has gone before' (Bolter and Grusin 1999: 270). Even though their concept deals only with technological remediation, where the change of the media landscape is seen as a result of particular characteristics granted to particular media, the concept can be used to understand how media users incorporate new technologies into their use of existing media. The role and uses of existing media are changing and are redistributed as a result of the incorporation of the new medium into the routines of everyday life and within the whole media ensemble available to the user. This re-negotiation is not an event, but a continuous process of the social use of media (Bakardjieva 2005; Kendall 2002). For example, Miller and Slater (2000: 12) show that rather than using 'the Internet', people create a personal set of 'various technical possibilities that add up to *their* Internet', a personalized understanding of the cluster of technologies that people access and use by means of their personal computers and mobile devices, to which they have attributed values and roles based on culturally and socially situated day-to-day encounters in their lives.

Social Use of Media Is Always Active

The social use of media is closely linked to the question of users' activity, the definition of activity as well as the question of whether it is determined by the medium or inseparable from any social use of media. Early media research saw the audience as a uniform mass that could be uniformly controlled and where the media message was injected into the viewers, hence 'a hypodermic needle model' (DeFleur and Ball-Rokeach 1989). Later, Bauer argued against the powerless audience, seeing media communication as 'an exchange of values between two or more parties; each gives in order to get' (1964: 327). It was Hall (1973) who argued that viewers/readers should be seen as an active part of the process of mediation and that the message encoded in the text does not necessarily have to be the same as the message decoded from the text. Morley (1980a, 1980b) then introduced the notion of a dialogue (struggle) between the text and the reader. Numerous studies demonstrate that the audience is not a uniform mass but that different media contents attract different audiences that use the content in particular ways (e.g. Ang 1985; Gillespie 1995; Katz and Liebes 1990; Morley 1986; Radway 1984). In those accounts, activity is understood primarily as a combination of cognitive and behavioural factors – selection, involvement, utility and intention (Biocca 1988).

In relation to digital media, activity is often understood as a contribution to media production, distribution and the circulation of information, rather than cross-media use and the reception of media content. Users are labelled 'active' because they not only receive and interpret the information but also create, transform or pass on original media content. Digital media have the potential to make activity more visible; however, this does not mean that the use of other media is less or not at all active. I would argue that activity is the dialogue between the content's and the media users' horizons as referred to by Gadamer. Seeing activity as a characteristic of the medium paradoxically defines the audience as passive, as if the reception of the particular content would not be possible without the technology. Similarly, Jenkins et al. (2009) in the white paper *If It Doesn't Spread, It's Dead*[2] refer to the circulation of media content. They point out that the metaphor that compares the original message to a virus hidden in a protein shell that can circulate unchanged despite the content, or form of the text, being transformed, repurposed, distorted and redistributed by the media users takes the agency away from the consumers and places it with the content:

> The winnowing down of cultural options is the product not of the strength of particular ideas but of many, many individual choices as people decide what ideas to reference, which to share with each other, decisions based on a range of different agendas and interests far beyond how compelling individual ideas may be. (Jenkins et al. 2009)[3]

Therefore, a definition of activity that places it in opposition to passivity does not really work, as there is no passive use of media (Biocca 1988). Indeed, activity is not characterized by the media nor the content. It is a process of understanding where the content encounters users' prior knowledge and context brought into the particular act of media use. Therefore, the social use of media always involves activity. Nonetheless, activity can be performed in different ways as it is a cognitive and behavioural act. It *can* lead to an actual contribution to media production, but it can similarly be performed on the couch by linking the content to the knowledge and references at hand. The way activity is performed does not relate to its profoundness or quality. The use of digital media might lead to certain expressions of activity becoming more visible, although such media do not create activity. The users are, however, active in different ways, and these differences are determined by their horizon of understanding, prior knowledge and system of references they bring into the encounter with the text.

Non-linear Texts

The structure of the text is another feature that is used as evidence for arguments in favour of activity achieved through digital media. Information that is distributed and circulated via the Internet is linked together, creating so-called hyperlinks or hypertexts – texts that have a non-linear structure. Aarseth defines a non-linear text as 'one in which the words or sequences of words may differ from reading to reading because of the shape, conventions, or mechanism of the text' (1994: 51). Therefore, a linear text is then seen as a specific case of non-linear text that is by convention read from the beginning to the end. Importantly, he makes a distinction between (non-)linearity of the narrative, in this case a story that a reader constructs from a text, and (non-)linearity of the text structure itself. The (non-)linearity of the text structure – called the physico-logical (non-)linearity – is understood as a set of textual elements offering its reader multiple possibilities of ordering these textual elements and their sequences. In the end, the reader creates a linear narrative from the text structure that might be one of many possible alternatives.

This characteristic, seen by scholars like Landow (2006) as the 'uniqueness' of the hypertext, leads to the tendency to see the text as authorless, giving all the power in the process of reception to readers or media users. Landow (2006: 56) states that hypertext 'does not permit a tyrannical, univocal voice' seeing the readers of a hypertext as becoming 'truly active'. If the reader is the one to whom the particular realization of the text belongs, then the notion of the author can be neglected. These conclusions are drawn merely on the basis that the text has a non-linear structure. However, the notion of hypertext is already present in much earlier writings in literary theory, such as Kristeva's (1980) concept of intertextuality where one text is linked to many others through a system of references and connections. Therefore, meaning is not constructed exclusively through the variable physical structure of the text – that would suggest that the understanding and construction of meaning is a linear process (one linear text structure equals one meaning). Rather, meaning results from interplay between the text and its explicit as well as implicit references and the reader's prior knowledge brought into the process of reading at various places. The same text can therefore be interpreted as a different story by different people as a result of the references they activate within the text as well as their knowledge at hand.

The linear text cannot be seen as a closed form in contrast to the hypertext, as neither of them is isolated from other texts. Importantly, regardless of whether the text is hypertext, the references available to the reader are not of the same relevance and intensity. Genette's (1997a, 1997b) concept of paratextuality suggests that text should be understood in a much broader sense than just the content between the opening and the closing line. Every text presents itself to the reader through paratextual features, which situate the text into a particular context. These could be the author's name, the blurb, the cover design or anything that frames the text. The paratext guides the reader on how to read and approach the text and co-creates the prejudice with which it is read. For their part, the readers are (un)consciously looking for those paratextual features to help them in the process of reading and to serve as a framework for the main text. Therefore, the reader is free (and not just in the encounter with the hypertext but equally with any text) but only within the space demarcated by the acknowledgement of particular paratextual features.

Texts form through a system of references, whether by clicking on links that appear on the screen of a media device or by activating previous knowledge, tradition and prejudice in the reader – the active process of choice making and evaluating those references is the same. It requires the reader to apply her own structure or categorization to the information, prioritizing certain aspects of the text over others to make meaning. It is the user who creates a culturally and contextually determined hierarchical relationship between particular textual parts, texts and sources – bringing her horizon into the process of use and interpretation and creating a final narrative and understanding.

Relationships between Users and Producers

Silverstone argues that the question of activity is not only 'whether an audience is active but whether that activity is significant' (1994: 153). The discourse of technological determinism that grants media technology the ability to make media users 'more' active and free of authors' domination sees the users' active contribution to media production and the hypertextual 'authorless' text as evidence for media users' empowerment in facing media producers. This applies to Web 2.0 in particular, which is often labelled as an environment where the roles of producers and consumers blend. One can argue that the Internet has been used by consumers for catching up on their own products, that the manufactured stories associated with media users and, in particular, fandom (Jenkins 2007) have become broadly accessible to other readers.

This view is refuted by de Certeau (1984), who sees the act of consumption in general as a different type of production. The distinction between the two is illustrated by a metaphor of belonging and by distinguishing between producers' strategies and consumers' tactics. Although the producers have their own 'land', the consumers always operate in a place that belongs to others. There is also an aspect of temporality in consumers' production that makes it distinct from that of producers. Therefore, the main distinction between producers and consumers is not the active production of meaning but the lack of land and resistance to the passing of time. When it comes to equality between the users and producers, the limits of place and space are still dependent on the 'land' owner. Media companies (content and/or service providers) not only set the rules but also determine how and which posts, videos or news feeds are promoted on the main page and who or what is given greater attention, exposure and recognition. The user–producer relationship is still unequal. And even though the ways that media are used by media users increasingly resemble the ways that media are used by producers, the distinction between the two remains and is recognized by users themselves.

Users' Engagement with the Subject of the Text

The key premise that the use of a particular medium is usually not isolated from the use of other media sources and rarely, if ever, isolated from other activities and social influences was examined further in an empirical study (Pavlíčková 2008) of cross-media consumption focusing on the access and use of mediated content circulated by the four main media channels. These were the press, radio, television and the Internet. The aim was to identify the patterns of media use of the particular respondents and thereby observe how media uses are linked to other practices and understanding in everyday life. The study employed qualitative research techniques, namely in-depth interviews and diaries, to analyse how various media are used as a source of news and mediated knowledge.

Interviews were carried out with 12 young adults with professional occupations from the Czech Republic and Great Britain. Participants were also asked to keep a media diary for a period of one week, to examine how the different horizons which people bring into the media use influence the role associated by the user with the particular medium across the entire media ensemble (Bausinger 1984). Each interview started with open questions that asked what media are used, when and for what purpose, before probing the interviewees' responses in greater depth. The coverage of topics in the interviews and the analysis that followed were guided by the interviewees' responses and their media diaries, rather than the prioritizing of particular media sources or content by the researcher. The study therefore explored how users' activity is expressed and the tactics that are employed by the users in their encounters with different media and contents.

Gadamer's account of interpretative understanding helped to comprehend the reader–text encounters as an active negotiation of meaning and to place the cross-media use within the broader context of the users' everyday lives, and 'routines', instead of focusing on isolated uses of the particular media or media content. The users' willingness to use, to critically evaluate, but also to produce – which is referred to here as 'engagement' – is closely bound to their expectations and knowledge at hand that were brought into the process of media use. The engagement with the subject areas of media content can be categorized using three categories of personal relationships to the content: *general knowledge*, *interest* and *passion*. This categorization does not intend to make distinctions between different types of information in the sense of their journalistic qualities or other formal features. This categorization describes users' relationships to particular information or media content.

The category of *general knowledge* covers content that is consumed simply because it is readily available. This does not imply that the consumption is passive. Rather, the content is not purposefully sought, and users make decisions about their consumption impulsively and spontaneously. The use of the content is satiated by the consumption itself. There is no perceived need to (re)search further or to evaluate the information against other sources. For example, the main Czech search engines and e-mail providers offer daily news (as well as gossip) from well-known and established Czech media institutions on their home pages. When users access their e-mail accounts, they often read the main news headlines as well. In the case of *general knowledge*, users mainly rely on known, trusted names (e.g. recognized media names and national news providers), and they rarely progress any further than those sources. The lack of familiarity with the particular subject area is therefore replaced by the familiarity with the source, while previous knowledge of the source helps media users to identify the relevance and reliability of the particular content.

Interest and *passion* are both associated with a greater degree of personal and emotional engagement. *Interest* is motivated by a need to solve something, looking for information that is determined by some pre-existing question, or a need to be prepared for a hypothetical situation in the future. This can also be initiated by the consumption of general knowledge, which provokes curiosity or hunger for more information, as well as by external non-media impulses, such as the requirement 'to solve' a problem. For instance, this category includes activity such as users' looking for recommendations about what coffee machine or Wii game to buy (problem solving) or a couple's search for information about in vitro fertilization when they are trying to conceive (preparing for a possible future scenario). No matter what the original reason for the user's search for information, interest in the subject disappears when the impulse to search ends too – when the 'right' answer or solution is found. The main aim of *interest* is to obtain information.

A search is performed to fulfil *passion*. This can be one's passion for film, literature, comics, music or for instance one's job, as in the case of this research. *Passion* is sought and used to broaden already existing knowledge. It is persistent and the search broadens with each new input of information. There is no 'right answer' that is sought, nor a final stop. All information is used and useful. The media users already have a certain expertise in the subject area at hand. They access new information and media content with the ability to be very critical and focused on details. The users are much more emotionally involved in the media use. The personal relationship to the specific subject of consumed content is independent of the presence or use of particular media outlets. This is also the category where media users are most likely to produce media content themselves. The term 'passion', as used here, overlaps with the notion of fandom (Gray, Sandvoss and Harrington 2007; Jenkins 1992).

The distinction based on users' engagement with the subject area is related not only to the use of media where content is consumed but also to the use where individuals are producing and distributing content. It needs to be stressed, however, that the engagement is not rigid but variable, changing over time in relation to the individual's continuous media consumption and the persistent presence of social and cultural contexts. The continual formation of passion or interest is a process of fusion of horizons where new impulses arrive, meet, change and develop the already existing and familiar knowledge. At the same time, new inspirations and novelties are evaluated against the already familiar ones.

The study showed that the way people use particular media content is determined by their pre-existing knowledge of the particular subject area, their familiarity with it and its relevance to the user within the media as well as the non-media environment. Media users are looking for familiar subject areas or paratextual features. This familiarity is the prior knowledge, the Gadamerian prejudice that people bring into the process of understanding. The less familiar that media users are with the subject area, the more they rely on the familiarity with the medium or media source and look for well-known names and brands. Similarly, with more profound prior knowledge of the particular subject, the willingness to consume new, unknown and unproven sources grows, as does the tendency to produce new content. Thus, the presence of familiarity (prior knowledge) is inevitable and inseparable from any reader–text encounter, but it also subsequently determines media users' understanding of the unknown.

Use of User-Produced Content

New technologies do not create a space for newly born activity and an impulse to produce content. Rather, users use media for expressing their existing opinions and to publish their pre-existing interests and passions. Are users' tactics of consumption the same when accessing known and unknown sources of content produced by other users? The study showed that the lack of one's familiarity with the source is replaced by social and cultural reputation, and hence recognition of the source. If that is missing, users will repetitively employ a hierarchy of their own values determined by their cultural and social context to recreate the recognition and reputation of the source which are otherwise lacking.

Authorship and prestige are values replicated from users' understanding of the content produced by the media industry. However, they retain their importance as values that users commonly search for or try to achieve themselves when producing as well as consuming user-generated media content. This can be well illustrated when one of the Czech respondents in the study talked about her use of the Czechoslovak film database (csfd.cz), a renowned website not only for Czech and Slovak films but also for all other films. It is the Czech equivalent of imdb.com (the Internet Movie Database). There, users can find film reviews, comments, information about actors, film-makers and other personalities related to the film and television industry. All texts in the database are written by users. The interesting characteristic of this website is that every reviewer has her own profile. Users can see other contributors' likes, dislikes and film ratings. However, to become a contributor, a user needs to pass a test of film knowledge, rate 500 films and answer general questions about films. Only then can the user also become a contributor to the website and be allowed to write reviews, bios, comments and create other types of content.

In this way, users themselves establish their own system of values and hierarchies that subsequently protect the 'prestige' of the source, creating particular interest groups and knowledge elites within the user base. This is also achieved by publishing a list of top reviewers on the home page, as users can give stars not only to films but to other reviewers as well. The website community reinforces the notion of familiar personalities and names by distinguishing those that are recognizable and connected with previous opinion and positive or negative recommendations within the community. The assumed anonymity of the contributors is replaced by a system of specific features that enable other users to classify the source, and even though the reviewers can only be identified by their nicknames and (anonymous) avatars, their identity is built via their continuously mapped contribution.

Conclusion

Recalling Gadamerian notions of tradition and prejudice is useful for comprehending that media users have been, and always will be, active in their media use and content reception by accessing and looking for media content through certain systems and hierarchies. These originate within users' particular social and cultural contexts as well as through prior knowledge of the subject area of the content. The medium is a tool used by users for expressing or realizing what has been shaped through other (non-)media uses and consumption. However, in the encounter with the particular content or medium, the users' knowledge, prejudices and horizons are shaped and reshaped. Familiarity with the medium, source or subject of the information is like Ariadne's thread, leading the user through the media landscape and media contents. Neither the users nor the media are 'winning' the battle for power. Both are entering the process of use within a certain context, with prior values and prejudices attributed to them, and therefore the negotiation is a never-ending process.

In debates about the digital media and their (hyper)texts, familiarity in this sense replaces the hierarchies through which the user could evaluate the relevance or reliability of texts in other media (Dreyfus 2001). Foucault (1980) writes of a hope that one day the agency behind the text that is always presented through paratextual features (Genette 1997b) will disappear. However, the reader or user still looks for the familiar characteristics and features that are presented in the text or medium to be guided through it and is always likely to do so. To agree with Cover (2006), the main actors in the power struggle over the meaning of the text have not changed. Author, producer, text, mediated content and audience all use and adapt old weapons in a new battlefield. The new media therefore do not substitute for the old, but the role of all media within the media ensemble is continuously socially and culturally renegotiated with the particular community or society, attributing new or shifted uses, roles and functions into different media.

References

Aarseth, E.J., 1994. Nonlinearity and literary theory. In G.P. Landow, ed., *Hyper/text/theory*. Baltimore, MD: Johns Hopkins University Press. pp. 51–86.

Ang, I., 1985. *Watching Dallas: Soap opera and the melodramatic imagination*. London: Methuen.

Bakardjieva, M., 2005. *Internet society: The Internet in everyday life*. London: Sage.

Bauer, R.A., 1964. The obstinate audience. *American Psychologist*, 19, pp. 319–328.

Bausinger, H., 1984. Media, technology and daily life. *Media, Culture & Society*, 6, pp. 343–351.

Berger, P. and Luckmann, T., 1971. *The social construction of reality*. New York: Penguin University Books.

Biocca, F.A., 1988. Opposing conceptions of the audience: The active and passive hemispheres of mass communication theory. In J.A. Anderson, ed., *Communication yearbook 11*. Newbury Park: Sage. pp. 51–80.

Boddy, W., 2004. *New media and popular imagination: Launching radio, television, and digital media in the United States.* Oxford: Oxford University Press.

Bolter, J.D. and Grusin, R.A., 1999. *Remediation: Understanding new media.* Cambridge, MA: MIT Press.

Carey, J.W., 1989. *Communication as culture: Essays on media and society.* Boston, MA: Unwin Hyman.

Cover, R., 2006. Audience inter/active: Interactive media, narrative control and reconceiving audience history. *New Media & Society,* 8, pp. 139–158.

de Certeau, M., 1984. *The practice of everyday life.* Berkeley, CA: University of California Press.

DeFleur, M.L. and Ball-Rokeach, S., 1989. *Theories of mass communication.* New York: Longman.

Dreyfus, H.L., 2001. *On the Internet.* London: Routledge.

Foucault, M., 1980. What is an author? In J.V. Harari, ed., *Textual strategies: Perspectives in post-structuralist criticism.* London: Methuen. pp. 141–160.

Gadamer, H.G., 2004. *Truth and method.* London: Continuum.

Genette, G.R., 1997a. *Palimpsests: Literature in the second degree.* Lincoln, NE: University of Nebraska Press.

—— 1997b. *Paratexts: Thresholds of interpretation.* Cambridge: Cambridge University Press.

Gillespie, M., 1995. *Television, ethnicity and cultural change.* London: Routledge.

Gitelman, L., 2006. *Always already new: Media, history and the data of culture.* Cambridge, MA: MIT.

Gray, J., Sandvoss, C. and Harrington, C.L., eds, 2007. *Fandom: Identities and communities in a mediated world.* New York: New York University Press.

Hall, S., 1973. Encoding/decoding. In M.G. Durham and D.M. Kellner, eds, 2001. *Media and cultural studies: Keyworks.* Oxford: Blackwell Publishing, pp. 166–176.

Iser, W., 1974. *The implied reader: Patterns of communication in prose fiction from Bunyan to Beckett.* Baltimore, MD: Johns Hopkins University Press.

—— 1978. *The act of reading: A theory of aesthetic response.* London: Routledge and Kegan Paul.

Jauss, H.R., 1982. *Toward an aesthetic of reception.* Brighton: Harvester.

Jenkins, H., 1992. *Textual poachers: Television fans and participatory culture.* London: Routledge.

—— 2007. The future of fandom. In J. Gray, C. Sandvoss and C.L. Harrington, eds, *Fandom: Identities and communities in a mediated world.* New York: New York University Press. pp. 357–364.

Jenkins, H., Li, X., Domb Krauskopf, A. and Green, J., 2009. If it doesn't spread, it's dead. *Confessions of an aca-fan: The official weblog of Henry Jenkins,* 11 February [blog]. Available at <http://www.henryjenkins.org/2009/02/if_it_doesnt_spread_its_dead_p.html> [Accessed 20 December 2010].

Katz, E. and Liebes, T., 1990. *The export of meaning: Cross-cultural readings of Dallas.* New York: Oxford University Press.

Kendall, L., 2002. *Hanging out in the virtual pub: Masculinities and relationships online.* Berkeley, CA: University of California Press.

Kristeva, R.J., 1980. *Desire in language: A semiotic approach to literature and art.* New York: Columbia University Press.

Landow, G.P., 2006. *Hypertext 3.0: Critical theory and new media in an era of globalization*. Baltimore, MD: Johns Hopkins University Press.

Marvin, C., 1988. *When old technologies were new: Thinking about electric communication in the late nineteenth century*. New York: Oxford University Press.

Miller, D. and Slater, D., 2000. *The Internet: An ethnographic approach*. Oxford, UK: Berg.

Morley, D., 1980a. *Nationwide audience: Structure and decoding*. London: British Film Institute.

—— 1980b. Texts, readers, subjects. In S. Hall, ed., *Culture, media, language*. London: Unwin Hyman. pp. 163–173.

—— 1986. *Family television: Cultural power and domestic leisure*. London: Comedia.

Pavlíčková, T., 2008. *Patterns of cross media consumption*. MRes dissertation, University of London.

Radway, J.A., 1984. *Reading the romance: Women, patriarchy, and popular literature*. Chapel Hill, NC: University of North Carolina Press.

Schütz, A., 1972. *The problem of social reality*. Hague: Nijhoff.

Silverstone, R., 1994. *Television and everyday life*. London: Routledge.

Warnke, G., 1987. *Gadamer: Hermeneutics, tradition and reason*. Cambridge: Polity.

Notes

1   First published in German in 1960, and in English in 1975. The third English edition from 2004 was used for the references in this chapter.

2   A white paper *If It Doesn't Spread, It's Dead* developed by the Convergence Culture Consortium was published by one of the co-authors, Henry Jenkins, and split into eight blog posts on his blog http://www.henryjenkins.org/ from 11th February to 27th February 2009.

3   Quoted from the first blog post of the series of eight blog posts entitled 'If It Doesn't Spread, It's Dead', published at the blog *Confessions of an Aca-Fan: The Official Weblog of Henry Jenkins*. Posted on 11 February 2009. Available at <http://www.henryjenkins.org/2009/02/if_it_doesnt_spread_its_dead_p.html> [Accessed 20 December 2010].

Chapter 3

Cultivated Performances: What Cultivation Analysis Says about Media, Binge Drinking and Gender

Andy Ruddock

Introduction: Alcohol, Advertising, Risk and Culture

In 2009, the World Health Organization (WHO) called for an international moratorium on alcohol advertising (WHO 2009). The organization maintained that advertising was a significant risk factor that contributed to unsafe levels of consumption, especially among the young, and that this was true irrespective of differences between drinking cultures. WHO's position is controversial for at least four reasons. First, advertising bans could make alcohol more accessible, should manufacturers seek new consumers by lowering prices (Cherrington, Chamberlain and Grixti 2006). Second, advertising may be a red herring because econometric analyses that compare total expenditure on advertising with total consumption within specific markets have not unambiguously corroborated its power (Ambler 1996; Broadbent 2008; Calfee and Scheraga 1994; Dorsett and Dickerson 2004; Duffy 1989, 1990; Nelson and Young 2001; Selvanathan 1989; Wilcox and Gangadharbatla 2006). Third, WHO's stance *appears* at odds with evidence that different audiences assign different meanings to media content according to the things that they already know. Fourth, calling for a ban seems anachronistic, given that so many of the images that associate drinking and fun today are made by young drinkers and are circulated through social networking. Whatever the merits of the first two objections, however, the belief that advertising bans have no place in media cultures where audiences actively interpret and make media content is mistaken.

This chapter explains why WHO's position is compatible with complex understandings of drinking cultures and the role of social media therein by using Gerbner's work on cultural indicators and cultivation analysis. Gerbner had a specific take on audience interpretation that helps explain how we can talk about media leverage without implying that young people are cultural dopes. This is especially important as successful advertising *counts* on active audiences. Because advertisers depend on audiences being creative with media content, anxieties about the influence of images that engagingly connect drinking and pleasure do not change when those images come from drinkers, even if those drinkers eschew the idea that the pictures they share are publicly significant. There is a gap between what social networkers say about the pictures they share and what those images come to mean once circulated. Gerbner's conviction that media content expresses the endemic values of message systems, and that quantitative content analysis leaves clues as to what these values are, helps explain why. Ultimately, this establishes a particular role for quantitative content analysis in exploring the changing role of media in drinking cultures, as a means of generating 'thick' descriptions that go beyond the *limitations* of audience interpretations as authoritative social accounts of media use.

Gerbner was a unique critical theorist who favoured quantitative content analysis and mass sample surveys. His ideas resonated with several positions in cultural studies (Ruddock, 2012), and intriguingly he used a qualitative reading of alcohol advertising in an early version of his signature point; that mass media fostered political inertia, and then channelled it into consumption:

> [Y]ou find that a large brewery advertises its beer by showing a man disgustedly throwing aside a newspaper full of European war horrors while the caption says that in times like these the only place to find peace, strength, and courage is at your own fireside drinking beer […] Why should people settle their social problems by action and sacrifice if they can serve the same ends by drinking a new brand of beer? […] From the aspect of more critical analysis, it becomes a dangerous sign of what a promotional culture might end up with. (Gerbner 1958: 100)

These early thoughts grounded the Cultural Indicators Project (Gerbner 1969) and Cultivation Analysis (Gerbner et al. 1980). By quantifying television content, then comparing viewing levels and political attitudes, Gerbner and his colleagues argued that repetitive images of similar people doing similar things affected audiences' perceptions of the world. Their first topic was media violence, which was approached in a fashion that was almost semiotic; media affected audiences by bombarding them with similar signifiers (lots of violent acts), uniformly arranged (mostly directed at women, the elderly and non-white characters, while white middle-class men were far more likely to escape unscathed or to use violence successfully). The more they saw these patterns, the more likely audiences were likely to feel endangered, and the more prone they were to want protection from others (Gerbner et al. 1980). Although he came to focus more on audience responses, as outlined in surveys, Gerbner's ideas were grounded in observations about the material aspects of media content; the power to control the supply and arrangement of signifiers was important because it set the terms of public debates and interpretations.

> I am concerned with the collective context within which, and in response to which, different individual and group selections and interpretations of messages take place. In that sense, a message (or message system) cultivates consciousness of the terms required for its meaningful perception. Whether I accept its 'meaning' or not, like it or not, or agree or disagree, is another problem. (Gerbner 1969: 139)

So interpretation did not matter *when the issue was how message systems set the parameters of public thought* (it *is* a scary world: what can be done?). French semiotician Roland Barthes, whose work became hugely influential in cultural studies, agreed. Barthes warned that the ability to decouple signifier (content) and signified (meaning) meant little set against the impossibility of escaping signification as a means of living.

> Any student can [...] denounce [...] such and such a form. The problem is not to reveal the (latent) meaning of an utterance [...] but to fissure the very representation of meaning. Languages are more or less thick; [...] the most social, the most mythical, present an unshakeable homogeneity. (Barthes 1977: 166–167)

Barthes insisted that the most social (widely used) languages were also the most 'mythical' (by which he meant ideological) and *homogenous*. Gerbner and Barthes focused on how media contained audience interpretation by controlling access to and sequencing of signifiers. Methodologically, this asserted the value of identifying denotative trends in the 'texts'. Gerbner was interested in how media encourage audiences to make reality through 'publication', and although he was writing about television, the ideas travel to social networking.

> The truly revolutionary significance of modern mass communication [...] is the ability to form historically new bases for collective thought and action quickly, continuously, and pervasively across previous boundaries of time, space, and culture. (Gerbner 1969: 140)

Media affected reality by making it easy for audiences to make it, to feel they were participating in something public.

Applying the Idea of 'Cultivation' to Drinking and Social Networking

Gerbner's conviction that social reality is, in many respects, something that media audiences *create* invites us to consider how his ideas might be applied to the content that young drinkers make and share through social media. Certainly, his message systems perspective affects how we understand the images that young drinkers make and share. Because young drinkers do not design social networks as 'public mechanisms', the significance of the images they share is, at least in part, determined elsewhere. And so these images become 'cultural indicators'. Facebook, for example, *is* part of the alcohol advertising conundrum because it *is* a valuable marketing tool for the drinks industry, especially among students, no matter what its users might say. Consider the UK Varsity Leisure Company's Carnage UK Fancy Dress Student Event. According to the company,

> The 'Carnage UK event is a social gathering by a cross social and racial network of students'. The object of the event is to bring together the broad cross section of students to encourage social engagement, understanding and friendship, which will assist the individual student to integrate within his/her new community.[1]

And according to one of its customers,

> Carnage UK is a [...] fancy dress bar crawl. [...] you buy a £10 t-shirt which gains you entry to bars and clubs around town. [...] After half an hour in each bar the students are moved on by the event stewards and this continues until the end venue.[2]

Carnage makes extensive use of the images that its customers voluntarily post on Facebook in its promotional arsenal. Its website links to customer-maintained pages, where students had uploaded over 9000 images by 2010. This outsourcing of marketing to consumers continues a UK tradition dating back to the nineteenth century. English brewers have long depended on social networks to prove that people drink because they want to (Reinarz 2007). The Carnage/Facebook pictures, so the story goes, are there because students like drinking when socializing, and always have. The question of whether either Carnage or its customers *mean* to exploit tradition is beside the point. Carnage shows that social networking *continues* a trend where drinking is glamorized by drinkers.

These images are not innocent pictures of people enjoying themselves, because UK advertising regulations make it clear that representing youth, alcohol and fun is always contentious. The Code of Advertising Practice (CAP) stipulates the following:

> Encouraging 'laddish' or 'laddette' behaviour is likely to be frowned upon [...] depicting conduct or actions that could be construed as drunken is likely to be unacceptable for encouraging excessive consumption and [...] condoning such behaviour might appeal to the young or daring. (CopyAdvice Alcohol, 2010)

Consider, then, the following picture. Two young women sit astride the back of a sofa, their legs draped over a man seated below. Both wear Carnage t-shirts bearing the moniker 'Dirty Porn Star', black knickers and hold-up stockings. One drinks directly from a bottle of champagne. Her colleague has 'bitch' written on her chest, and a man's mobile number scrawled in large red text over her thigh. If this was an ad, the image, in isolation, could violate CAP, depending on the inferences the viewer attached to it, or not; and that is the point. The inference depends on the viewer making the connections. As such, the image exemplifies the view that successful alcohol advertising avoids the letter of regulation by saying one thing and meaning another (Leiss, Kline and Jhally 1997). Faced with such systemic irony, it makes sense to ask how often young drinkers are given the chance to make such connections with images shared though social networking. These images are used to promote events organised by the alcohol industry, and they do speak a language that advertising regulation prohibits.

The picture is one of 64 portrayed on a Carnage page from Southampton, an English coastal town that is home to a large student population. In what follows, I use this small sample, taken from a particular page, that can be taken as a particular 'culture' with a particular story, to argue that quantitative methods enhance a 'thick' cultural understanding of why Carnage matters within the global trends that concern WHO. The case study shows how user-generated content (UGC) helps the drinks industry evade advertising regulations, by explaining why the denotative aspects of social media content are more important than any meanings advertisers may intend.

Gerbner's take on interpretation is especially relevant to the analysis of 'attractive' messages about drinking for two reasons. First, the idea that interpretation and audience action *is not* a defence against persuasion is pointed because successful alcohol advertising depends on audiences making inferences about the social benefits of drinking (Leiss, Kline and Jhally 1997). In the case study presented here, social networking is an extension of this 'inference' process. Second, Elms' (2009) analysis of how young people represent their bodies online notes that young women tend to present themselves stereotypically, even if, as individuals, this is not their intention. Images assume independent public lives, as they draw on unreflective literacies with unintended consequences. Ultimately, comparing critical insights on alcohol marketing with Gerbner's thoughts on media content, the role of interpretation in determining media power and the location of that power as a social and cultural force leads back to the importance of quantitative content analysis. This fills a particular gap in critical writing on drinking and gender, where qualitative researchers do feel there are several reasons to worry about the harm done by attractive media images of alcohol.

Media and Public Health

In the United Kingdom, health experts worry that 'the aggressive marketing of drinks towards young people' (Moriarty and Gilmore 2006: 94) exacerbates rising consumption and disease levels. Gilmore believes that young women are particularly vulnerable because they are encouraged to associate drinking with equality and independence (Gilmore 2008). Although Gilmore (2010) is principally concerned with price and availability, he thinks drinking has something to do with the production of gendered identities.

Historically, women have often taken centre stage when Britain imagines intoxication. From gin-soaked negligent mothers of the eighteenth century through to the 'flappers' of the 1920s to late twentieth-century 'ladettes' (Jackson and Tinckler 2007; Nicholls 2006), news drawings and photographs of drunken women have long conjured the tensions of social change. Even when women invest their own desires in public intoxication, they still suffer. McRobbie (2007) believes that media-induced gendered performances continue to frame women as sexualized second-class citizens. Consequently, any pleasure women get from them is less relevant than the forces that frame their choices. Drinking is an indicator of a general social contract that offers young women autonomy, as long as they conform to traditional positions of sexual subservience that the media still celebrate. The mediated visibility of 'phallic girls', who can drink and carouse just as wildly as young men, is nothing to cheer:

[Because it is] made available by the logic of the consumer culture, which [...] consolidates patriarchal privilege and masculine hegemony by apportioning some limited features of this privilege to young women, within specified conditions that they [...] are complicit with the norms of the new leisure culture where sexuality is redefined within the tabloid language of masculinist pleasures. (McRobbie 2007: 733)

McRobbie has come to criticize the focus on interpretation and resistance because

[t]he failure to interrogate the conditions upon which such an embracing of seeming female freedoms was predicated by media organizations meant that the relations of power underpinning and overseeing such a move remained worryingly invisible. (McRobbie 2008: 535)

That is, surveying the contemporary media representations of gender, McRobbie has come to agree with Gerbner's position that what matters most is how message systems encourage audiences and media users to make meanings that favour the interests of hegemonic institutions. With its methods for showing how media storytelling naturalizes gender inequality (by identifying repetitive features of media content), cultivation theory is a valuable triangulation device that explains the necessity of moving beyond users' accounts of mediated social experiences to further detail how drinking assumes particular meanings within historical traditions. Reading gender images as expressions of an industrial order that exists above anything meant by particular representations, or the interpretation of them, was a key argument put forward by cultivation analysis (Gerbner et al. 1980). Naturally, this argument has to be located within a critical understanding of audiences that explains why interpretation is not necessarily a buffer to the allure of alcohol messages. To understand this, we need to consider common elements crossing qualitative and quantitative studies on drinking and media influence.

Outlining a Critical Consensus on Media and Drinking

A critical view of how media affect drinking can be summarized as follows: media normalize drinking through many genres. The diversity and ubiquity of positive drinking messages mean that these messages have become a part of our material environment in all sorts of ways. Media effects are therefore conditional and pervasive. Positive drinks images are everywhere: soap operas (Pitt et al. 2005), sports (Horne and Whannel 2009; Zwarun and Farrar 2005), newspaper content (Rouner et al. 2009), films directed at underage teen audiences (Sargeant et al. 2006; Stern 2005) and even Disney movies (Ryan and Hoen'ner 2004). Advertising is part of a general trend where drinking is normalized through the colonization of popular culture, the appropriation of cultural traditions, the sponsoring of community events and even the regeneration of urban spaces (Jette et al. 2009; Measham and Brain 2005; Wenner and Jackson 2009). In Asia, social networking has been explicitly targeted as a means of breaking into new youth consumer markets (Blecken 2009). Young people find great pleasure in the language of alcohol advertising, even if they do not view drinking as something they want to do (Aitkin 1989). It is unsurprising, then, that young drinkers seem happy to make free advertising, as promotional language around alcohol is a recurrent feature of their cultural environment. Indeed, Cherrington, Chamberlain and Grixti (2006) argue that drinks marketing has always recruited drinkers by appropriating their traditions, then selling these same traditions back to the communities that own them through altered drinking practices. Carnage's monopolization of UK student drinking is a case in point.

Scholars agree that alcohol marketing 'works' because it works *with* audiences. Interpretation is the start, and not the end, of debates on how media images about alcohol successfully make drinking attractive. Although media literacy has been advanced as one way of dealing with the targeting of advertising at young drinkers (Austin 2006), others counter that literacy is no prophylactic to persuasion. Indeed, even proponents of this view note that 'resisting so many appealing messages has to require some effort, especially for those young people already at risk for drinking alcohol' (Austin and Hust 2005: 782). In doing so, they acknowledged the importance of accounting for *quantities* of media content.

The fact that audience interpretations vary does not imply that advertising has no general effects, especially when marketing adeptly addresses niche markets in a language that takes media literacy into account (Livingstone and Helsper 2006). 'Literacy inoculation' ignores the observation that advertising only works *because* audiences make inferences. Writing about Canadian alcohol advertising regulation, Leiss, Kline and Jhally (1997) argued that advertising rises or falls on the fantasies that audiences assemble from the sounds, images and implied associations that advertisements provide them. They wrote,

> [The problem of modern advertising policy] is that the ground upon which the issue of dishonesty first rested has shifted, from the matter of over-verbalized deceptions [...] to the implied claims [...] that a viewer is led to make as a result of the complex language and imagery used in advertising. (Leiss, Kline and Jhally 1997: 364)

Advertising regulation is a near-impossible effort to 'operationalize honesty' that endeavours to answer imponderables about what advertisers intend and what audiences think they mean. UK alcohol advertising regulation reflects this dilemma. The United Kingdom's Advertising Standards Authority (ASA) acts according to what they think audiences see, and sometimes this *helps* advertisers. Take, as an example, the adjudication on a magazine advertisement for Bishop's Finger Kentish Ale in October 2006.

> [The ad in question] featured an image of a woman in a low-cut mediaeval costume sitting provocatively on a bale of hay. Headline text stated 'I love a good session on the Bishop's Finger'. In the bottom right corner of the ad, text below an image of a bottle of Bishops Finger Kentish Ale stated 'At 5.4% it's near the knuckle'. (ASA 2006)

The decision on the 'offensiveness' at play here shows why polysemy favours industry. Shepherd Neame's defence rested on the audience's knowledge of popular culture. The company had focus group data showing that viewers 'compared the image of the woman in mediaeval costume to similar images in historical comedies such as Carry On films and Blackadder' (ASA, 2006, no page), acknowledging the innuendo as more intertextual nod than sexist slur. The ASA agreed, dismissing the complaint of sexism because the intended audience was likely to get the joke.

Social Networking and Drinking: Carnage on Facebook

A critical view of why alcohol marketing matters therefore needs to move beyond polysemy to understand social outcomes. One way to negotiate the intricacies over what media do is to change the emphasis. What sorts of debates does the content of social networking open about how drinking works as a social event? This rethinks the relationship between content, interpretation and outcome. Gerbner is important here because his early work on what media content *is* actually fits social networking well, even though it was written in the 1950s. Gerbner defined media content as a 'formally coded or representative social event' (1958: 86) whose effect *demanded* interpretation because what that content 'does' is to make 'possible inferences about states, relationships, processes not directly observed [...] The content of communication is the sum total of warranted inferences that can be made about relationships involved in the communication event' (Gerbner 1958: 86). The idea of the 'communication event' explains why the question of what young drinkers think when they take and distribute images of themselves having fun might be less important than the matter of how those images come to be and what they represent to other audiences. This, in the end, relates drinking to the social conditions that encourage drinking.

Gerbner allows us to think through the problems of qualitative analysis on how young women choose to represent their bodies on the Internet. In her study of Swedish teens, Elms (2009) maintains the importance of considering why users publish their images online, but her comments about stereotyping and risk concede that focusing on the user limits our ability to discuss these images as social phenomena. Elms notes, for example, that many young women use the language of pornography when representing themselves online. A full understanding of these images must, therefore, ask how this language becomes a public resource. One can only conclude that user accounts follow the understanding of ideology as 'necessarily partial, offering an incomplete and abstract picture of the world to the group that lives within the world as described by those ideas' (Bennett, Grossberg and Morris 2005: 176). The Southampton pictures have been selected because they make this case. They are significant because we know what some of the people in the images thought about how they and the event were represented in the media, but evidence from the site itself shows how these views only give a partial account of what the site came to mean as a public artefact.

One of the women featured in the photographs is an aspiring advertising and public relations executive who runs her own blog.[3] Here, 'Rosie T' criticized what she saw as media panics about Carnage events. The evenings are, in her view, professionally managed occasions that enable safe fun and let women enjoy the pleasures of dressing up in the company of other women. More importantly, the company had employed her to promote the event and had therefore provided the first step into her chosen career.

Evidence specific to the Southampton pictures suggests that 'Rosie T' failed to consider a number of pertinent issues connecting images with real economic and social conditions. McRobbie (2008) argues that women are visible as key drivers across a range of cultural practices through economic injunction, and this becomes clear when we compare the choices that western women make with those forced on others in the developing world, who must respond to neo-liberal demands with fewer resources. Bearing this in mind, the Southampton pictures are significant because in October 2009 the first four photographs the viewer saw were of women who were *not* Carnage customers, but who were struggling with different economic realities. On that date, the viewer was greeted by modelling shots of young women, who were purportedly seeking western husbands, from a Ukrainian 'dating' website. Whether the women really were Ukrainian, or knew their images were being used, is beside the point. Their presence made the site more than a souvenir of the fun a group of students had on a particular night out, locating it within the international flow of images of young women.

By 12th of October 2009, these images had been removed, but the fact that they were ever there says much about how UGC speaks a visual language that is prohibited by UK advertising regulations that prevent the articulation of drinking and sex. As a result, we must appreciate that these images are another example of how media content naturalizes gender inequality. Durham (2008) writes that young women are caught in the crossfire of media cultures that induce highly sexualized performances and then pillory women who respond in kind. This has real effects. Meyer's (2010) content analysis of British news on drinking and sexual assault shows a connection between the visibility of sexualized drinking performances and the legal argument that women shoulder the burden of responsibility for what fate befalls them should they drink excessively when scantily dressed. Carnage is quite clear on its policy to promote responsible drinking, but whether the practices that surround its online presence share their commitment is a different matter. The Southampton Facebook page boasts a crude gender division. Where male customers were simply encouraged to 'get ready for the BIGGEST night of uni', women were put to work, being told that the organizers 'wanna see how sexy you can make these t-shirts'.[4] The sexualized display of female flesh was part of the 'preferred' architecture of the event. To what extent, then, was this an injunction that scripted how Carnage-goers eventually displayed themselves?

This question can be answered by enumerating denotative aspects of the pictures. What is the visual evidence that the women in them are bound by the social contract McRobbie specifies, and does this mean that they do advertising work by making associations between drinking, sex and pleasure? The 64 pictures were coded to enumerate the number of women and men they depict and the numbers of images that (1) actually feature drinking, (2) show women in various forms of underwear, (3) make written references to sexual activity, (4) show simulated scenes of sexual activity and (5) show drinkers suffering some sort of harm.

Denotatively, perhaps the most important observation is the simple fact that it is women rather than men who are on show. The images are consistent with the understanding that the event was mostly about how sexy women look in Carnage t-shirts. Men are absent from 66 per cent of the images, whereas women feature in all but 11 per cent. Over half of those women (59) are in their underwear.[5] Almost one-third of the images (20) feature some written reference to sex, either on t-shirts of the graffiti that adorns the bodies (the former make reference to 'sexy schoolgirls' and 'dirty pornstars', while one women has 'I heart gash' daubed across her chest). Intriguingly, the denotative features of the images cumulatively absorb the 'responsible drinking' message, whatever suspicions they might raise about the amounts actually consumed on the night. Alcohol is invisible in 64 per cent of the pictures, and only two feature people who appear to be unambiguously drunk (a man is shown unconscious on the floor of what looks like a student flat, with his trousers around his knees; a young women falls to the ground, legs akimbo in the air). According to the numbers, then, these 'amateur' images speak the familiar professional language of alcohol advertising, where powerful links between sex and drinking are suggestively advanced without being explicitly stated (Hacker 1998).

Discussion

Interpretation of these images is evidently contentious, but the purpose of these simple empirical observations is to point out that, whatever their motives, the Southampton pictures were not *just* about the fun that a certain group of women decided to have on a given night. The co-presence of students with women on the international sex-trade circuit implicated UK student drinking traditions with global gender politics through media. The gendered alcohol discourses were naturalized because they appeared to be driven by tradition and the desire of media users. Privileging the interpretations of young drinkers limits an account of why these photographs mattered.

The point here is simply that public health research acknowledges that studies of media and gender matter, and that there is a compelling convergence between McRobbie's thoughts and Gerbner's work on cultural indicators and the cultivation of gender roles. McRobbie questions how young women like 'Rosie T' explain their drinking, on the grounds that these explanations fail to consider how such cultural practices reflect broader forms of economic oppression directed at women. Despite her role in championing the need to respect how young women understand popular culture, McRobbie has come to conclude that many do substantially *misunderstand* how their opinions on media content reflect ongoing forms of patriarchal hegemony. Certainly, advertising regulations are less troublesome when young people are happy to associate drinking with sex and fun free of charge. Such images often draw on the visual language of alcohol advertising, which is often a source of pleasure for young people (Aitken 1989; Meng-Jinn et al. 2005). In the United Kingdom at least, polysemy is a boon to advertisers when it comes to regulating content. The challenge to critical media scholars is in explaining the general trends in media influence that develop through audiences and users who are diverse in thought, action and reaction. In this regard, general patterns of signification say something about the industrial and historical structures of gendered media experiences. This is why Gerbner's work is important, as it defines the role of quantitative content analysis in describing the cultural significance of drinking images that young people circulate through social networks.

Close attention to the Southampton page contextualizes the Facebook site within the controversy surrounding Carnage as a symbol of binge culture and the perception that drinking represents a social dynamic that induces women to assert their independence through sexualized performances. The case for investigating patterns of 'cultural indication' across a wider sample of UGC becomes clear, as does the value of cultivation theory in conceiving binge drinking as a social phenomenon *involving* media representation. Using Gerbner's original thoughts on what media content represents, social networking appears as an *event* where a social analysis uses numbers to situate denotative media content in a global historical context, rather than the interpretations of the people who make them. This specifies the critical contribution that media studies makes to the controversy around WHO's call for an advertising ban. Against the charge that there is no evidence that advertising makes people drink, we can at least point to the reasons for expanding the field of effects to include a broader range of texts and practices that celebrate drinking in diverse ways, considering how UGC represents a *continuation* of marketing traditions and asking if effects are hard to see because they are self-inflicted.

References

Aitken, P., 1989. Television alcohol commercials and under-age drinking. *International Journal of Advertising*, 8(1), pp. 133–150.

Ambler, T., 1996. Can alcohol misuse be reduced by banning advertising? *International Journal of Advertising*, 15(2), pp. 167–174.

ASA, 2006. *ASA adjudication on Shepherd Neame Ltd* [e-book]. London: Advertising Standards Authority. Available through Advertising Standards Authority website: http://www.asa.org.uk/ASA-action/Adjudications/2006/10/Shepherd-Neame-Ltd/TF_ADJ_41865.aspx [Accessed 19 April 2011].

Austin, E., 2006. Why advertisers and researchers should focus on media literacy to respond to the effects of alcohol advertising on youth. *International Journal of Advertising*, 25(4), pp. 541–544.

Austin, E. and Hust, S., 2005. Targeting adolescents? The content and frequency of alcoholic and nonalcoholic beverage ads in magazine and video formats. *Journal of Health Communication*, 10(8), pp. 769–785.

Barthes, R., 1977. *Image, music, text*. New York: Noonday.

Bennett, T. Grossberg, L. and Morris, M., eds, 2005. *New keywords: A revised vocabulary of culture and society*. London: Wiley-Blackwell.

Blecken, D., 2009. Building a beer brand in the blogosphere. *Campaign Asia-Pacific* [online]. Available at: http://www.campaignasia.com/Article/211612,case-study-building-a-beer-brand-in-the-blogosphere.aspx [Accessed 27 April 2010].

Broadbent, T., 2008. Does advertising grow markets? *International Journal of Advertising*, 27(5), pp. 745–770.

Calfee, J. and Scheraga, C., 1994. The influence of advertising on alcohol consumption: A literature review and an econometric analysis of four European nations. *International Journal of Advertising*, 13(4), pp. 287–310.

Cherrington, J., Chamberlain, K. and Grixti, J., 2006. Relocating alcohol advertising research: Examining socially mediated relationships with alcohol. *Journal of Health Psychology*, 11(2), pp. 209–222.

CopyAdvice Alcohol, 2010. *Irreverent or laddish behaviour* [e-book]. London: CopyAdvice. Available through CopyAdvice website: http://copyadvice.co.uk/Ad-Advice/Advice-Online-Database/Alcohol-Irreverent-or-laddish-behaviour.aspx [Accessed 15 November 2010].

Dorsett, J. and Dickerson, S., 2004. Advertising and alcohol consumption in the UK. *International Journal of Advertising*, 23(2), pp. 149–171.

Duffy, M., 1989. The effect of advertising on the total consumption of alcoholic drinks in the United Kingdom: Some econometric estimates. *International Journal of Advertising*, 1(2), pp. 105–117.

—— 1990. Advertising and alcoholic drink demand in the UK: Some further Rotterdam model estimates. *International Journal of Advertising*, 9(3), pp. 247–257.

Durham, M., 2008. Girls' sexuality. *Journal of Children and Media*, 2(1), pp. 79–80.

Elms, M., 2009. Teenagers get undressed on the Internet. *Nordicom Review*, 30(2), pp. 87–103.

Gerbner, G., 1958. On content analysis and critical research in mass communication. *AV Communication Review*, 6(2), pp. 85–108.

—— 1969. Toward 'cultural indicators': The analysis of mass mediated public message. *AV Communication Review*, 17(2), pp. 137–148.

Gerbner, G., Gross, L., Morgan, M. and Signorelli, N., 1980. The mainstreaming of America: Violence profile #11. *Journal of Communication*, 30, pp. 10–29.

Gilmore, I.T., 2008. Not just a lifestyle disease. *British Medical Journal*, 336, pp. 952–953.

—— 2010. Alcohol misuse and its consequences – An overview and a European perspective. *European Review*, 18(1), pp. 47–56.

Hacker, G., 1998. Liquor advertisements on television: Just say no. *Journal of Public Policy & Marketing*, 17(1), pp. 139–142.

Horne, J. and Whannel, G., 2009. Beer sponsors football: What could go wrong? In L. Wenner and S. Jackson, eds, *Sport, beer & gender*. New York: Peter Lang. pp. 55–74.

Jackson, T. and Tinckler, P., 2007. Ladettes and modern girls: Troublesome young femininities. *The Sociological Review,* 55(2), pp. 251–272.

Jette, S., Sparks, R., Pinsky, I., Castaneda, L. and Haines, R., 2009. Youth, sports and the culture of beer drinking: Global alcohol sponsorship of sports and cultural events in Latin America. In L. Wenner and S. Jackson, eds, *Sport, beer & gender.* New York: Peter Lang. pp. 75–96.

Leiss, W., Kline, S. and Jhally, S., 1997. *Social communication in advertising.* 2nd ed. London: Routledge.

Livingstone, S. and Helsper, E., 2006. Does advertising literacy mediate the effects of advertising to children? *Journal of Communication,* 56, pp. 560–584.

McRobbie, A., 2007. Top girls? *Cultural Studies,* 21(4), pp. 718–737.

———— 2008. Young women and consumer culture. *Cultural Studies,* 22(5), pp. 531–550.

Measham, F. and Brain, K., 2005. 'Binge' drinking, British alcohol policy and the new culture of intoxication. *Crime Media and Culture,* 1, pp. 263–284.

Meng-Jinn, C., Grube, J., Bersamin, M., Waiters, E. and Keefe, D., 2005. Alcohol advertising: What makes it attractive to youth? *Journal of Health Communication,* 10(6), pp. 553–565.

Meyer, A., 2010. Too drunk to say no. *Feminist Media Studies,* 10(1), pp. 19–34.

Moriarty, K. and Gilmore, I., 2006. Licensing Britain's alcohol epidemic. *Journal of Epidemiological Community Health,* 60(2), p. 94.

Nelson, J. and Young, D., 2011. Do advertising bans work? An international comparison. *International Journal of Advertising,* 20(3), pp. 273–296.

Nicholls, J., 2006. Liberties and licences: Alcohol in liberal thought. *International Journal of Cultural Studies,* 9(2), pp. 131–151.

Pitt, G., Forrest, D., Hughes, K. and Bellis, M., 2005. *Young people's exposure to alcohol: The role of radio and television.* Centre for Public Health. Liverpool, UK: LJMU.

Reinarz, J., 2007. Promoting the pint: Ale and advertising in late Victorian and Edwardian England. *Social History of Alcohol Review,* 22(1), pp. 26–44.

Rouner, D., Slater, M., Long, M. and Stapel, L., 2009. The relationship between editorial and advertising content about tobacco and alcohol in United States newspapers: An exploratory study. *Journalism & Mass Communication Quarterly,* 86(1), pp. 103–118.

Ruddock, A. (2012). Cultivation analysis and ritual theory. In J. Shanahan, M. Morgan and N. Signorelli, eds, *The cultivation differential.* New York: Peter Lang. pp. 366–385.

Ryan, E. and Hoen'ner, K., 2004. Let your conscience be your guide: Smoking and drinking in Disney's animated classics. *Mass Communication & Society,* 7(3), pp. 261–278.

Sargeant, J., Wills, T., Stoolmiller, M., Gibson, J. and Gibbons, F., 2006. Alcohol use in motion pictures and its relation to early-onset teen drinking. *Journal of Studies on Alcohol,* 67(1), pp. 55–65.

Selvanathan, E., 1989. Advertising and alcohol demand in the UK: Further results. *International Journal of Advertising,* 8(2), pp. 181–188.

Stern, S., 2005. Messages from teens on the big screen: Smoking, drinking, and drug use in teen-centered films. *Journal of Health Communication,* 10(4), pp. 331–346.

Wenner, L. and Jackson, S., 2009. Sport, beer and gender in promotional culture: On the dynamics of the Holy Trinity. In L. Wenner and S. Jackson, eds, *Sport, beer & gender.* New York: Peter Lang. pp. 1–34.

Wilcox, G. and Gangadharbatla, H., 2006. What's changed? Does beer advertising affect consumption in the United States? *International Journal of Advertising*, 25(1), pp. 35–50.

World Health Organization (WHO), 2009. *Global strategy to reduce harmful use of alcohol.* Geneva: World Health Organization.

Zwarun, L. and Farrar, K., 2005. Doing what they say, saying what they mean: Self-regulatory compliance and depictions of drinking in alcohol commercials in televised sports. *Mass Communication & Society*, 8(4), pp. 347–371.

Notes

1   This quote is taken from a company response to allegations that Carnage UK encourages binge drinking. This can be found at http://image.guardian.co.uk/sys-files/Education/documents/2008/09/16/carnageresponse.pdf.

2   See http://rosietonline.blogspot.com/search?q=Carnage.

3   The Grad: The Life and Musings of an Ad Grad in London: http://rosietonline.blogspot.com/.

4   See http://www.facebook.com/group.php?gid=60356168738&ref=search&sid=511492903.3650201251.

5   Underwear was coded as visible bras, panties, stockings and garter belts.

Chapter 4

Motivations to Participate in an Online Violent Gaming Community:
Uses and Gratifications in an Ethnographic Approach

María T. Soto-Sanfiel

Introduction

The consumption of media violence, and its effect on aggressiveness, has not only generated interest but also many controversies. Parents, educators, audiovisual professionals and legislators ask whether the violence represented in the media produces negative effects on individual and social behaviour. Those who manifestly enjoy violent content are sometimes regarded with curiosity and distrust, in search of signals that confirm such hidden aggressiveness.

Researchers have sought certainties, but although a large number of studies present contradictory results, some studies have confirmed the public's suspicions. Most of the evidence (basically obtained under experimental laboratory conditions) reveals that, when there is individual disposition, a positive relationship emerges between the consumption of audiovisual violence and aggressive behaviour (Christensen and Wood 2007: 145–146).

The debate has also reached video games. It has been claimed that active participation in video games could produce effects similar to other violent media content. And even though the results are contradictory, again most of them confirm the effect of violent games on aggression (albeit lower than for television) (Sherry 2007).

Violent Gaming in a Virtual Community

Recently, there has been a proliferation on the Internet of interactive gaming communities, many of which involve violent games. However, researchers have paid scant attention to them (perhaps because of the difficulty of conducting systematic studies in live social environments or due to limited access to them). Hence, there is a need for research not only into the consequences of team-based violent gaming on individual gamer's attitudes and behaviours (with respect to the game, content, other gamers in the community and competitors) but also to identify the existing dynamics in these new forms of entertainment. Virtual communities are meeting places in cyberspace where exchanges are produced around a specific interest that symbolically frames and glues its members' activities together. Moreover, these communities encourage the formation of relationships because the participants make repeated contact with each other over more or less prolonged periods of time (Fernback and Thompson 1995; Porter 2004; Rheingold 1993). So, according to these assumptions, the violent game is not only the reason for union between the members of these virtual communities but also the factor that streamlines gaming activities and could influence real-world behaviour. Nevertheless, there is a lack of data to confirm these ideas.

Uses and Gratifications

How can we observe the effects produced by a violent game in one of these complex, multivariable and highly dynamic communicative realities where the game itself coexists alongside individual, interpersonal and group communication processes that are sometimes synchronic and difficult to reproduce in the laboratory? In a community there can be, for example, different types of activity that are simultaneous to the game and related to it (e.g. chats, participation in forums and exchange of files).

Communication research has the ideal theoretical perspective for dealing with such problems, the Uses-and-Gratifications (U&G) approach. The paradigm has supported numerous works designed to explain both the social and psychological needs to use media, and their effects and associated communicative practices (Jensen 2002). The variety of these works has given it the flexibility required to explore new communicative problems. Also, it conceptually defines certain suppositions on which a study of the effects on the members of virtual communities can be framed. Those theoretical assumptions are outlined next.

U&G approach seeks to explain what audiences do with the media (what functions it serves in their lives). Katz, Blumler and Gurevitch (1974) summarized their objectives as explaining how people use media, understanding the motives for media behaviour and defining the functions that explain audiences' needs, motives and behaviours. Researchers have found that uses, attitudes, behaviours and effects are associated with each other and have demonstrated how individuals, media and their messages interrelate.

The basic assumptions of the paradigm (Katz, Blumler and Gurevitch 1974) are still valid instruments for organizing observations of the relevant factors in the study of a virtual community. To begin with, U&G approach conceives audiences as active. It considers that the initiative in linking needs gratification and media choices during the communication process mainly lies in the audience member. It believes that media compete with other sources of needs satisfaction. A further assumption is that individuals can report their reasons for using the media. Finally, U&G approach assumes that audience orientations must be explored on their own terms before making value judgements about the cultural significance of the communication process.

A U&G approach is valid for a study of uses and effects of a violent game in a community because it supports the joint influence of social, psychological and structural factors. In fact, it proposes considering the influence of the social context in the definition of the communication problem (Dobos 1992) and postulates that both the individual and the social structure influence uses and effects (Rosengren and Windahl 1989). It also considers that individuals are able to reflect on the gratifications they seek (motivations), and those that they really obtain, from playing a violent game and actively participating in the community. Following the paradigm, then, the starting point could be that, in the increasingly more diverse communications world of the present day, forming part of a virtual violent entertainment community is a voluntary action, which is actively selected over other leisure options and that has psychological and social antecedents and consequences (on the intra-game or extra-game groups in which they participate).

A Proposal for the Study of Virtual (Violent) Gaming Communities from the U&G Perspective

The first U&G studies were basically descriptive and sought to classify audiences' responses into significant categories (for which, to some extent, qualitative methodologies were used (e.g. Berelson 1949; Lazarsfeld and Stanton 1942, 1944, 1949). It was only later that researchers started to conduct more theory-driven research. From this early period, we have inherited guidelines and also typologies that may still be valid today, at least as a starting point. For example, the study of the effects of violent gaming in virtual communities might assume that gamers' ultimate needs and motivations are limited to and represent those essentials that were sufficiently observed in earlier studies. As there are only few studies that identify categories for the motivations and/or gratifications of video games (Myers 1990; Raney, Smith and Baker 2006; Selnow 1984; Sherry et al. 2006; Wigand, Borstelmann and Boster 1985), the first phase of this research will be to verify that the motivations and/or gratifications of virtual violent gaming communities can be aligned with gratification typologies of other media use.

The Application of Ethnography

Nevertheless, simply applying the gratification typologies developed so far in U&G approach to video gaming prevents finding dimensions that are specific for gaming. In fact, exploratory research may attempt to open up new debates and propose new routes. One inspiring method, because it enables the identification of patterns that enrich observations, is ethnography. However, the application of this approach in association to U&G is unusual, although it is in line with the recommendations that Ruggiero (2000) formulated in his seminal article on the challenges of researching the paradigm in the twenty-first century: it adds information about the qualitative and interpersonal aspects of the recent realities of media communication.

An ethnographic approach to the study of the motivations, attitudes and behaviours of gamers belonging to an online violent gaming community gets us close to our subjects in a non-invasive way, thus minimizing circumspection or rejection. It avoids obtaining conditioned and/or artificial statements (such as those that might be obtained from questionnaire answers). It also sends us in a parallel direction to so many studies of this nature, which are supported by self-reporting and which reflect the tendency to consider the audience to be constantly aware of its behaviour: 'highly superrational', as Windahl (1981) would say. Ethnography enables us to deal with variabilities between ritualistic and instrumental participation and between rationalised and non-deliberate behaviour. Actually, the reports and testimonies supplied by the protagonists of a phenomenon are complemented (and compared) with the observations of context, which enables new explanations and relations to emerge.

By ethnography, we mean the set of qualitative methods that, admitting the influence of the context and the need to observe the actions within it, seeks to understand these actions through a rich description of the lives and values of the subjects (Morley and Silverstone 1991: 150). An ethnographic view supposes an understanding of violent gaming in a virtual community by observing the structures and dynamics (of the action itself) to understand the processes by which the game, and participation in a community that plays it, acquires meaning.

Technically, ethnographic researchers participate in their subjects' lives for prolonged periods, observing their culture, directly questioning the protagonists and generally gathering as much data as they can, with different methods, with the sole objective of finding clues that might explain the problem they are researching (Hammersley and Atkinson 1983: 2). The design of the techniques they use is derived from the case being studied (Morley and Silverstone 1991: 150).

Ethnography concentrates on describing the dynamics of the actions produced in particular contexts. It involves placating the immediate desire to reach definitive conclusions. In fact, the approach expects the knowledge to emerge when the descriptions have been exhausted and the data accumulated from particular cases really enable the definition of the general lines that explain the phenomenon being studied. So an ethnographic proposal can be considered the starting point for debate, as its aim is for future studies to cooperate in the validation of its observations in other contexts and also using other methods.

To summarize, the ethnographic approach implies acceptance of the researcher's subjectivity as an element of the process of obtaining and analysing the phenomena. In fact, qualitative scientists obtain inspiration from the different specific views that the study of a phenomenon can adopt. Being aware of researchers' motivations to study a phenomenon, they empathically seek to understand the nature of each contribution. Ethnography allows the voice of the phenomenon, and of the researchers, to be heard.

Observing a Specific Violent Gaming Community

To determine the effects of violent gaming on the members of a virtual community and, specifically, to break new ground in the identification of gamers' motivations and gratifications, both in relation to the violent game and to membership of these communities, an ethnographic intervention was conducted with the Compañía Easy (CE), a clan of Spanish *Call of Duty* (*CoD*) players. As mentioned, the initial research question, and therefore the basic motivation for the study, was to observe the consequences of the violence of the game on the members. In particular, the study explored the specific dynamics detected among the members of virtual violent gaming communities.

The intervention, which was longitudinal in nature, was conducted over three years (2008–2010), when data were obtained about life in the community, its history, its manifestations, its behaviours, its types of game and the gamers' individual perceptions with respect to the game and the community. The data basically cover six group sessions (four virtual and two face-to-face), each of which was attended by an average of five members. All of these meetings were chaired by a researcher, who used unstructured questionnaires containing open-ended questions. The virtual sessions were conducted through a chat programme that the clan members commonly used to communicate. Their answers were recorded, transcribed and qualitatively analysed. These data were complemented with participant observation by the researcher in the community's work and activities (e.g. website, chats, forums, videos), in particular, by attending the gaming and entertainment sessions as a spectator.

But aside from the above, information was also obtained from the community's extraordinary face-to-face meeting of 20 gamers. During this activity, the researcher also conducted unstructured interviews, asking open-ended questions of small groups (six gamers in each session). These were also recorded, transcribed and incorporated in the qualitative analysis.

Later, the researcher held individual interviews (one virtual and two face-to-face) with three different gamers to obtain information about specific aspects of the way the community works and to verify the correctness of the data obtained from previous sessions.

With the help of one gamer, a questionnaire was administered that contained open-ended questions to detect the motivations and gratifications in relation to the game and participation in the community.

The answers were treated qualitatively (organized into categories derived from existing research). This analysis confirmed that the motivations and gratifications declared by the gamers did ultimately fit with those already revealed by previous research in the field of U&G dedicated to other media and/or audiovisual products. Because of its tautological nature and for reasons of space, this part is not included in this chapter.

The CE community was created in 2003 and had an average of 25 members for half a decade and was runner-up in a European league (DL). Its membership remained stable until 2009, when it started descending, and by the end of the following year, had fallen by half. In 2008, when this research began, approximately a quarter of its members had a primary education, almost half had a secondary education and just over a quarter had a higher education. The average age was about 38 years (of a total range of between 22 and 42 years). There was only one female member. The gamers had a variety of different professions (e.g. students (secondary and university), a soldier, a policeman, a paramedic, a mechanic, a train driver, a software developer, a university lecturer and a slaughterhouse worker). Group members, to communicate during the game and in all forms of exchange between the community, used text messages and voice communication (with microphone and headphones), and the software TeamSpeak (TS).

CoD, the community's game, was a first-person shooter, published in 2003, that spawned a series of video games. It dealt with the experiences of soldiers and was set, with some exceptions, in real-life conflicts (e.g. World War II). The player took on the subjective perspective of a soldier in a virtual three-dimensional world and controlled everything through him. The game put the player in situations where antagonists had to be eliminated and was basically focused on killing enemies. CE was organized around the first version; it later switched to *Call of Duty 2* and, finally, *Call of Duty 4: Modern Warfare*. The latter, unlike the previous two, was not based on World War II, but on modern-day conflicts, although the game worked the same way. CE played different multiplayer modes with a variety of objectives (e.g. search and destroy, capture the flag).

The following section presents and comments on a selection of facts that the members of CE make to report both on their life in the community and the gaming experience when they meet as a group. Coherent with U&G, it has been considered that this set of expressions configures the clan's social context and therefore its symbolic ontology, and also that their testimonies suggest needs (shortcomings to be satisfied) as they work towards achieving ultimate individual targets (the experience of entertainment) through participation in the community. In fact, the testimonies (the gamers' reports) are treated as indicators of needs (some manifest and others latent) that motivate behaviour. Ethnography brings these hidden elements to light. Although there is a rich history of research into needs and motivations in psychology, an exploratory approach was employed directed by the phenomenon itself. The aim was for the qualities of the observed subjects to emerge.

The Manifest Reality of a Virtual Community

As opposed to what might be expected (given the cited literature and presumptions), an online violent gaming community is not necessarily a violent place where manifestly aggressive people meet or where aggressive behaviour is produced, but can actually be quite the opposite. CE is a meeting place in which, paradoxically, fighting, discipline, authority and competition have not (as the metaphor of the game they play might suggest) been the means by which the group has survived and been able to achieve its objectives. It members behave in an orderly and ethical manner because they have come to understand that peace and harmony are the means by which enjoyment in the game can be achieved and maintained.

The following section presents and analyses the circumstances that arise among the community's membership. As stated earlier, they are observed as indicators of (basically latent) needs within the community.

Need for Standards (for Order and Stability) and Harmony
CE has survived over time, which is unusual for such groups. We assume that this survival is the result of its members observing standards of behaviour that guarantee harmonious

coexistence. And not only do the members voluntarily choose to follow the rules for non-aggression and respect for others at meetings, but they are also keepers of the same. The regulations, and the penalties in case of violation, are public and available in the community's forum.

This shows that there is primary need for permanence, that the ultimate aim is to ensure that CE persists over time (to assure, conduct and promote entertainment). To satisfy this need, subsidiary social goals are generated: of organization, of order and of establishing clear standards of behaviour to ensure the efficacy of their activities. And, as a result of this, strategies are derived to establish their own atmosphere, to bring individual desires into line with the group's aims, for democracy or participation under equal conditions, and for defence-justice (to oversee the others). All of these form part of the general motivation to generate a political-administrative system for the group.

CE, as stated earlier, has defined an ideology formed around the principles of peace, cooperation, dialogue and respect. These principles go against the game's metaphor, which is based on the military, war, cunning and the imposition of force to achieve objectives. So the gamers need to keep the metaphor (fantasy) of the game down to reasonable limits, even if there were a primary tendency to extend it to reality. The members' behaviour suggests that the affective link between them regulates their behaviour. Affection is used as a regulatory guide for action, given that there is a need to foster emotional ties between the members to foster the permanence of the community and the entertainment.

The clan's survival, through voluntary submission to the standards (which were spontaneously generated upon formation), causes feelings of gratifying pride. Moreover, bragging about this, explicitly commenting on it and experiencing it as a collective achievement are pleasant ways of finding consensus. The members actually present the regulations to persuade others about the need to maintain them. By invoking the regulations, they are reinforced (through positive connotations) as the yardstick for judging fellow members. So the gamers have an individual need to influence others (and themselves) to satisfy their need for entertainment. To do this, they use the community's achievements as an argument. This attitude shows, on the one hand, the existence of hidden doubts regarding the total compliance by the other members and, on the other, the fear of the group, and the structure designed to maintain it, failing and CE disappearing.

Need for Narration and Histories

The meetings generate memories of past and shared events, which the members look back on nostalgically. But this behaviour is ritualized; it is a common feature of meetings. The events are narrated in the form of an interactively performed story (involving everybody's participation). The versions of the events between sessions are similar.

The above reveals both the need to (collectively) create narratives and for these to trace a shared history. The need to describe a past history, memories of which in the present produce positive feelings and influence the construction of the future, is indicated by the use of narrative for regulatory purposes.

In general, the narrations allude to pleasurable circumstances. The story involves a need for security and group identity. It is a collective creation that seeks mutual respect and explains personal motivations for power, affiliation, achievement and avoidance of situations that are also produced among the membership. The story follows the next pattern: the good guys (kind, community-oriented and friendly) together won over the bad guys (those who had become problematic, tyrannical and selfish) and have established a renewed harmonious environment. They will defend their creation from any opposition, based on the idea that fun is only possible to exist through peace and good manners.

However, apart from the above, the group's history features the inherent structural elements of narrative texts (e.g. Aristotle 2002; Propp 1968; Todorov 1969). For example, and following Propp (1968), a history like the one told here is adapted to a typical sequence of classic narrative motives (something alters a balanced situation; the hero appears to restore the balance; the hero faces difficulties; the hero completes the mission; the situation is re-established and the hero is rewarded). Also, Propp's typical characters are distinguished in the narration (e.g. villain, donor, dispatcher, hero and false hero): the excesses of the founder and leader of the clan (so-called dictator) in his behaviour caused discontent among the members, who promoted a 'rebellion' to the 'dictatorship'. After a definitive confrontation, he left. The members made profound changes to the clan. They decided to encourage friendship among its members, rather than competitiveness. As a result, they respect each other, leave in harmony and are all friends.

On the Community's Official Narrative

CE went through two crises related with the exercise of authority that led to two transformations in the social life of the members. Both these moments were called 'schisms' by the group. The use of this significant name alludes to ruptures that are the result of intense disagreements and are associated to institutional revolutions (it is a response to the need to make the community, and its activities, important). It also suggests a tense atmosphere surrounding the circumstances that led to the eventual changes (it evokes negative emotions associated to these events). Finally, it dramatically marks the key moments in the clan's history and offers a semantic field for member interpretation. The following section includes this history not only because it reveals the evolution of the community but also because it shows the notion of change and mutability that these groups experience. This notion, in turn, emphasizes the importance of longitudinal studies to explain these phenomena in a balanced way, as processes. The idea of process implies, on the one hand, considering the duration of the actions and, on the other, their objectives, causes, means and consequences.

The first organized activities were led by a figure known as the founder. The organization was necessarily created for the game (to act competitively and efficiently) and for the other activities. The first form of organization was militarily inspired, with ranks and hierarchies, following the game's metaphor. The structure worked until the leader's excesses in administering power caused discontent. The members of CE call this first period 'the dictatorship'. This stage ended when the leader left the clan he had created. The members that did not go with him implanted major reforms.

All of this shows an attempt to raise the metaphor of the game to real life, a need to extend the fantasy to aspects of the group's reality that was considered plausible as a prolongation of the game (and its enjoyable effects) until it was proven ineffective (when it violated the individual and collective conception not just of entertainment but also of appropriate inter-group behaviour). This, as a whole, confirms the need among the members of the group for vigilance, for healthy behaviour among the group to be monitored, for its effects to be regulated and, in general, to stay in contact with reality. It also shows a need to move away from negative feelings and affections (which, in turn, explains the group concept of entertainment associated to emotions and situations with positive values).

However, the above also suggests that in virtual violent gaming communities, the violence of the content can come to contaminate the attitudes and behaviours of certain individuals (that are predisposed to the same) and lead them to produce aggressive gestures, as sustained by most previous research of conventional media (Christensen and Wood 2007) and video games (Sherry 2007). But it should be added that these effects (bad behaviour), at least in the history of this community, are occasional and momentary. A negative emotional climate (of tension) associated to the use of force and authority is not desirable, even though it may be tolerated in sporadic situations as a way of achieving superior goals.

The 'rebellion' caused members to reconsider the community's real objectives, which led to a new organizational model and moral agreement. There was a need to learn lessons. The trauma led CE to decide to encourage friendship rather than competitiveness among its members. From being a community that sought to promote the game as entertainment, it became a space of social exchange for entertainment. It was understood that the game in itself was not enough to ensure fun; there was a need to foster links and organize structures. First, CE got rid of its military metaphors and was organized into 'departments', a form of distribution inspired by formal democratic structures. Tasks were voluntary and agreed upon by CE. Collectively, a need was generated for the members to cooperate, which incited an individual need to participate in the construction of the community (of entertainment). Responsibility was acquired on the basis of the members' skills and interests. This phase of expanding the clan and its activities was the longest (four years). Membership increased. Decision-making was done via 'assemblies' where everybody had speaking rights.

This organization proved to be efficient, and the social climate was stable. The game became secondary and what the members really valued were the interpersonal exchanges. In spite of that, new circumstances arose: not everybody liked the later versions of *CoD* (which shows a need for stability, for conservation and for resistance to change in the way that some people acquire entertainment). Others were bored with *CoD* (need for change, for variation, which contradicts the former need). Also, personal circumstances prevented some members from regularly visiting the meeting space (a need to adapt to new external conditions). Finally, it became difficult to attract new members due to the proliferation of other games (showing the need to incorporate elements to revive the sense of entertainment, given the internal deterioration). So CE promoted the change by adopting a massively multiplayer online role-playing game (MMORPG). The violent game was abandoned and was replaced, without major difficulties, with another of a different genre. The new game follows the market trend. There is, therefore, no collective need related to dependence on the game.

The new game, being cooperative, does not need leaders, but the leader of the second phase maintained his domineering attitude. After disagreements, he left CE, along with others. There was, therefore, another schism or purge (catharsis). This phase sought the reconstruction and re-balancing of the clan.

The previous situation also reveals the existence of group orientation behaviours (that subordinate the group's individual needs) and other individual needs (that reward individual needs over group needs), in the search for permanence (for entertainment). These behaviours would, in turn, be related to the acceptance of the community's process cycles and the role that each individual plays in them: a period of stability was followed by one of reorganization. Selfish behaviours, which reveal insufficient adaptation to change (a need to maintain power, authority and the role assumed over time), led members to refuse to participate in the construction of a new phase of entertainment (because that would imply accepting a position that some would consider diminished) and to the break-up of the community. Behaviours that seek to annul immediate needs for selfish satisfaction and that are adaptative (the hope that new entertainment situations will be generated) lead to the survival of the entertainment. In whatever case, although there were tense moments during this transition, none of these incidents are described as violent (rather as merely uncomfortable).

Today there are still 12 active members. Some play the new game and others only attend the social exchanges. CE maintains the organization and harmonic climate described earlier. Some members think the group is struggling because there are other arenas for free gaming. The game has definitively stopped being the reason for union; it has given way to interpersonal relations.

Need for Recognition, to Compete, Play and Lead

During the growth and expansion of the clan, there was a collective need to compete and win. Winning, and being good players, attracts competition and/or gamers, which means maintaining and improving the playing level; it guarantees survival. Winning also provides emotional experiences that are individually and collectively motivating.

The leader selects the first choice and substitute competitors based on the skills detected. Depending on the gamers' personalities and motivations, this can lead to conflicts. Among the gamers, the needs to be recognized and to be led converge. This is a field that requires further scholarly attention: the behaviour of the leaders and the led in these gaming groups, possibly to be scrutinized with theories of leadership, authority and persuasion (credibility).

In times of competition, gamers are selected as they are for a sports team and must train. The sporting metaphor is not only normative and regulatory of the internal conduct of the members of the clan but also generates cohesion among them and establishes memories of the creation, exchange and achievement of common targets. It also reappraises the gaming activities (making them a sport) and gives them a different referential framework in which they are reinterpreted. It also helps to understand one's own behaviour and justify it against others. There is hence a need to justify time spent on the game and to develop competitiveness in the play. Entertainments, in turn, are necessary for revealing qualities in the gamers and adjusting them to their playing positions.

Need for Face-to-Face Meetings, Intimacy and Closeness

Soon, a few members, from nearby geographic areas, felt the need to meet in person. Their virtual relations were not enough. The meeting showed that the links forged in CE could be extended to face-to-face encounters. It also generated the desire to increase personal contact outside of the game. From then on, CE started organizing group activities, all for fun, to take advantage of and promote their good social climate: the virtual was nourishing the face-to-face (and vice versa).

Prominent among the new activities are their 'gatherings', which reveal how the community is part of personal life. For four summers, the members shared a week's holiday; they travelled hundreds of miles (along with their families) to a campsite. The gamers felt the need to discover their true identities (for security and control). They did not play *CoD* at the gatherings. There was therefore a need for change, to share new leisure experiences. They also wanted to show their families that they were not dependent on *CoD*. However, what was especially noted was a need to increase social capital through the exchange of actions, resources and ideas by different means. The following are the three aspects that, according to Wellman et al. (2001), explain the construction of social capital converging at the gatherings: an increase in relations with family and friends, capital participation and a voluntary link with the organization, and commitment to the community (a strong attitude towards the community and a desire to mobilize social capital).

To conclude this report on some of the activities arranged by the members, and which imply violent play, and life in a community, it is observed that in CE there is a need to innovate and create. The members design other activities that allow them to share the enjoyment of leisure, overcome distance and challenge the virtual world. For example, they arrange joint film sessions (each member plays the film simultaneously) and watch and comment on it together using TS. They also create and show videos of members' best plays. They even sing Christmas carols together.

Discussion

This virtual violent gaming community was approached in search of the aggressive effects of media violence, but these were only encountered in few specific situations. Instead, a community was formed that aimed at maintaining the entertainment and pleasure through creative activities that are unrelated to the semantic sphere of the game (which was only the main original nexus of union); activities that explicitly sought to prevent aggressive and dominant behaviour. Its history also reveals the complex processes between the effects of the game and the gamers' own motivations and gratifications over time.

Meanwhile, the relationship between ethnography and U&G, in this study, is beneficial. The information provided by the descriptions shows how the individual reflections offered by the subjects are deliberate action strategies for interpreting the existing dynamics in violent gaming communities, which is coherent with a heterodox application of U&G. However, these descriptions, when inserted in the social context, analysed and observed over time, also allow latent, non-ritualized and non-deliberate qualities to emerge, which are not usually detected in spoken reports or in the typical data-collection designs and U&G techniques. They also enable progress in the determination of the weight of the context in individual belief. Ethnography applied to the study of motivations and gratifications hence leads to the emergence of hidden patterns and aspects for reappraising the analysis of effects.

References

Aristotle, 2002. *On poetics*. Translated by S. Bernadete and M. Davis. South Bend, IN: St. Augustine's Press.

Berelson, B., 1949. What 'missing the newspaper' means. In P. Lazarsfeld and F. Stanton, eds, *Communications research, 1948–1949*. New York: Harper & Brothers. pp. 111–128.

Christensen, P. and Wood, W., 2007. Effects of media violence on viewer's aggression in unconstrained social interaction: An updated meta-analysis. In R. Preiss, B. Gayle, N. Burrell, M. Allen and J. Bryant, eds, *Mass media effects research: Advances through meta-analysis*. Mahwah, NJ: Lawrence Erlbaum. pp. 145–168.

Dobos, J., 1992. Gratification models of satisfaction and choice of communication channels in organizations. *Communication Research*, 19, pp. 29–51.

Fernback, J. and Thompson, B., 1995. *Virtual communities: Abort, retry, failure?* [online]. Available at: http://www.rheingold.com/texts/techpolitix/VCcivil.html [Accessed 1 November 2010].

Hammersley, M. and Atkinson, P., 1983. *Ethnography: Principles in practice*. London: Tavistock.

Jensen, K.B., 2002. Media effects: Quantitative traditions. In K. Jensen, ed., *A handbook of media and communication research: Qualitative and quantitative methodologies*. London: Routledge. pp. 138–155.

Katz, E., Blumler, J.G. and Gurevitch, M., 1974. Uses and gratifications research. *The Public Opinion Quarterly*, 37(4), pp. 509–523.

Lazarsfeld, P. and Stanton, F., eds, 1942. *Radio research, 1941*. New York: Duell, Solan and Pearce.

——— 1944. *Radio research, 1942–3*. New York: Duell, Solan and Pearce.

——— 1949. *Communication research, 1948–9*. New York: Harper.

Morley, D. and Silverstone, R., 1991. Communication and context: Ethnographic perspectives on media audience. In K. Jensen and N. Jankowski, eds, *A handbook of qualitative methodologies for mass communication research*. London: Routledge. pp. 149–162.

Myers, D., 1990. Computer game genres. *Play & Culture*, 3, pp. 286–301.

Porter, C., 2004. A typology of virtual communities: A multi-disciplinary foundation for future research. *Journal of Computer-Mediated Communication* [online]. Available at: http://jcmc. indiana.edu/vol10/issue1/porter.html [Accessed 1 November 2010].

Propp, V., 1968. *Morphology of the folktale*. Austin, TX: University of Texas Press.

Raney, A., Smith, J. and Baker, K., 2006. Adolescents and the appeal of video games. In P. Vorderer and J. Bryant, eds, *Playing video games: Motives, responses, and consequences*. Mahwah, NJ: Lawrence Erlbaum. pp. 165–179.

Rheingold, H., 1993. *The virtual community: Homesteading on the electronic frontier*. New York: Addison-Wesley.

Rosengren, K. and Windahl, S., 1989. *Media matter: TV use in childhood and adolescence*. Norwood, NJ: Ablex.

Ruggiero, T., 2000. Uses and gratifications theory in the 21st century. *Mass Communication & Society*, 3(1), pp. 3–37.

Selnow, G.W., 1984. Playing videogames: The electronic friend. *Journal of Communication*, 34(2), pp. 148–156.

Sherry, J.L., 2007. Violent video games and aggression: Why can't we find effects? In R. Preiss, B. Gayle, N. Burrell, M. Allen and J. Bryant, eds, *Mass media effects research: Advances through meta-analysis*. Mahwah, NJ: Lawrence Erlbaum. pp. 245–262.

Sherry, L., Lucas, K., Greenberg, B. and Lachlan, K., 2006. Video game uses and gratifications as predictors of use and game preference. In P. Vorderer and J. Bryant, eds, *Playing video games: Motives, responses, and consequences*. Mahwah, NJ: Lawrence Erlbaum. pp. 213–224.

Todorov, T., 1969. Structural analysis of narrative. *Novel: A forum on fiction*, 3(1), pp. 70–76.

Wellman, B., Quan-Haase, A., Witte, J. and Hampton, K., 2001. Does the Internet increase, decrease, or supplement social capital? Social networks, participation, and community commitment. *American Behavioral Scientist*, 45(3), pp. 437–456.

Wigand, R., Borstelmann, S. and Boster, F., 1985. Electronic leisure: Video game usage and the communication climate of video arcades. In M.L. McLaughlin, eds, *Communication yearbook* 9. Beverly Hills, CA: Sage. pp. 275–293.

Windahl, S., 1981. Uses and gratifications at the crossroads. In G. Wilhoit, ed., *Mass communication review yearbook: Volume 2*. Beverly Hills, CA: Sage. pp. 174–185.

PART II

Media Use as Social and Cultural Practice

Chapter 5

Imagined Communities of Television Viewers: Reception Research on National and Ethnic Minority Audiences

Alexander Dhoest

Introduction

Television audiences are often described as 'imagined' or 'interpretive' communities, sharing interpretive frameworks and using television to form or confirm their group identities. Undeniably, as the prime mass medium, television always was and still primarily is a shared medium: shared within families but also shared across wide (often national) territories. Even today, most of the time television implies large groups of people watching the same programme at the same time. But how exactly should we conceive those communities? And how do the delineations of those communities change in the contemporary context of multichannel TV and multiethnic societies?

This chapter first discusses the notion of the imagined community, linking it in particular to national audiences. Then, the notion of ethnic (minority) audiences is discussed, drawing on research into diasporic media use and questioning the notion of homogeneous interpretive communities. Both of these theoretical strands are further developed in a methodological reflection on research into national and ethnic audiences, focusing in particular on reception analyses. As an illustration, reference will be made to original research drawing on in-depth interviews and focus groups with ethnic majority and minority audiences in Flanders, Belgium. This research will be used to reflect on the conceptualization of and underlying assumptions about viewing communities.

Imagined and Interpretive Communities of Viewers

Benedict Anderson (1991) probably gave the single most influential definition of nations as 'imagined communities', referring to the bond between people who do not know each other personally and to the constructed nature of the nation. Although Anderson focuses mostly on the roots of the modern western nation, which he links to the rise of print capitalism and standardized languages, his argument can be extended to modern mass media. Television, in particular, has often been described as a national medium, especially in Europe where public broadcasting was conceived as a national institution meant to contribute to unity within the nation state (Newcomb 1997). Apart from its national organization, television also provides programmes referring to and spreading national culture, 'making the nation one man' (Cardiff and Scannell 1987: 157). Media representations, images, narratives and discourses all contribute to the everyday construction of nations as imagined communities (Edensor 2002: 20–21; Hall 1992: 292–295).

The television audience, particularly in the early years, was conceived as 'the nation', one imagined community of viewers (Scannell 1996). Even when they are diffused in reality, audience members are deemed to be connected to each other while sharing viewing experiences (Abercrombie and Longhurst 1998: 114–117; Livingstone 2004: 51; Silverstone 1994: 21). Television viewing is described as a 'national ritual' (Morley and Robins 1989: 29), providing 'symbolic membership' of the nation, linking dispersed members to its centre and promoting a sense of communal identity (Morley 2004). However, there are some problems with this conception of the audience as a national imagined community. To start, like all conceptions of audiences it is a discursive and historical construct, aiming to limit and contain the complexity and variability of everyday interactions with television (Ang 1991, 1995). As such, it may lead to reification, essentialism and reductionism, assuming homogeneity rather than acknowledging the actual diversity of interactions with television. Indeed, like 'the nation', the 'national audience' is first and foremost a discursive construct. It may be (or have been) the broadcaster's intention to unify national audiences, but the actual nationalizing character of television viewing has hardly been documented in audience research.

Of course, industrial audience research is mostly effectuated at the national level. Ratings and market shares are generally collected within national television markets, often – particularly at the time of European public broadcasting monopolies – disclosing massive audiences for national programmes. This suggests that television provides shared experiences for large groups of viewers, the co-presence of other viewers creating a sense of community. However, this national framework is not as natural as it seems, for it is very much the product of the institutional organization of commercial audience research, which in turn reflects the (still predominant) national organization of television. Based on this research, we do know that people within national boundaries often watch the same programmes at the same time, but we have no idea whether they actually share an awareness of this national experience, nor do we know if television watching correlates with a sense of national identification. Smith and Phillips (2006) tried to empirically check the latter proposition, using a nationwide survey in Australia to research the links between media usage and national identity. They found that television use strengthened a sense of national identity, highbrow genres correlating with inclusive views of the nation and lowbrow genres with more exclusive views, but they have to admit that it is difficult to adequately research such culturally sensitive matters.

Academic audience research, too, often takes place within a national framework, but it seldom explicitly addresses the assumptions inherent in this modus operandi. As indicated by Ang (1991), academic research all too easily takes over the institutional, taxonomic view on audiences as abstract, decontextualized groups. Comparative research could help to achieve clearer insights into the actual national character of audiences, but such research is scarce, partly due to the great challenges it faces (Livingstone 2003). This being said, there is some evidence that audience tastes actually do differ across national contexts. For instance, one consistent finding concerns the preference of audiences for their own national channels and programmes. This is mostly linked to the notion of 'cultural proximity', which implies that viewers prefer productions that are culturally familiar, primarily national productions but also local or regional ones (Straubhaar 1991, 2007). This is particularly clear in the field of TV fiction, where American productions are liked by European audiences but generally less so than domestic productions (Silj 1988). As Buonanno states, 'people expect and are pleased to recognize themselves, their own social, individual and collective world, their customs and lifestyles, accents, faces, landscapes and everything else that they perceive as close and familiar' (Buonanno 2008: 96). Based on the analysis of schedules and audience ratings, Ksiazek and Webster (2008) found that language is the prime indicator of proximity, audiences mostly preferring programmes in their own language. However, they also found that bilingual groups have a 'multicultural fluency' which allows them to enjoy programmes in different languages, thus questioning the inherent idea of cultural polarization in cultural proximity theory. Instead, they point at the current reality of mixed and multilayered identities which makes for multiple levels of proximity.

Apart from its limited empirical support, this is another key criticism on the notion of national imagined communities of viewers: it does not take into account the current reality of complex identities in a multiethnic society. With globalization, alternative (ethnic and other) allegiances increasingly fragment the formerly homogeneous nation state, making for multiple levels of cultural identity (Hartley 2004; Sinclair 2004). The ensuing postmodern view of identity as a continuous process of identification more closely matches the current media-saturated society with different television channels and platforms as well as other media competing for attention. In this context, media – such as television – can be regarded as one among many sources providing materials used in the construction of identities (Barker 1999). Drawing on the insights of social psychology, we can conceive social identity as a repertoire of identifications, which are context dependent and therefore become salient in particular circumstances (Hogg and Vaughan 2002). However, as was the case for national imagined communities, this fragmentation of identities and the concomitant weakening of national viewing communities are not strongly supported by empirical research. Indeed, many point at the consistently national organization of the medium which remains embedded in everyday life in the nation and continues to create a sense of national 'co-presence' (Turner 2009; Waisbord 2004).

There is a growing awareness of the internal diversity of these national viewing communities, in particular in terms of ethnicity. As indicated by Morley (2004), the imagined community constructed by television implies a notion of ethnic 'normality' and is implicitly racialized, as it is (at least in the West) self-evidently white. Building on earlier research into issues of underrepresentation and stereotyping, research on ethnic minority audiences bloomed in the past decades. It discloses the (increasing) ethnic diversity of the supposedly homogenous nation state, pointing at alternative sources of cultural identification. This focus on ethnic identities and diversity seems to completely question former thinking on national imagined communities; however, there are some interesting continuities and similarities. To start, we should be careful not to completely dismiss the national framework in current globalized media and society, where we still witness a strong degree of 'banal', taken-for-granted nationalism (Billig 1995) as well as a retreat into ethnic nationalism (Ross and Playdon 2001). Second, the underlying dynamics of ethnic identification are very much related to (and often the foundation of) national identification. Both are based on the need for group cohesion and community formation, focusing on in-group similarities and out-group contrasts. In this way, both are social and discursive constructions, based on processes of boundary formation. Like national identity, ethnicity is subject to essentialist thinking and reification, as historical and changeable boundaries are fixed and hardened (Cottle 2000; Harindranath 2005; Ogan 2001). Therefore, we should avoid considering ethnic (e.g. 'black') communities as homogeneous (Ross 2001). Perhaps 'identification' is better suited to describe the processes involved than 'identity', for the latter always implies a sense of fixedness (Silva 2010).

Although they are seldom described as such, research often implicitly builds on a notion of ethnic groups as interpretive communities. Indeed, as we will further elaborate in the methodological discussion, empirical research on these issues generally seeks out media uses and readings which are specific to ethnic (minority) groups. As elaborated in reception theory, the notion of interpretive communities refers to groups with common purposes and practices in media use, members sharing common readings and ideologies, or 'interpretive repertoires' (Carragee 1990; Jensen 1993). Like the concepts discussed above, interpretive communities threaten to become reified and essentialized as they tend to be seen as stable entities determining media use. In this spirit, and commenting on his research where class was too strongly emphasized and isolated, Morley (1981) states that we should avoid seeing media use as 'determined' by ethnic (or any other social group) belonging, rather considering it as one among many factors in media uses and readings (Morley 2006: 107–109). Therefore, the imagined community is a useful concept to transcend micro-accounts of audience readings. As Schrøder indicates, we should look for a middle way and 'conceive of actual audiences in a somewhat more tangible and generalizing manner, without ending up with the sort of empiricist objectification that Ang sets out to combat' (Schrøder 1994: 341).

One term often used to describe the complexity of contemporary ethnicities is 'diasporic identities', conceptualized as networks of transnational identification, encompassing different imagined communities (Barker 2000). Such identities are conceived as contingent, changing and hybrid in their glocal mix of different cultures (Kraidy 1999). Another way to describe such contemporary forms of identity is to point at their intersectional nature, as they encompass different and intersecting sources or axes of identification which become salient in particular contexts (Brah 1996; Gillespie 2007; Lind 2004). This is confirmed, among others, by Müller and Hermes (2010), who did audience research on multicultural television drama and found that actual engagement with cultural identity, or what they call 'cultural citizenship', is contingent and only emerges in certain contexts. More concretely,

Fujioka (2005: 452) found that ethnic identity is particularly salient among African American audiences when they are assessing 'distasteful presentations of Blacks'.

Studying National and Ethnic Audiences

The second part of this chapter will provide a more ample overview of empirical research on national and ethnic television audiences, not aiming for completeness but rather focusing on some conceptual and methodological issues. Although some quantitative research is done in this field, I will focus here on qualitative research as this constitutes the majority of the published research. The methods most used in this field are in-depth individual or focus group interviews, sometimes supplemented with ethnographic participant observation. Although it is not the place here to review these methods in depth, in general terms they generate rich data about the micro-processes of television use and the meanings attached to it. However, one of the problems with these methods is that they often use small and unrepresentative samples, which leads to findings which are not very reliable or broadly generalizable. Although some, in this light, plead for a radical embrace of audience heterogeneity and against any form of generalization (e.g. Ang 1991), Schrøder states there is a need for patterns and categories to avoid ending up, as Morley puts it, in 'an endless realm of contextual specificity' (Morley as cited in Schrøder 1999: 47). Morley also warns against anecdotalism: 'we should not mistake the vividness of the examples it offers us for their general applicability' (Morley 2006: 106). For Höijer (2008), informants in qualitative research are often considered as representative of a particular social group, the researcher assuming some degree of homogeneity within a subculture. Although generalization is not explicitly the aim of this kind of research, there is some interest in prevalence within particular social strata: 'The focus is on collective or culturally established social phenomena, and often there is also an interest in studying differences between social cases, institutions and groups of people' (Höijer 2008: 283). Therefore, it is worth reflecting on this assumption, to avoid hasty generalization and to pay attention to the selection of informants.

There is not that much empirical research on national audiences conceived as imagined communities. Overall, the national framework is mostly taken for granted in academic audience research, as it is in commercial audience research. Most television audience research uses informants representing (a specific subgroup of) the national population but hardly ever reflects on the potential national specificity of responses (nor, it should be said, explicitly generalizing to the whole national population). Wimmer and Schiller (2002) call this tendency to naturalize the nation as a research framework 'methodological nationalism'. Drawing on Billig (1995), we could also call this a sort of 'banal nationalism', the national context always being present in a taken-for-granted and hardly noticeable way. Similarly, when 'the national' is explicitly addressed, it often turns out that viewers do not really have well-defined ideas about the issue. For instance, based on in-depth interviews, Moran (1998: 145–153) found that young German viewers did think that German soaps were 'German', but they could not quite pinpoint why or how, apart from the language used. They did not consider them as 'typically' German but just as 'German', which Moran attributes to the fact that these soaps deal with national elements that are unexceptional, taken for granted and therefore generally invisible for domestic audiences.

If the specificity of 'own' national programmes is generally hard to define as such, contrastive definitions come more easily. For instance, based on group interviews with students, Griffiths (1996) found that they strongly identified with one Welsh soap, which they considered to be realistic, positively comparing it to another, 'too American' soap. Bilitereyst (1991), comparing the reception of a Flemish and an American sitcom by Flemish viewers, equally found a stronger involvement in the domestic show, which was more referentially read and linked to the viewers' own world and identities. Just like the comparison of programmes from different origins more clearly brings out their 'national' character, comparing the reception of the same programme by different cultural groups brings out different national or ethnic readings. In the classic study by Liebes and Katz (1990), focus groups with people from different ethnic origins were used to assess the reception of *Dallas*, thereby disclosing different referential (linking the show to the real world) and critical (more distanced and analytical) readings in different groups. In this research, the informants were explicitly considered as members of a particular ethnic group. According to Harindranath (2005), the notion of ethnicity is defined monolithically here in an essentialist way, contradicting the variable and fluid nature of actual ethnic belonging. To him, such research is self-fulfilling: 'certain ethnic groups watch particular programmes and films that then contribute to the maintenance of a collective identity of those ethnic groups' (Harindranath 2005).

Gillespie (1995), in her ethnographic research on the television use of young Punjabi Londoners, uses a more dynamic definition of ethnicity, taking into account its changeable nature as well as the negotiation involved in 'dual identities'. She finds that her informants actively engage with television, in the process negotiating between different cultures. However, according to Harindranath (2005), there is also a problem of circularity, as the reading of certain texts is deemed to simultaneously be influenced by ethnicity and to construct a sense of ethnic identity. Also, he claims that the audience response is considered here as unified and singular, not taking into account their multiple positions in terms of gender, class, language, religion and so on. These, however, are all factors Gillespie herself acknowledges in her theoretical introduction (where she also warns against ethnic determinism) but which indeed do not get equal attention in the actual research report. This illustrates how hard it is to translate the current, nuanced visions on the complexity of cultural and social identities into empirical research, even in ethnographic research where individuals are analysed so closely. By focusing on one particular group or one particular aspect of identity, research tends to overemphasize its importance and isolate it from the complex intersection with other sources of identity.

A similar point is made by Tsagarousianou (2001), who also comments on the danger of reification and the reduction of complexity in studying 'ethnic communities'. She states that the identification of different ethnic communities is partly the product of the research process stressing ethnicity and the minority status of the researched: 'describing the responses of such "interpretive communities" artificially isolates individuals into categories that may have little reality in the flux and flow of social life' (Tsagarousianou 2001: 22). Reflecting on her own research using focus groups with South Asian and Greek Cypriot Londoners, she comments on the importance of generational differences within those groups. Such generational differences, often linked to varying language skills, are also found by many others (e.g. Elias and Lemish 2008; Ross 2001). Sreberny (2000) makes a similar point when reflecting on her research on Iranians in London, stating that we should avoid constructing a community in our research which does not exist in a coherent form outside of it. Like many others, she considers 'diaspora' to be the term most fit to destabilize assumptions about the national boundedness of ethnic experience, defining diasporic communities as follows:

> [They] are caught, or live, between at least two and often more places, their original homes of dispersal and their new homes of arrival, neither fully at home in nor totally detached from either and often creating a significant third space of globalized diasporic connections. (Sreberny 2000: 180)

This involves multiple identifications and complex interrelations between generation, gender, political differences, language as well as ethnicity.

In short, we should be aware of the simplification and threat of essentialism inherent in the use of ethnic labels. Nevertheless, it does make sense to focus on ethnicity in the analysis of media responses, for media turn out to be an important source of identifications and negotiations around ethnic and cultural identity. Soaps, in particular, are often studied as sources of representations used in the negotiation of hybrid cultural identities, particularly among younger viewers (e.g. Barker 1999: 119–130; de Bruin 2005; Strelitz 2002). At the same time, a lot of discontent is found among ethnic minority viewers, whose ethnic identification indeed (as mentioned above) comes to the fore when confronted with representations of ethnic minorities, both in non-fiction and in fiction on TV (e.g. de Leeuw 2005; Devroe, Driessens and Verstraeten 2010). But then again, although ethnicity does become salient in certain contexts, television preferences are often found to be generally similar among ethnic majority and minority viewers, particularly in the younger generation who share 'global' media products (e.g. Elias and Lemish 2008; Tufte 2001). In many ways, then, the distinction between ethnic groups is artificial as it focuses on differences rather than similarities between groups while ignoring other (e.g. gender, age or class) differences which are more important. Indeed, recent research increasingly points at the dismissal of ethnic labels by informants (e.g. d'Haenens, El Sghiar and Golaszewski 2010), which brings us back to the essentialism and determinism inherent in such labels.

Flemish Interpretive Communities

To illustrate these points, in the final part of this chapter, I will discuss my own research on the reception of television fiction by ethnic majority and minority viewers in Flanders, the Dutch-speaking northern part of Belgium, focusing on the issues raised above. In a first project, 80 'emerging adults' (18–25 years old; Arnett 2004) were interviewed, 40 ethnic majority and 40 ethnic minority members (see Dhoest 2009a). Semi-structured, in-depth interviews were used to ascertain a systematic coverage of particular issues. An equal division across gender (50/50 male/female) and education (50/50 higher/lower education) combined with diverse recruiting strategies helped to get a good mix of informants, so it seems justified to make (cautious) claims about the prevalence of the findings in the broader population. The aim of this research was to analyse whether domestic fiction was part of a shared Flemish culture. Did these young people identify with it? Did they use it to construct a sense of identity?

To start with the ethnic majority Flemish viewers, the preference for imported, American fiction is clear. Most respondents think it is better made and more entertaining, but they do think Flemish fiction is more 'recognisable' and 'realist', two key terms in the appreciation of domestic fiction. For instance, Inne comments on the domestic soap opera *Thuis*: 'I also quite like Flemish series like *Thuis* and the like because it's so realist, because most of that could really happen here. But if I do have to choose, it would be foreign series like *Friends* and the like.' Although they do not recognize themselves in Flemish fiction, let alone (admit to) identify with it, they do think it gives a good representation of everyday life in Flanders. Most informants consider Flemish fiction (in particular soaps) to be 'typically Flemish', but they have a hard time explaining why or how, linking it mostly to 'ordinariness'. In this way, they reinforce the above-mentioned notion of 'banal', everyday and unnoticeable (Flemish) nationalism, both in programmes and in audience responses (Dhoest 2009b).

The response of ethnic minority viewers (mostly of Moroccan descent) is quite similar. They also prefer American fiction and they neither watch nor like Flemish fiction very much, which confirms the point made above about the importance of age above ethnicity and the sharing of global culture among younger viewers. Their motivations are generally similar to those of the ethnic majority viewers: American fiction is better made and more entertaining; Flemish fiction (in particular soaps) has lower production values and tends to be boring. Still, they also think that Flemish soaps give a recognisable and realist portrayal of Flanders, perhaps even more so than the ethnic majority respondents. However, the ethnic minority viewers do not think Flemish fiction gives an accurate representation of their *own* world, as they feel they are under-represented and marginalized in Flemish fiction. One respondent's comment typifies this perception: 'No offence, but they're almost all Belgians acting in that and hardly ever a Moroccan or a Turk, while there are many of them in reality. That should be addressed more.'

Across both groups, there is a similar mechanism involved in judging domestic fiction: it is mostly read referentially, comparing it to one's own world. Ethnic majority viewers think such programming provides a recognizable portrayal of Flanders in general but not of themselves. Nor do they identify with the characters. Ethnic minority viewers also think Flemish fiction gives an accurate portrayal of Flanders but not of their own world. Although Flemish fiction makes an effort at representing ethnic minorities positively, these respondents are unhappy with the number and the unrepresentative nature of ethnic minority characters. Although overall their ethnic identity is not 'salient' in discussing television, it does come to the fore when discussing the representation of ethnicity. This illustrates not only the intersectional nature of identifications but also the predominance of minority identifications (Dhoest 2009a).

Looking back on this research, one point of criticism could be that, although it points out quite a few similarities across both groups, it does reinforce the binary distinction between ethnic groups in its methodological set-up. Also, it generalizes across ethnic minorities although only a few respondents are not of Moroccan origin. To remedy this, in a second, follow-up project a broader range of ethnic groups was included. In this research, we used focus groups with emerging adults (18- to 20-year-olds) to better grasp the social character of viewing and evaluating television and to tease out in-group similarities and differences (Dhoest and Simons 2009). We conducted 12 focus group interviews of five to six members with members of six different ethnic groups in Flanders (a total of 63 respondents). Most Flemish research on ethnic minority media use focuses on the largest groups, Moroccans and Turks, which are often grouped under the umbrella term *allochtonen* (allochthones, people born abroad). However, one important finding is that Turkish and Moroccan viewers differ quite radically on a number of accounts (e.g. Devroe, Driesen and Saeys 2005; d'Haenens et al. 2004). To widen the range, beside these two groups and ethnic majority Flemings, we also included Dutch people, black people of African descent and Jews, all important groups in the population of Antwerp where the research was effectuated. The aim was not to generalize to the broader groups but to explore similarities and differences both within and across these groups. To cover potential gender differences and to prevent possible uneasiness in mixed groups, homogeneous male and female groups were interviewed for each ethnic group. Clips were used in this follow-up research to provoke more spontaneous responses and to more closely approximate normal processes of television viewing than in traditional interviews. The clips were selected to include different kinds of portrayal of ethnic minorities, both in Flemish and in American fiction.

As in the first project, we found strong similarities across all groups in terms of the preferred channels and programmes, American fiction in particular constituting a clear *lingua franca*. When talking about television in general terms, ethnicity is not a salient issue, nor does it make for different patterns of television uses and preferences: entertainment is what the respondents look for. They all watch the same American shows on the same Flemish channels, apart from the Turks who tend to have more access to and also watch more 'own' (Turkish) TV.

Q: Why do you watch more Turkish television?
Elif: For instance because that's our own language.
Hadise: So we feel more at home.
Elif: You also recognize more, all the things that happen there. In Turkish series you see yourself more, as in 'oh yes that also happened with me'.

These findings illustrate the similarities between ethnic majority and minority groups as well as the diversity within the (supposedly homogeneous) ethnic minority community.

As in the first project, opinions start to diverge more clearly between ethnic majority and minority viewers when the representation of ethnicity is discussed. It is important to note that the research was not introduced as being *about* ethnic minorities. Although the clips were chosen to illustrate different portrayals of ethnic minorities in Flemish and American fiction, many respondents did not pick up on that. In the discussion after each clip, most groups did not spontaneously comment on this issue, which confirms the point made above: in general, ethnic identity is not that salient in watching television. Therefore, we should be careful not to frame our research too clearly in terms of ethnicity as this may lead to an overestimation of the discontentment among ethnic minority viewers, which is generally found in this kind of research.

Space limitations do not allow for detailed discussion of responses to the different video clips and ethnic minority representations (Dhoest and Simons 2009). However, as in the earlier project, opinions clearly diverge on this topic. The more complex set-up of this research discloses a wider and more complex variety of responses, illustrating the similarities and differences across and within ethnic groups. For instance, the responses in the Turkish focus groups differ more strongly from the Flemish ethnic majority ones, whereas the Moroccan and in particular Jewish groups are more similar. Overall, the ethnic minority groups are more sensitive to issues of stereotyping and negative portrayals, but their opinions are mixed, also within groups. For instance, there is disagreement in the group of Jewish boys:

Q: Do you think there are enough allochthonous people on TV here?
Beau: No, not enough, otherwise it wouldn't draw our attention when there is one in it. Many programmes try to remedy that, but because you're not used to it, it's quite difficult to change that.
Dino: Well, I think they get on TV often enough. A bit like in real life so it's realistic.

Clearly, being part of an ethnic minority does not make for one unified reading position or 'interpretive repertoire'. Although the overall evaluation is negative, as in earlier research, many respondents do not seem to be very worried about issues of representation. Even problematic representations are often not spontaneously criticized, as the respondents claim to focus on entertainment rather than representation when watching TV.

Conclusion

Returning to the core issue of this chapter, the existence and workings of national or ethnic imagined communities of viewers, it is clear that there is some distance between theory and empirical research. Although theoretically the notion of national and ethnic communities has been deconstructed and the intersectionality of identities has been disclosed, in actual research it is often hard to take all this complexity on board. Even ethnographic research, and certainly less micro-level accounts of reality based on individual or group interviews, tends to look for patterns, to set up narrative and explanatory frameworks and to use group labels and categories. Although this is problematic because of the simplifications and generalizations it implies, it is also necessary for a better understanding of audience behaviour.

As a whole, the kind of micro-research discussed in this chapter is an interesting complement to the overly abstract, theoretical macro-accounts of national and ethnic viewing communities and identities. It allows for a better understanding of the actual diversity in everyday interactions with television, with its complex interaction of different sources of identity. It also shows how our appraisals of reality are very much the product of academic discourse, sometimes overemphasizing unity (in the literature on imagined communities and interpretive communities) but also, I would claim, sometimes overemphasizing individuality (in the more recent literature on intersectional identities). Imagined or interpretive communities have never been as homogeneous as we are sometimes led to believe, but television viewers do belong to national and ethnic groups, and they do share significant characteristics with fellow group members.

References

Abercrombie, N. and Longhurst, B., 1998. *Audiences: A sociological theory of performance and imagination.* London: Sage.

Anderson, B., 1991. *Imagined communities: Reflections on the origin and spread of nationalism.* Revised. London: Verso.

Ang, I., 1991. *Desperately seeking the audience.* London: Routledge.

———— 1995. *Living room wars: Rethinking media audiences for a postmodern world.* London: Routledge.

Arnett, J., 2004. *Emerging adulthood: The winding road from late teens through the twenties.* Oxford: Oxford University Press.

Barker, C., 1999. *Television, globalization and cultural identities.* Buckingham: Open University Press.

———— 2000. *Cultural studies. Theory and practice.* London: Sage

Billig, M., 1995. *Banal nationalism.* London: Sage.

Biltereyst, D., 1991. Resisting American hegemony: A comparative analysis of the reception of domestic and US fiction. *European Journal of Communication,* 6, pp. 469–497.

Brah, A., 1996. *Cartographies of diaspora: Contesting identities.* London: Routledge.

Buonanno, M., 2008. *The age of television: Experiences and theories.* Bristol: Intellect.

Cardiff, D. and Scannell, P., 1987. Broadcasting and national unity. In J. Curran and A. Smith, eds, *Impacts and influences: Essays on media power in the twentieth century.* London: Methuen. pp. 156–173.

Carragee, K.M., 1990. Interpretive media study and interpretive social science. *Critical Studies in Mass Communication,* 7(2), pp. 81–96.

Cottle, S., 2000. Introduction: Media research and ethnic minorities: Mapping the field. In S. Cottle, ed., *Ethnic minorities and the media: Changing cultural boundaries.* Buckingham: Open University Press. pp. 1–30.

de Bruin, J., 2005. *Multicultureel drama: Populair Nederlands televisiedrama, jeugd en etniciteit.* Amsterdam: Otto Cramwinckel.

de Leeuw, S., 2005. Television fiction and cultural diversity: Strategies for cultural change. In L. Højberg and H. Søndergaard, eds, *European film and media culture.* Copenhagen: Museum Tusculanum Press. pp. 91–111.

Devroe, I., Driesen, D. and Saeys, F., 2005. *Beschikbaarheid en gebruik van traditionele en nieuwe media bij allochtone jongeren in Vlaanderen.* U.A. & L.U.C: Steunpunt Gelijkekansenbeleid.

Devroe, I., Driessens, O. and Verstraeten, H., 2010. Minority report: Ethnic minorities' diasporic news consumption and news reading. In S. Van Bauwel, E. Van Damme and H. Verstraeten, eds, *Diverse mediawerelden: Hedendaagse reflecties gebaseerd op het onderzoek van Frieda Saeys.* Gent: Academia Press. pp. 233–249.

d'Haenens, L., El Sghiar, H. and Golaszewski, S., 2010. Media en etnisch-cultureleminderheden in de Lage Landen: Trends in 15 jaar onderzoek. In S. Van Bauwel, E. Van Damme and H. Verstraeten, eds, *Diverse mediawerelden: Hedendaagse reflecties gebaseerd op het onderzoek van Frieda Saeys.* Gent: Academia Press. pp. 210–232.

d'Haenens, L., van Summeren, C., Saeys, F. and Koeman, J., 2004. *Integratie of identiteit? Mediamenu's van Turkse en Marokkaanse jongeren.* Amsterdam: Boom.

Dhoest, A., 2009a. Establishing a multi-ethnic imagined community? Ethnic minority audiences watching Flemish soaps. *European Journal of Communication,* 24(3), pp. 305–323.

——— 2009b. Do we really use soaps to construct our identities? Everyday nationalism in TV fiction: The audience's view. In E. Castelló, A. Dhoest and H. O'Donnell, eds, *The nation on screen. Discourses of the national on global television.* Cambridge: Cambridge Scholars Publishing. pp. 79–96.

Dhoest, A. and Simons, N., 2009. One nation, one audience? Ethnic diversity on and in front of Flemish TV. *Quotidian: Dutch Journal for the Study of Everyday Life* [online]. Available at: http://www.quotidian.nl/vol01/nr01/a04, 2009. [Accessed 14 June 2011].

Edensor, T., 2002. *National identity, popular culture and everyday life.* Oxford: Berg.

Elias, N. and Lemish, D., 2008. Media uses in immigrant families: Torn between 'inward' and 'outward' paths of integration. *International Communication Gazette,* 70(1), pp. 21–40.

Fujioka, Y., 2005. Black images as a perceived threat to African American ethnic identity: Coping responses, perceived public perception, and attitudes towards affirmative action. *Journal of Broadcasting and Electronic Media,* 49(4), pp. 450–467.

Gillespie, M., 1995. *Television, ethnicity and cultural change.* London: Routledge.

———— 2007. Security, media and multicultural citizenship: A collaborative ethnography. *European Journal of Cultural Studies*, 10(3), pp. 275–293.

Griffiths, A., 1996. National and cultural identity in a Welsh-language soap opera. In R. Allen, ed., *To be continued … Soap operas around the world.* London: Routledge. pp. 81–97.

Hall, S., 1992. The question of cultural identity. In S. Hall, D. Held and T. McGrew, eds, *Modernity and its futures.* Cambridge: Polity Press & Open University. pp. 273–325.

Harindranath, R., 2005. Ethnicity and cultural difference: Some thematic and political issues in global audience research. *Particip@tions* [online]. Available at: http://www.participations.org/volume%202/issue%202/2_02_harindranath.htm [Accessed 14 June 2011].

Hartley, J., 2004. Television, nation, and indigenous media. *Television & New Media*, 5(1), pp. 7–25.

Hogg, M.A. and Vaughan, G.M., 2002. *Social psychology.* 3rd ed. Harlow, UK: Pearson Education Limited.

Höijer, B., 2008. Ontological assumptions and generalizations in qualitative (audience) research. *European Journal of Communication*, 23(3), pp. 275–294.

Jensen, K.B., 1993. Media audiences. Reception analysis: Mass communication as the social production of meaning. In K.B. Jensen and N.W. Jankowski, eds, *A handbook of qualitative methodologies for mass communication research.* London: Routledge. pp. 135–148.

Kraidy, M.M., 1999. The global, the local, and the hybrid: A native ethnography of glocalization. *Critical Studies in Mass Communication*, 16, pp. 456–476.

Ksiazek, T. and Webster, J., 2008. Cultural proximity and audience behavior: The role of language in patterns of polarization and multicultural fluency. *Journal of Broadcasting and Electronic Media*, 52(3), pp. 485–503.

Liebes, T. and Katz, E., 1990. *The export of meaning. Cross-cultural readings of Dalla.* New York: Oxford University Press.

Lind, R.A., 2004. Laying a foundation for studying race, gender, and the media. In R.A. Lind, ed., *Race/gender/media: Considering diversity across audiences, content, and producers.* Boston: Pearson Education. pp. 1–10.

Livingstone, S., 2003. On the challenges of cross-national comparative media research. *European Journal of Communication*, 18(4), pp. 477–500.

———— 2004. Television and the active audience. In N. Carpentier, C. Pauwels and O. van Oost, eds, *Het on(be)grijpbare publiek: Een communicatiewetenschappelijke verkenning van het publiek.* Brussel: VUB Press. pp. 49–66.

Moran, A., 1998. *Copycat TV. Globalisation, program formats and cultural identity.* Luton, UK: University of Luton Press.

Morley, D., 1981. 'The nationwide audience' – A critical postscript. *Screen Education*, 39, pp. 3–14.

———— 2004. Broadcasting and the construction of the national family. In R.C. Allen and A. Hill, eds, *The television studies reader.* London: Routledge. pp. 418–441.

———— 2006. Unanswered questions in audience research. *The Communication Review*, 9(2), pp. 101–121.

Morley, D. and Robins, K., 1989. Spaces of identity: Communication technologies and the reconfiguration of Europe. *Screen*, 30(4), pp. 10–31.

Müller, F. and Hermes, J., 2010. The performance of cultural citizenship: Audiences and the politics of multicultural television drama. *Critical Studies in Media Communication*, 27(2), pp. 193–208.

Newcomb, H., 1997. National identity/national industry: Television in the new media contexts. In G. Bechelloni and M. Buonanno, eds, *Television fiction and identities: America, Europe, nation*. Napoli, Italy: Ipermedium. pp. 3–19.

Ogan, C., 2001. *Communication and identity in the diaspora. Turkish migrants in Amsterdam and their use of media*. Lanham, MD: Lexington Books.

Ross, K., 2001. White media, black audience: Diversity and dissonance on British television. In K. Ross and P. Playdon, eds, *Black marks: Minority ethnic audiences and media*. Aldershot, UK: Ashgate. pp. 3–14.

Ross, K. and Playdon, P., eds, 2001. *Black marks: Minority ethnic audiences and media*. Aldershot, UK: Ashgate.

Scannell, P., 1996. Britain: Public service broadcasting, from national culture to multiculturalism. In M. Raboy, ed., *Public broadcasting for the 21st century*. Luton, UK: University of Luton Press. pp. 23–41.

Schrøder, K.C., 1994. Audience semiotics, interpretive communities and the 'ethnographic turn' in media research. *Media, Culture & Society*, 16, pp. 337–347.

——— 1999. The best of both worlds? Media audience research between rival paradigms. In P. Alasuutari, ed., *Rethinking the media audience: The new agenda*. London: Sage. pp. 38–68.

Silj, A., 1988. *East of Dallas. The European challenge to American television*. London: BFI.

Silva, K., 2010. Brown: From identity to identification. *Cultural Studies*, 24(2), pp. 167–182.

Silverstone, R., 1994. *Television and everyday life*. London: Routledge.

Sinclair, J., 2004. Globalization, supranational institutions, and media. In J. Downing, ed., *The Sage handbook of media studies*. Thousand Oaks: Sage. pp. 65–82.

Smith, P. and Phillips, T., 2006. Collective belonging and mass media consumption: Unraveling how technological medium and cultural genre shape the national imaginings of Australians. *The Sociological Review*, 43(4), pp. 818–846.

Sreberny, A., 2000. Media and diasporic consciousness: An exploration among Iranians in London. In S. Cottle, ed., *Ethnic minorities and the media: Changing cultural boundaries*. Buckingham, UK: Open University Press. pp. 179–196.

Straubhaar, J.D., 1991. Beyond media imperialism: Asymmetrical interdependence and cultural proximity. *Critical Studies in Mass Communication*, 8, pp. 39–59.

——— 2007. *World television: From global to local*. Thousand Oaks, CA: Sage.

Strelitz, L.N., 2002. Media consumption and identity formation: The case of the 'homeland' viewers. *Media, Culture & Society*, 24, pp. 459–480.

Tsagarousianou, R., 2001. Ethnic minority media audiences, community and identity: The case of London's South Asian and Greek-Cypriot communities. In K. Ross and P. Playdon, eds, *Black marks: Minority ethnic audiences and media*. Aldershot, UK: Ashgate. pp. 17–32.

Tufte, T., 2001. Minority youth, media uses and identity struggle: The role of the media in the production of locality. In K. Ross and P. Playdon, eds, *Black marks: Minority ethnic audiences and media*. Aldershot, UK: Ashgate. pp. 33–48.

Turner, G., 2009. Television and the nation: Does this matter any more? In G. Turner and J. Tay, eds, *Television studies after TV. Understanding television in the post-broadcast era*. London: Routledge. pp. 54–64.

Waisbord, S., 2004. Media and the reinvention of the nation. In J. Downing, ed., *The Sage handbook of media studies*. Thousand Oaks, CA: Sage. pp. 375–392.

Wimmer, A. and Schiller, N.G., 2002. Methodological nationalism and beyond: Nation-state building, migration and the social sciences. *Global Networks*, 2(4), pp. 301–334.

Chapter 6

Exploring Media Ethnography: Pop Songs, Text Messages and Lessons in a British School

Caroline Dover

Introduction

Imagine the scene: an English lesson in a large secondary school in London. The students are mostly attending to classwork but also chatting among themselves. Habibah and Nadia (not their real names) do not normally sit near each other as they are not friends, but the teacher has put them together and instructed Nadia to keep Habibah 'on task' in a small group poetry exercise. As Habibah takes a seat next to Nadia, the following greeting is exchanged:

> **N:** I'm so hyper, I'm so bored!
> **H:** This lesson is shit!

This conversation opener establishes a degree of camaraderie although Nadia proceeds to do some work while Habibah does not. At the same time, talk between the girls turns to boyfriends and to Habibah's sister getting into trouble with her parents. Continuing to complain about her sister, Habibah says,

> **H:** She's so rude to me you know. She knows my [social network] password, I'm gonna have to change my password. Bitch. She changed my screen name and everything!
> **N:** I know.
> **Girl:** Why don't you just change your password?
> **H:** Yeah, I'm gonna do that today. I can't be bothered.
> **N:** I can't change my password […] But I don't care cos no one is going to find out my password […] hopefully.
> **H:** I hacked into [X's] account. I deleted all his contacts and made his life hell.
> **N:** Why?
> **H:** Cos I don't like his friends.
> **N:** […] You know his password?
> **H:** His secret answer, I guessed it.
> **N:** Oh.
> **H:** And what was it? His surname. Stupid! … How dumb!

Then about half a minute later, Nadia initiates a new discussion:

N: [Looking at her mobile phone] If this bastard doesn't text me back, I'm going to hurt him, I swear to god! [laughs]. He must think he's smart, you know!
H: I don't even have a phone, fuckin' 'ell.
N: How come?
H: I'm not allowed.
N: Why?
H: [Sigh] I'm too young. [In mock parental voice] 'I'm not responsible!'
Girl: How does your boyfriend contact you?
H: Oh. Online, innit. Chat to him online and when my dad's not home 'Quickly! Phone my home!' And […] but they know what times not to phone.
Girl: Boys weren't allowed to phone my home, but now they are […] Some of my friends can phone my house phone […].
H: But it has to depend on what they're calling about, yeah?

This interactional episode represents just 3 minutes from approximately 180 hours of audio data recorded periodically during 2 years of ethnographic research in the school. It illustrates how talk about online activities is discussed almost simultaneously with talk about other kinds of media use and also other non-media, offline activities. And highlighted in this particular excerpt are the importance and insecurity of online representations of identity, the power of transgressions in social media etiquette, the significance of social media in negotiating relationships and the negotiation of parental control and access. Across the recordings, references facilitated a variety of processes: friendships, relationships with teachers, involvement in and disaffection from curricular activities and performance of taste. Indeed, in its potential to both heighten the sociability of some young people and also denigrate the peer status of others, popular/media culture (PMC) was significant in the ongoing negotiations of local power relations between pupils.

Such an exploration of media use (or, more broadly, media culture) is not primarily focused on the texts consumed, or the moment of encounter with texts or technology (although the latter does have relevance). Instead, the emphasis is placed on the use of popular culture references and media technology in facilitating talk and social relationships and the negotiation of peer status. This kind of 'identities-in-interaction' research reflects 'a shift in interest from category bound research with a demographic basis, to practice-based research' (Georgakopoulou 2008). Of value here is the conception of identity as contingent that has for a long time been incorporated in symbolic-interactionist social anthropology – notably the work of Anthony P. Cohen (1985) – and more recently in studies of young people and media (Buckingham 2008), sociology (Back 1996; Lawler 2008), youth culture studies (Laughey 2006) and sociolinguistics (Rampton 2005; Zimmerman 1998) to cite just a few examples. From such a perspective, identity invokes perceived boundaries of similarity and difference between individuals and (imagined) communities, and 'identity is constituted through interaction with friends' (Livingstone 2009: 117). The shift away from a concern with media texts as well as the interest in social processes suggested here also relate my approach to a growing field of studies that looks beyond audiences towards an understanding of everyday media experience (Bird 2003, 2010) and media-related practices (Hobart 2010). In the following sections, the theoretical framework shaping this research will be explored before considering the appropriate research methods and, finally, illustrating the aims and potential insights offered by such an approach, using the school-based research as a case study.

From Media Texts to Social Practices

Over the past 30 years important research has been undertaken within media and cultural studies into the processes of media consumption and everyday life (examples are numerous but include Gillespie 1995; Livingstone 2002; Mackay 1997; Moores 2000; Morley 1992, 2000; Radway 1984; Silverstone 1994). These studies have been crucial for the development of audience studies and our understanding of the complex ways in which media products have significance within our lives. Critics of such approaches have (unjustly, I would argue) feared the lack of politics in everyday life studies and derided their findings as simply telling us that people do the ironing whilst watching the television. But to fully evaluate the breadth of understanding such studies have offered, it is necessary to examine more closely what actual processes have been investigated by empirical media research. It is not the mundane and everyday emphasis of such studies that limit their reach (for such is the fabric of life) but their specificity. Although many audience studies continue to offer insights into the context of and motivations for media reception and use, a useful supplementary approach is to adopt a 'wide-angle lens' (Spitulnik 2010) to examine a broader range of social practices. The urge is not to replace but '*add to* [my emphasis] existing strands of media theory' (Postill 2010: 2).

In the past, the focus of research into the role of media in everyday life has overwhelmingly been on the interaction between the text/medium and the consumer, or the text/medium and a group of consumers located in the same reception space such as the household (Algan 2003). This emphasis within audience studies on people's encounters with media objects is hardly surprising. It has framed the site of research (a great advantage in conducting empirical work) and has allowed theorists to claim conceptual space within the social sciences – space that is explicitly and tangibly media related, rather than space already occupied by sociologists, anthropologists and others (Dover 2007). The persistent separation of production, text and consumption as areas to study makes sense in terms of the pragmatics of research but implies a linear relationship between the three. As Peterson points out 'audience studies, although shifting attention from texts to the processes and situations of their interpretation, have nonetheless tended to reproduce this paradigm by putting the text and its interpretation at the centre of meaning making' (2005: 136). This emphasis on issues of interpretation has been reflected in and compounded by the methods of asking people about texts. With the rise of information and communication technologies, media academics have become increasingly interested in media hardware as objects of study, as opposed to media content (Livingstone 2002: 9). Although such attention to the materiality of media consumption and the 'double articulation' of media (Silverstone 1994: 286) is a useful extension of audience studies, the rarefying of media technologies as textual objects is consistent with the dominant paradigm cited above.

Meanwhile, there has been a growing interest in 'media' within anthropology but relatively little crossover between the two disciplines. 'Media anthropologists have regarded media practices not as objects of study in their own right but rather as conduits through which to reach other research objects' (Postill 2010: 4). Those of us located within media studies can learn from media anthropology (as urged by Bird 2010; Couldry 2010). A more holistic look at media consumption and re-production in everyday life would be 'an ethnographic approach that prioritizes the audience in its unique geographical, cultural and social environment, rather than the media text or genre' (Algan 2003: 25). In other words, the impetus becomes to conduct media consumption ethnographies, rather than ethnographic reception studies. A distinction is that the former 'take as their analytical point of departure a particular group of people, not a particular type of medium' (Drotner 2000: 172), and the (potentially messy) focus is on 'the kaleidoscope of daily life' (Radway 1988: 366). Through a broader engagement with everyday life beyond moments of reception, this 'third generation of studies' (Bird 2003: 4) will analyse other ways in which media are embedded in and reconstituted through everyday life and some of the consequences of living in a media world.[1] Such an approach engages with media as a cultural frame (Bird 2003: 3). Within this cultural frame, or 'circuits of media culture' (Osgerby 2004: 6), media texts do, of course, remain significant (not least as resources) but are not necessarily the pivotal concern of the researcher.

Ethnography

Widely (though not always appropriately) used in audience studies, the term 'ethnography' has become rather ambiguous within this field. It sometimes signals little more than the use of observational methods or in-depth interviews but ought to be undertaken as more than a set of methods. Ethnography is a methodology that stands out from others in its appreciation of everyday living, its empathy with others and the commitment to lengthy research. Conducted well, it is able to explore the minutiae of everyday life and, at the same time, engage with the broader social issues cross-cutting different people's experiences.

Within anthropology, a 'crisis of representation' gained ground in the 1980s with the publication of a number of critiques (cf. Clifford and Marcus 1986; Geertz 1988). The ways in which anthropologists assert their objective authority in written ethnographies were central to the criticisms and, consequently, ethnographers have been encouraged to be more reflexive about the (postcolonial) power relations implicit in the research and writing process. It is ironic that just as anthropologists were in the midst of a heated debate as to the efficacy of ethnography, it was increasingly claimed as a means of research within media and cultural studies – particularly within audience studies. As Morley points out, 'the boom in ethnographic media audience research in the 1980s was, in part, the result of the critique of overly structuralist approaches, which had taken patterns of media consumption to be the always-ready-determined effect of some more fundamental structure' (1997: 126).

The 'field' within which we have conducted our enquiry is a physically bounded site (i.e. a school) and, inevitably, our focus is on the activities in that location. But, as far as possible, the project does try to incorporate (or, at the very least, acknowledge) the cross-cutting influence of other areas of our subjects' lives: family, community, the media industry and so forth. This is facilitated by the employment of a variety of research methods (discussed later in the chapter) and by focusing on the interrelationship of identities with media consumption. The tastes, preferences and uses of consumption found among the research participants will reflect the individual's cultural and financial capital and also his/ her location in a north London school.[2]

Media consumption ethnography does then involve the seemingly impossible task of multi-level analysis. It will never be feasible – or necessarily even desirable – to encompass all macro-industry factors (such as the range of media products available to our informants at any one time). However, the ethnographic task becomes more manageable if it is accepted that the political and the structural are manifested in and recreated through everyday social processes and interactions. Laughey's argument about engagement with music applies equally to other areas of PMC:

Learning how to consume and produce [music] on an everyday basis, for example, occurs in localized contexts such as schools and homes, and is articulated through personal narratives either about the self or significant others in which – even if global media appear to dominate the agenda about what is available – co-present influences ultimately shape literacies and tastes. (Laughey 2006: 111)

There are many ways of investigating 'circuits of media culture' (Osgerby 2004: 6). Our own emphasis on interpersonal interaction developed out of the involvement of sociolinguists in the project and our shared interest in the locally learnt literacies and tastes, referenced by Laughey. These foci are compatible with the identities-in-interaction perspective outlined in the introduction.

Social Interaction and Media Intertextuality

Broadcasting and other areas of media and popular culture offer significant resources for everyday social interaction and act as markers of taste and identity (Moores 2000). Implicated are the negotiation and/or confirmation of identities and, by extension, power relations between people within particular local settings. The processes involved can occur at any time, not just during moments of interactions with media texts and technology. So, how can we capture them?

A possible starting point is to employ ethnographic methods to reveal and investigate moments of social interaction framed by media culture, such as those described briefly at the beginning of this chapter (Dover 2007). As Couldry points out, one concrete question that can be asked about media culture is, 'what types of things do people say in relation to media?' (2010: 41). As a topic of conversation, media may be incidental but as an integral part of our lives, '[new] media appear in the stories we tell each other about what happened during our day' (Baym 2010: 22). Moreover, as Peterson argues,

> Media intertextuality, the interweaving of bits and pieces of dialogue, actions, or other symbols from mass media texts into everyday speech and action [...] has much to teach us about how people attend to media texts and how media enter into the practices of everyday life. (2005: 130)

Although intertextuality has been widely studied by media scholars as a characteristic of texts, much less attention has been given to its place as an interaction strategy. In attempting to investigate the efficacy of media resources for confirming or renegotiating a person's status within different settings, our research project draws on sociolinguistic studies concerned with the performance and negotiation of identities through interaction (cf. Goffman 1959; Zimmerman 1998). The performer requires the knowledge of appropriate media culture references and how and when to use them. This knowledge is used strategically even if habitually and unreflexively. Equally, the audience requires the cultural knowledge to interpret these references (although meanings may not always be shared by speaker and listener).

Intertextual moments can offer a significant point of entry for investigating media consumption and identity, but it is necessary to reach beyond such fleeting moments and connect them to a broader profile of the subjects' engagement with media culture. This is achievable partly through the use of interviews and surveys but also through the collation of moments of media performance over a period of time. Here, the employment of ethnographic methods is key, for not only is the researcher engaged in interpretive analysis, attempting to understand other people's meanings (Geertz 1975), but is also seeking to understand a topic through the analysis of patterns of everyday processes. To further explore the kind of research suggested here, I will present some of the aims and methods of a school-based project and then provide a brief description of some of the findings.

Media-Related Practices in a British Secondary School

The thoroughly multidisciplinary nature of the project is relatively unusual, but we were all interested in employing ethnographic methods to explore issues of identity negotiation and performance among British urban teenagers. Building on an earlier, similar study

(Rampton, Harris and Dover 2002), and also some team members' interest in educational issues, we located our study in a school. Given that they tend to be the locus for most young people's relationships in the United Kingdom, schools also offer a valuable opportunity for exploration of their peer interaction.

Research Methods

The fieldwork for our research was a large community secondary school in London that draws its students from the local area. Over 2 years the researcher made more than 100 visits and was able to get to know the environment and our key participants, and in turn, she became very familiar to them. Furthermore, her field-notes, along with other written and recorded materials, enabled a mediated ethnographic understanding of the field by the other research team members. Although this school cannot be taken to represent all London schools, the ethnographic detail possible from focusing longitudinal research on one location offers insights into everyday practices in context. As part of the project, we also presented our findings to a group of 39 teachers from schools across London and gained feedback as to how familiar or not different scenarios were.

Two tutor groups were chosen for the research. In Phase 1 of our study, the year 9 class members were 13 to 14 years old. In Phase 2, we then followed their progression from year 9 to year 10 (when they were 14 to 15 years old). After spending some time getting to know the classes, the research officer identified nine students who could offer interesting insights as key research participants. The reasons variously included his/her gender, ethnic and religious background, language, academic ability, newness to the school and peer position (size and range of friendship groups and so forth). With the additional permission of their parents, all nine students agreed to be audio-recorded (and some of them video-recorded) for the research.

As argued in the previous section, it is productive to think about media consumption as in articulation with other areas of everyday life. One means of exploring it is through opportunistic ethnography (Bird 2003), which focuses on moments of interaction where consumption is referenced. To enable audio-recordings of such spontaneous activities, our nine focal students wore radio microphones on different days. The researcher listening through headphones was able to discreetly stay within range and was not in close proximity to the informant unless invited by the student himself or herself. If the informants wanted to conceal something, they were free to switch off the microphone. In practice this rarely happened, not least because the confidentiality of all material recorded was assured. The recordings (over 180 hours in total) and observations gave us access to the ways that different kinds of PMC practices and resources are interwoven in everyday social interaction in school and provide insight into unofficial backstage talk (Goffman 1981) not normally captured in research in schools or among young people more generally.

Working closely in conjunction with the radio microphone recordings are playback interviews where the informants listened to and commented on extracts from the radio microphone recordings of themselves. The sessions increased understanding 'of the participants' sense-making devices and local theories' (Dover 2007: 14) and also allowed the research participants to have greater involvement in the project. In contrast, the semi-formal interviews separately conducted with informants provide data about issues that informants do not routinely talk about in everyday activity, some contextual information about, for example, their lives outside school and 'accounts of a reflexive nature [involving] normative expectations, moral judgements and self- and other- ascriptions' (Dover 2007: 14). Interviews with some members of staff were also conducted and, in combination with school documents, offered insights into the official discourses within the school. The combination of all these methods enabled a wide range of material to be gathered and usefully highlighted 'conflicts' in the findings. Indeed, as Hobart argues, 'this disjuncture between how people understand or represent themselves (for example during interview) as against how their practices appear to the outside analyst, is arguably the *raison d'être* of anthropology' (2010: 67).

The School

The school has approximately 1000 students drawn from the densely populated and ethnically diverse neighbourhood. Although the number of students from middle-class families has increased in the lower years of the school, there were still a large proportion of children eligible for free school meals (an indication of the number of students from low-income families). The disciplinary ethos of the school emphasized openness, negotiation, adult responsibilities and resolutions. Mobile phones were not officially allowed in school, but everyone worked to the understanding that many of the kids had mobiles as parents like to keep in touch and, in practice, there was even quite a lot of phone use during lessons (often for texting or for listening to music through headphones). The presence and use of MP3 players also proved difficult to control. As parts of the curriculum were available for the students to download from the school website, they were encouraged to have USB memory sticks but some used MP3 players instead (and so carried their music around too).

Lessons at this school were often relatively informal, with students interacting with teachers and/or each other in class. Teachers sometimes had to negotiate for the students' attention.

The Descriptive Survey

One of the approaches to analysis that we have adopted in our research project, and the first level of analysis I want to introduce here, is a descriptive survey of the audio data. The aim of the survey is to count the number of naturally occurring episodes captured on the radio-mic recordings of our key informants where some form of PMC is talked about or is referenced through performance (singing, humming or mimicry). Our concept of PMC encompasses references to fashion and body-care as a narrower (more media-centric) focus used in our previous study was found to be limiting given our interest in self-identity (Rampton, Harris and Dover 2002). Also counted in the survey are identifiable moments where PMC hardware and software, such as mobile phones, MP3 players and the Internet, are physically used. The intention is not to reduce essentially qualitative material to a series of statistics, but as we have a large data set, the descriptive survey helps us to map what kinds of orientation to PMC are displayed by whom, their frequency and if this changes over the two periods of fieldwork.

There is not the space here to outline all of the patterns that arose, but a few key points can be introduced. Overall, PMC references were frequent. It was found that our informants audibly engaged with PMC on average seven times an hour.[3] Various factors influenced the occurrence of any one episode: opportunities for talk in a particular class, access to computers in a particular class, ownership of mobile phones, how much an individual tends to talk as well as an individual's relative engagement with PMC. The frequency and nature of PMC episodes also relates to an individual's friendship groups and peer status within class. Although it was not directly measurable in the survey, some individuals had more freedom than others to pursue (and impose) their own interests, had wider and more varied audiences than others and were more likely to be initiators of conversations.

The relative frequency of PMC engagement by the informants remained consistent over the two phases of fieldwork. However, for certain individuals, there were contrasts between Phases 1 and 2 of the fieldwork, in terms of the types of textual resource referenced. Digital (interactive) media such as mobiles, PSPs (PlayStation Portables) and MP3 players became more significant in the second phase of fieldwork partly because their greater prevalence in the market (compared to Phase 1, a year earlier) was reflected in their physical presence in the classroom. It is also evident that *talk* about this use and about the textual content of digital media can be significant for these young people, regardless of the opportunities and desire to use the technology at that moment in time.

It is also important to note that during the period of our study, some students did not have access to digital technologies (other than class computers). For some, lack of financial capital prevented access (and availability of credit is definitely a factor limiting phone use even for those who have a handset). For others, parental disapproval was a factor. But it should not be assumed that all students are interested in digital culture. As a proportion of the total conversational references to PMC recorded, one-third related to locally (i.e. self or peer) produced content (text messages, personal web pages etc.), whereas two-thirds of the PMC talk referenced industry-produced popular culture (TV, film, fashion, computer games, pop music etc.). More specifically, it was found that 10 per cent of all conversational PMC episodes included references to television programmes.[4]

There is little evidence of definite gender differences in the descriptive survey. However, qualitative analysis can reveal more nuanced differences, such as a tendency for the girls to talk about their *use* of interactive technologies in relationships, compared with boys who were more likely to talk about the actual technology. Similarly, associations of ethnicity are not measurable in the survey but are invoked in some of the PMC references (in relation to different genres of music, for example). These complex relationships need to be explored through the qualitative analysis conducted in parallel with the broader sweep of the survey. There are a variety of starting points possible in approaching the qualitative analysis. This can be done by looking for references to particular genres (e.g. music) or by highlighting themes such as demonstrations of knowledge/competence and of social rules surrounding media use. The process can also start with each of the focal students.

By taking an individual and a chronological period as one of the initial units of analysis, the researcher can consider how media references are used in the presentation of 'narratives of the self' (Finnegan 1997; Giddens 1991). To illustrate the kind of empirical 'data' that can be subjected to such analysis and some of the themes that begin to emerge, I will briefly present a snapshot of one of our students (without including the detailed transcriptions we have).

Nadia

Nadia (not her real name) has a South African mother and Armenian father and her home language is English. She was popular, lively and talkative, central to the action in most of her lessons and was also officially categorized by the school as a 'gifted and talented' student (a relative label). Shared music tastes helped to define the friendship network of the popular group (as well as shared attitudes to school). In the descriptive survey of our recorded data, Nadia emerged as the most prolific user of PMC references in conversation and performances. The recordings of Nadia introduced here are from a single morning in the Spring term in the second year of our fieldwork.

On her way to the first lesson, Nadia asked a boy to send a video of a fight among some of the boys. Comments were briefly made about the quality of the filming but not about the fight itself. During the English lesson, Nadia combined participating in the lesson, interacting with the teacher (asking impertinent questions about the permanence of his position as the class teacher) and chatting with friends. The cheeky nature of Nadia's interaction with the teacher was fairly typical for her and was indicative of her position as a vocal student who was allowed transgressions of student–teacher relationships because she was relatively successful academically. All students had to work out relationships with teachers within the context of a school culture that emphasized open negotiation of responsibilities. All were not equal however, and some of Nadia's classmates would not have been allowed to sustain such behaviour by teachers striving for authority.

Nadia also frequently sang, hummed and tapped a beat on the desk. Sometimes she did this while getting on with class work, and it served as an accompaniment. At other times, there was a more self-conscious performance of boredom. There was also a competence demonstrated in having a repertoire of popular songs available to her, and this was emphasized when she was able to sing short bursts of lyrics that reflected the topic of conversation at that moment in time. Although these lyrical resources were often drawn from memory, on this day Nadia was listening through headphones to the radio on her mobile phone. At one point she shared her headphones with a friend. Such activities were not officially sanctioned in the school but tended to be ignored by teachers if not too disruptive to classwork.

During the lesson, chat with friends included new clothes bought and songs and TV series liked. Her friend M said that her home computer was broken. Nadia teased her for being an MSN addict and claimed that she did not care about using MSN as she could phone anyone she needed to speak to.[5] She then went on to complain about not receiving a call or text message from a certain boy and said she would be rude to him next time she was online. She may have been joking but an important aspect of mobile communication for many young people is the ability to always be available to friends (Mizuko et al. 2008; Stald 2008), and a failure to respond can represent a transgression of friendships. Nadia was someone who used her phone frequently, and on her way to the next lesson she said she was late to school that day because she was on her phone until 4 a.m.

The third lesson of the day was media studies, where students were given the task of comparing stories in tabloid and broadsheet newspapers. They were also involved in a project to create online fan sites. Nadia continued to sing along with the radio (which was playing mainstream pop songs) whilst she and her friends attended to the classwork. At one point she shared her headphones with a friend. Later in the lesson, there was a discussion about eyebrows (a surprisingly recurrent topic among the girls), and Nadia asserted that she would never shave a ('tram') line into hers, as her brothers would not like it. This was yet another fleeting comment, but it does allude to culture and ethnicity as 'tram lines' are a fashion associated with black 'street' culture and Nadia indicated the potential conflict between her position as a girl who was fashionable, of mixed race and also from a family with conservative gender politics.

During the morning break time, Nadia tried to call the radio station to enter a competition to win CDs. She gave up after a while but her friends then tried while she continued listening to the radio. Some of the girls complained (for the first time) about her choice of music, but the criticism was not off-putting for Nadia who was able to continue filling most of the gaps between her talk with her singing. Singing for Nadia often reconfirmed her relatively assured peer position. For another of our female students, who was struggling academically and also relatively unpopular among her peers, singing was often a form of defensive retreat (a disengagement from class activities and others), reaffirming her own *un*-assured position.

Nadia continued singing intermittently during the following lessons and at lunchtime. During the lunch break, chat included references to the content of a website, the plot of a television show and the cost of some DVDs one girl was trying to sell to another. There was also a discussion about local gangs ('crews') and their websites. L told Nadia she read on one crew's website about someone wanting to 'shank' (stab) someone else. Nadia commented that they should use their websites for music purposes only and that they were stupid to advertise a potential 'beef' (fight). Just as in the conversation earlier in the day about the mobile phone video of a fight, critical comments focused on the incompetent or inappropriate use of media technology. It was the transgression of 'rules' surrounding online behaviour that were often (ironically) the focus of conversation, although local social group values are also performed here (the implied normality of physical fights – or, at least, the normality of the threat of fights).

At the end of lunchtime, Nadia bumped into a boy, D, and angrily accused him of having a picture of her on his phone that he had passed on to others. She said her picture was on Face-pic and Hi5 (social network sites) without her permission and became increasingly angry about this, repeating the story to others, including a teacher. She also claimed that some girls were pretending to be her on various websites, and by offering to do things with boys they would get her labelled 'a slag' (sexually permissive). Such old-fashioned and derogatory gender labels were still pervasive among these young people, and Nadia's friend advised her to stop sending photos of herself to people but she dismissed this idea. Although the dangers in using social/communication media were recognized by Nadia and her friends, they seemed unlikely to stop their use or even to be more careful in their use. Problems were seen as arising from others' misuse, rather than from the public nature of these digital networks. Again, the emphasis is placed on social norms attending the use of digital technologies that are learnt (boyd 2008; Stald 2008).

These and further events during this one morning, as well as elsewhere in the project recordings, demonstrated that Nadia often asserted her popularity in her references to PMC and use of technologies such as mobiles and MSN. Although each person's relative position is contestable, Nadia, for example, seemed able to maintain a position of authority within her peer group partly through her engagement with and knowledge of PMC resources, particularly pop music. Someone else less keyed in with the cultural capital locally deemed appropriate could be labelled (however temporarily) as stupid. Such ascriptions are far from stable as they are continually negotiated, inverted and reassigned, but they are a significant aspect of an individual's experience of school. Although there has not been the space to explore all the possible factors implied in Nadia's PMC use, this description of episodes occurring during one morning has indicated the relevance of media literacy, peer hierarchies, school culture, family and local community culture.

In Nadia's case, it is also seen that engagement with PMC during lessons does not necessarily occur in reverse proportion to the engagement with the curriculum. Spontaneous music making, for example, most commonly occurs in interludes between periods of officially focused classwork (Rampton, Harris and Dover 2002). In other words, it takes place in 'open states of talk' (Goffman 1981: 134) when low levels of informal chat are licensed by the teacher. As a result, it normally poses no direct threat to curriculum order.

So student engagement with PMC during lessons should not be assumed to be an emblem of opposition to, and a means of opting out from, the learning activities imposed by the school – although this can of course happen.

Conclusion

So, why are the kinds of fleeting encounters and practices referenced here significant? Well, first, and in relation to the specific context of our research, I would argue that student relationships are made and sustained over many hours every week, for many years and should be recognized as an important part of the education system, worthy of research and understanding alongside issues such as curriculum and pedagogy.

Second, and more broadly, as the data from our initial research show, there are many subtle ways in which media products are embedded in and reconstituted through everyday life. Relevant is not only people's physical uses of media hardware and their engagement with texts but also their use of media (both old and new) as a resource for negotiating local power relations and identities. For some of our research participants, new media and popular culture involved networking and enhanced sociability, whereas for others popular cultural references could be cumbersome and unreciprocated, with new media talk focusing on prohibition and lack of access (Rampton et al. 2008). Although not focused on here, an interest in the more nebulous aspects of media culture can also inform our understanding of 'non-media' practices such as the negotiation of authority by teachers or the maintenance of young people's peer relationships within the home. These interactions and processes can reveal the difference media use makes in small everyday activities that could otherwise escape us.

Although questions of who consumes what and when in relation to market possibilities necessarily remain important in studies of media and popular culture consumption, there are also many questions to ask about what happens beyond the initial act of consumption. Adopting a multidisciplinary approach and also an ethnographic research model that engages with social interactions is one way to move beyond text-centred reception studies and explore media-related practices in everyday life.

References

Algan, E., 2003. The problem of textuality in ethnographic audience research: Lessons learned in Southeast Turkey. In P.D. Murphy and M.M. Kraidy, eds, *Global media studies: Ethnographic perspectives*. London: Routledge. pp. 23–39.

Back, L., 1996. *New ethnicities and urban culture: Racisms and multiculture in young lives*. London: UCL Press.

Baym, N.K., 2010. *Personal connections in the digital age*. Cambridge, UK: Polity Press.

Bennett, A., 2000. *Popular music and youth culture: Music, identity and place*. London: Palgrave.

Bird, S.E., 2003. *The audience in everyday life*. London: Routledge.

—— 2010. From fan practice to mediated moments: The value of practice theory in the understanding of media audiences. In B. Brauchler and J. Postill, eds, *Theorising media and practice*. Oxford, UK: Berghahn Books. pp. 85–104.

boyd, D., 2008. Why youth love social network sites: The role of networked publics in teenage social life. In D. Buckingham, ed., *Youth, identity, and digital media*. Cambridge, MA: The MIT Press. pp. 119–142.

Buckingham, D., 2008. Introducing identity. In D. Buckingham, ed., *Youth, identity, and digital media*. Cambridge, MA: The MIT Press. pp. 1–24.

Clifford, J. and Marcus, G., eds, 1986. *Writing culture: The poetics and politics of ethnography*. Berkeley, CA: University of California Press.

Cohen, A.P., 1985. *The symbolic construction of community*. London: Routledge.

Couldry, N., 2010. Theorising media as practice (reprinted). In B. Brauchler and J. Postill, eds, *Theorising media and practice*. Oxford, UK: Berghahn Books. pp. 35–54.

Dover, C., 2007. Everyday talk: Investigating media consumption and identity amongst school children. *Participations*, 4(1) [online]. Available at: http://www.participations.org/Volume 4/ Issue 1/4_01_dover.htm [Accessed 27 December 2011].

Drotner, K., 2000. Less is more: Media ethnography and its limits. In I. Hagen and J. Wasko, eds, *Consuming audiences? Production and reception in media research*. Cresskill, NJ: Hampton Press. pp. 165–188.

Finnegan, R., 1997. Storying the self: Personal narratives and identity. In H. Mackay, ed., *Consumption and everyday life*. London: Sage/OU. pp. 65–112.

Geertz, C., 1975. *The interpretation of cultures*. London: Hutchinson.

—— 1988. *Works and lives: The anthropologist as author*. Cambridge, UK: Polity Press.

Georgakopoulou, A., 2008. On the MSN with buff boys: Self- and other-identity claims in the context of small stories. *Journal of Sociolinguistics*, 12(5), pp. 597–626.

Giddens, A., 1991. *Modernity and self-identity: Self and society in the late modern age*. Cambridge, UK: Polity Press.

Gillespie, M., 1995. *Television, ethnicity and cultural Change*. London: Routledge.

Goffman, E., 1959. *The presentation of self in everyday life*. New York: Anchor Books.

—— 1981. *Forms of talk*. Oxford, UK: Blackwell.

Hobart, M., 2010. What do we mean by 'media practices'? In B. Brauchler and J. Postill, eds, *Theorising media and practice*. Oxford, UK: Berghahn Books. pp. 55–76.

Laughey, D., 2006. *Music and youth culture*. Edinburgh, Scotland: Edinburgh University Press.

Lawler, S., 2008. *Identity: Sociological perspectives*. Cambridge, UK: Polity Press.

Livingstone, S., 2002. *Young people and new media*. London: Sage.

—— 2009. *Children and the Internet*. Cambridge, UK: Polity Press.

Mackay, H., ed., 1997. *Consumption and everyday life*. London: Sage/OU.

Mizuko, I. et al., 2008. Living and learning with new media: Summary of findings from the digital youth project (White Paper). Chicago, IL: The John D. and Catherine T. MacArthur Foundation Reports on Digital Media and Learning.

Moores, S., 2000. *Media & everyday life in modern society*. Edinburgh, UK: Edinburgh University Press.

Morley, D., 1992. *Television, audiences and cultural studies*. London: Routledge.

—— 1997. Theoretical orthodoxies: Textualism, constructivism and the 'new ethnography' in cultural studies. In M. Ferguson and P. Golding, eds, *Cultural studies in question*. London: Sage. pp. 121–137.

—— 2000. *Home territories: Media, mobility and identity*. London: Routledge.

Osgerby, B., 2004. *Youth media*. London: Routledge.

Peterson, M.A., 2005. Performing media: Toward an ethnography of intertextuality. In E.W. Rothenbuhler and M. Coman, eds, *Media anthropology*. London: Sage. pp. 129–138.

Postill, J., 2010. Introduction: Theorising media and practice. In B. Brauchler and J. Postill, eds, *Theorising media and practice*. Oxford, UK: Berghahn Books. pp. 1–34.

Radway, J., 1984. *Reading the romance*. Chapel Hill, NC: University of North Carolina Press.

—— 1988. Reception study: Ethnography and the problems of dispersed audiences and nomadic subjects. *Cultural Studies*, 2(3), pp. 359–376.

Rampton, B., 2005. *Language in late modernity: Interaction in an urban school*. Cambridge, UK: Cambridge University Press.

Rampton, B., Harris, R. and Dover, C., 2002. Interaction, media culture and adolescents at school. Working Papers in Urban Language & Literacies, 20. King's College London [online]. Available at: http://www.kcl.ac.uk/projects/ldc/publications/workingpapers/download.aspx [Accessed 1/6/11].

Rampton, B., Harris, R., Leung, C., Georgakopoulou, A. and Dover, C., 2008. Urban classroom culture & interaction. Working Papers in Urban Language & Literacies, 53. King's College London [online]. Available at: http://www.kcl.ac.uk/projects/ldc/publications/workingpapers/download.aspx [Accessed 1/6 /11].

Silverstone, R., 1994. *Television and everyday life*. London: Routledge.

Spitulnik, D., 2010. Thick context, deep epistemology: A mediation on wide-angle lenses on media, knowledge production and the concept of culture. In B. Brauchler and J. Postill, eds, *Theorising media and practice*. Oxford, UK: Berghahn Books. pp. 105–126.

Stald, G., 2008. Mobile identity: Youth, identity and mobile communication media. In D. Buckingham, ed., *Youth, identity, and digital media*. Cambridge, MA: The MIT Press. pp. 143–166.

Zimmerman, D., 1998. Identity, context and interaction. In C. Antaki and S. Widdicombe, eds, *Identities in talk*. London: Sage. pp. 87–106.

Notes

1   In this characterization of three generations of audience studies, we can say that the first generation involved the reappraisal of audiences as 'active' interpreters (decoders) of texts, and the second generation of studies began to consider the domestic setting and social relationships involved in media reception, through the use of ethnographic methods.

2   For a discussion of the importance of locality in relation to young people's cultural consumption, see Bennett 2000.
3   In the survey, an 'episode' was defined as a sequence of talk introducing and often sustaining a media-cultural theme, bounded by periods of talk and activity devoted to other matters.
4   My own further, initial research suggests that this picture has changed in the few years since this fieldwork was conducted with the increasing use of social networks, but that industry-produced media culture is still very significant for young people. The rise in popularity of, for example, YouTube further complicates this issue as most users are watching rather than producing videos, and some YouTube content is produced by industry broadcasters, film companies and so on.
5   Among our students, it was quite often implied that having phone contact with someone was regarded more highly than having online contact, rendering the relationship more authentic.

Chapter 7

Film Audiences in Perspective: The Social Practices of Cinema-Going

Philippe Meers and Daniel Biltereyst

Introduction

> There is more to cinema-going than seeing films. There is going out at night and the sense of relaxation combined with the sense of fun and excitement. The very name 'picture palace', by which cinemas were known for a long time, captures an important part of that experience. Rather than selling individual films, cinema is best understood as having sold a habit, a certain type of socialised experience. [...] Any analysis of the film subject which does not take on board these issues of the context within which the film is consumed is, to my mind, insufficient.
>
> Morley 1992: 157–158

Twenty years ago renowned British media scholar Morley called attention to the important but often neglected aspect of the social in the study of film audiences. In the same period, the American film and television historian Allen wrote a polemical article against the dominant text-oriented tradition within film studies, arguing that 'film history has been written as if films had no audiences' (Allen 1990: 348). Criticizing the often theoretical or textually inscribed approach of audiences within mainstream film studies, a wide range of scholars have shown a growing interest in the lived experiences of film audiences and the social experience of cinema-going. Over the past two decades, a broad stream of empirical research on the 'real audience' (Stacey 1994: 54) contributed to the emergence of *film audience studies* as a broad perspective where different traditions, concepts and methodologies of (film) audience research meet. This includes the usage of perspectives, which were often neglected within film studies so far like ethnographic research into film audiences (e.g. Meers 2004; Richards 2003; Taylor 1989). This interesting 'rapprochement' and interdisciplinary exchanges lead to the awareness that the history of film (or cinema as a social institution) is actually being rewritten (cf. the concept 'new cinema history' in Maltby, Biltereyst and Meers 2011).

The aim of this chapter is not to isolate the field of film audience studies but to contextualize it within broader media research and point to interactions and exchanges with other subfields of audience research. The chapter will discuss the paradigmatic integration of traditions on audience research within cinema studies, cultural studies research on audiences as well as political economy insights on film audience formation to build new, integrative perspectives on contemporary and historical film audiences.

After this overview of paradigms and approaches on film audience research, we focus on a case study on historical cinema-going audiences in two Belgian cities. Using oral histories we argue that the social practice of cinema-going was less inspired by movies, stars and programming strategies than it was a significant social routine, strongly inspired by community identity formation, class and social distinction.

Theoretical, Conceptual and Methodological Issues

Film audience research does not come out of a historical vacuum. There have always been researchers interested in film audiences, albeit in the margins of disciplines. Suffice it to reference some of the studies dating from the beginning of the twentieth century (e.g. Altenloh 1914; Blumer 1933; see overview in Gripsrud 1998). In the late 1960s, when the study of film was institutionalized and became an academic discipline firmly located within the humanities, film studies mainly concentrated on aesthetics, ideology and auteur theory (Lapsley and Westlake 2006) and neglected the empirical study of audiences. In the 1970s, the audience reappeared within psychoanalytic film theory (e.g. Metz 1975), albeit as an abstract, universal and ideal 'spectator'. It meant that the analysis was restricted to the film text and to how the film constructed the (passive) spectator. Screen theory, as this perspective is often referred to, conceptualized the spectator as a victim of the 'cinematic apparatus' that impregnated him or her with the dominant ideology, through the process of identification (Gripsrud 1998: 206).

Towards Film Audience Research: Major Influences

Only since the late 1980s has the field of film audience studies known major developments. This was partly due to the growing attention for film audiences, reception or spectatorship within film studies itself, mainly under the influence of feminist film theory, revisionist film history, cognitive film theory and some other currents which focused on a more active and socially contextualized viewer (e.g. semiopragmatic film theory; Casetti 1998). But the re-emergence of the field of film audience studies was also strongly inspired by other disciplines, including those coming from media studies and the broader social sciences, most prominently cultural studies-inspired television audience research, communication research and political economy. This does not mean the evolution was a fast and easy one. The efficiency of the 'disciplinary fire wall' around film studies is not to be underestimated (Austin 2002: 1).

The largest impact on film audience studies undoubtedly came from (British) cultural studies and its concept of audiences as consisting of socially, culturally and historically located individuals who actively negotiate hegemonic discourses in society. As Stacey (1994: 24) described, there were significant debates between cultural studies and mainstream film studies when it came to audiences: for example, regarding focus (spectator positioning vs. audience readings), methods (textual analysis vs. ethnographic methods), the status of the viewer (passive vs. active) and the level of analysis (unconscious vs. conscious). But there were good reasons why film studies scholars engaged the debate. There was a growing interest in the pleasure experienced by cinema audiences, who were no longer considered ideological victims (Turner 2002). Examining the social context of the public became the key to grasp the meaning and relevance of popular film (Willis 1995: 175). Because of the hegemony of screen theory, however, film studies offered little or no scope to analyse social context and the pleasure of movie watching. Hence, researchers found inspiration in cultural studies that did not see viewers as passive dupes (Turner 2002: 4–5), and some argued for 'a cinematic version of David Morley's work in family television' (Klinger 1997: 125, Note 50). The contributions of cultural studies are manifold. The approach pays attention to the 'viewer agency', the active role of viewers in the production of meanings of media texts and the experience of pleasure (Austin 2002: 21). Besides the textual determinants of the viewer, structural determinants are also included. So it is no longer solely the text that builds the identity of viewers. There are social identities such as class, gender, ethnicity or nationality that shape the viewing experience (Stacey 1994: 73). The cultural studies approach was particularly fruitful in the field of qualitative research on television audiences and their reception. Film audience researchers therefore acknowledge that film studies had a lot to learn from the area of television studies (Klinger 1997: 113, Note 18; Prince 1996: 77). Just as television is a social ritual, 'going to the movies' is seen as a social activity rather than an opportunity to watch particular films. The contribution of television studies is particularly relevant as watching films is no longer bound to the cinema. A lot of film viewing is taking place in people's 'domestic media centers' (Allen 1999) on television, DVD, computer or even mobile phone.

Also from within film studies, questions were raised about how mainstream film theory conceptualized the audience. Feminist film theorists, for instance, began to question the untenable position of the female film viewer in *Screen*-dominated film theory dominated the film theory, questioning why cinema was mainly conceived as 'pleasurable to the male viewer, but not the female' (Pribam 1988: 1).

The problem of female viewers having to identify with the 'male gaze' gave the need to conceptualize a female viewer out of the psychoanalytic framework. Authors such as Hansen (1991: 5) put the emphasis on variable cultural and historical aspects of reception, whereas Kuhn (1984: 23) stressed the important distinction between a theoretical *film spectator* and the actual *cinematic social audience*. Feminist writers later tried to bring reconciliation between psychoanalysis and empirical approaches to film audiences (Bobo 1988; Hansen 1991; Stacey 1994; Staiger 1992; Taylor 1989).

Another impulse came from the historical turn within film studies. In the 1970s, film history was pushed into the background by ahistorical and text-oriented 'high theory'. Researchers interested in non-textual historical issues, such as economic structures, the relationship between film and other entertainment forms, the technology or the reception, were classified as 'damned empiricists' (Allen 1990: 347–348). As Barker (1999: 132) notes, this gap was filled over the past two decades, largely by revisionist film historians from 'new film historiography' (e.g. Bordwell, Thompson and Staiger 1985) and more recently by 'new cinema history' (e.g. Biltereyst, Maltby and Meers 2012; Maltby, Biltereyst and Meers 2011). The usual methods were revised through detailed empirical studies. The primacy of the canon was put aside to focus on cinema as an economic and social institution. The viewer is addressed in these studies as 'a consumer, as a member of a demographically diverse audience' (Hansen 1991: 5). Many authors (e.g. Stokes 1999) are now emphasizing that the major historical significance of film can be found in its reception rather than in its production.

Cognitive film theory, another influencing strand, heavily based on developments in cognitive psychology, came to the fore in the 1980s with scholars such as Bordwell, Thompson and Carroll. Cognitive film theory looked at the viewer as an autonomous rational being who follows 'schemata' and 'mental sets' in the interpretation of a film. The focus is on the rational mental processes that occur for an individual viewer while watching a movie. The greatest contribution undoubtedly is that it no longer perceives the viewer as a passive consumer of film but as an active meaning maker. Bordwell (1985) takes as a starting point the 'hypothetical viewer' who should actively cooperate for a film experience to emerge. This is a competent viewer that performs the operations necessary to construct a story from the representations of the film:

> [T]he 'spectator' is not a particular person, not even me. I adopt the term 'viewer' or 'spectator' to name a hypothetical entity executing the operations relevant to constructing a story out of the film's representation [...] Insofar as an empirical viewer makes sense of the story, his or her activities coincide with the process I will be describing. (Bordwell 1985: 30)

From a totally different angle and paradigm, contemporary political economy media scholars recently focused their attention on the film audience. As is common in the political economy approach, the focus is on audience control and consumer surveillance. Maxwell (2000), for instance, used the metaphor of a 'second cold war of culture' which expresses that market research puts people into categories of audiences and consumers to extend corporate control over the infrastructure of consumption. In their analysis of political economy of audiences for global Hollywood, Miller et al. (2001) stressed the crucial role of marketing. Arguing that 'audiences are an untamed labour force that must be domesticated for consumption', Miller et al. (2001) referred to the role of film marketing as a tool for an 'ever deepening surveillance of people's feelings, opinions, loves and hates in a much more intense, even righteous, quest for knowledge of the film-going experience'. Inspired by previous work from Smythe (2001), Miller et al. called for 'a labour theory of consumption', whereby the 'labour of audiences owned by market research and protected by IP laws deny the research subjects access to the very speech acts that constitute the labour of reception' and where 'consumers *themselves* become the product' (emphasis in original, 2001: 210). More recent political economy perspectives on audiences are provided by Biltereyst and Meers (2011).

Finally, within traditional communication science research, a series of studies are worth mentioning, especially Austin's work from the 1980s onwards. Besides his own studies and the extensive bibliography which he composed (Austin 1983), he was editor of a book series called *Current Research in Film* that regularly published contributions on film audiences (e.g. Palmgreen et al. 1988).

Under the influence of the above-mentioned conceptualizations of audiences, different strands of research have developed. We focus on historical research on film audiences, reception studies of contemporary audiences, studies of contemporary film consumption as social practice and political economy analyses of audience formation.

Historical Research on Film Audiences

Within research on movie audiences, historical film audience studies have a prominent place (see, for example, Stokes and Maltby 1999a; 1999b; 2001). Historical studies of film audiences are not only quantitatively dominant. Film historical approaches to cinema-going were also highly insightful because they allowed to confront earlier abstractions of the film viewer with real audience's experiences (Jenkins 2000: 172).

Making a distinction between film and cinema history, Maltby has argued that while the first deals with 'an aesthetic history of textual relations', the latter focuses on the 'social history of a cultural institution', in which he diagnoses a need for 'detailed historical maps of cinema exhibition, telling us what cinemas were where and when' (Maltby 2006: 91). This 'new cinema history' project includes the 'experience that will ground quantitative generalisations in the concrete particulars of microhistorical studies of local situations, effects and infrastructure' (Maltby 2006: 91; Maltby, Biltereyst and Meers 2011). This broad scholarly examination of film reception has gone hand in hand with an empirical, historical and spatial turn in film studies. Work by Kuhn (2002) and others on bottom-up experiences and memories of cinema-going not only reconfirmed ideas of audience activity, selectivity and power in a historical context but also underlined the extent to which cinema-going was remembered as part of the fabric and routine of social life, thereby questioning the relevance of the movies themselves. In a recent collection of case studies dealing with various historical European contexts on film exhibition and audiences, all addressing everyday film culture, the role of the audience is a key issue in the critical reconsideration of cinematic modernity and its relation to tradition, community and everyday life (Biltereyst, Maltby and Meers 2012). Summarizing criticism of the modernity thesis' conceptualization of spectatorship, Fuller-Seeley and Potamianos have argued that it tends 'to transform viewers and their culture, the surrounding theatres and streets, into a vast, anonymous, homogeneous, mass audience' (2008: 5).

Looking back, it is quite remarkable how the early research agenda defined by Allen (1990: 349–354) remains useful to categorize current developments in the contemporary research field on historical audiences. Allen proposed research on exhibition, reception, social composition and discourses, and finally, cinema-going as social practice. Economic exhibition history analyses and describes the structural and institutional context in which the film consumption occurs. It is a necessary step in the direction of film audience research, with 'Shared Pleasures' by Gomery (1992) as pioneering study, which gives a clear view of the evolution of film exhibition in the United States from the start to the advent of the video. But in the end it remains an institutional history, which gives particular attention to economic and industrial aspects of the screening and not to the meaning of going to the movies for real moviegoers (Jancovich, Faire and Stubbings 2003: 4).

Second are historical reception studies that examine how specific audiences give meaning and experience pleasure in specific film moments. By far the best-known and most widespread approach is that of historical reception studies such as those launched by Staiger (1986, 1992, 2000, 2005) or Davis (2001). Staiger's (1992: 89) 'historical materialist reception research' analyses and reconstructs the viewing strategies available to the viewer in a specific historical period through a contextual analysis of public discourses about a film. This provides insights into the range of possible readings in specific historical periods (Staiger 1986: 20). Staiger (2000: 1) specifies that contextual factors, more than textual factors, determine the experience viewers have while watching a movie and how they use these experiences in daily life. The horizon of expectation is reconstructed on the basis of surrounding texts. These are not just fiction films but include the historical, political and scientific discourses. Her classical sources are press reviews, interviews, articles and letters to the editor.

Third, research addresses the social 'composition of the audience' and the 'discursive construction' of film audiences. This perspective centres on how cinema has become a part of everyday life and deals with the social composition of the audience of the early cinema. One of the topics that initiated a fierce debate about movie audiences was the assumption that the cinema audiences mainly consisted of lower social classes, workers and mainly immigrants (Stokes 1999: 1). One argument in this debate is that the narrative form and the genres that developed did not reflect the tradition of the working class and ethnic cultures but rather that of the middle class (Hansen 1991: 60; Staiger 1992: 101–123). Some authors focus on the discursive construction of the cinema audience in a specific historical context (often early cinema) and by special organizations such as political and cultural elites. These are often discourses on 'vulnerable' groups such as immigrant workers who could pose a threat to social order (Grieveson 1999; Uricchio and Pearson 1999: 73). Hansen's (1991) study of spectatorship in American silent film is another milestone in film audience research. Hansen stays close to historical materialist reception but adds an extra conceptual dimension, considering the cinema as an (alternative) public sphere. This public dimension of the reception goes beyond existing social and textual descriptions of 'spectatorship' because it allows for 'a dynamic whereby social formations are formed around specific films, stars, or types of performances' (Hansen 1991: 6). For female moviegoers, the cinema signifies a (social) space for women regardless of marital status, age or background. The cinema was a place where women could go alone, as consumers, to participate in any other form of collectivity than the family (Hansen 1991: 118).

Fourth, the last category of historical studies (which is also illustrated in the case study of this chapter) analyses the event of 'going to the movies' as a social phenomenon. Their contribution is that they draw attention to the location of the exhibition and the context. A number of studies are often described as 'ethnographic', in the broad sense of media ethnography. In their historical study of movie consumption in the city of Nottingham, Jancovich, Faire and Stubbings (2003: 4, Note 2) deliberately use the term 'consumption' because the movie is not only about going to the movies but it also relates to activities associated with other forms of distribution and exhibition including but not limited to television (broadcast, satellite and cable), video rental and sales, and Internet. Jancovich, Faire and Stubbings (2003: 216) point out that, in Britain since the 1970s, television is the main place for film consumption. For the interviewees, the choice between cinema and television related to the difference between going out and staying in, a choice between different social activities with different meanings that may be appropriate or inappropriate at different times. The Nottingham study also involved the mapping of the cultural geography of cinema where each cinema is associated with a specific form of consumption. These forms are organized hierarchically and evaluated.

Some of these studies focus on stars and 'fandom'. Dyer (1986) was among the first to do a study on the reception of film star Judy Garland by gay audiences. Stacey's *Star Gazing* (1994) is perhaps the best-known pioneering work in this trend of audience research within 'star studies'. Stacey combines theories of spectatorship in feminist film criticism with cultural studies work on gender and audiences. Stacey gives a new positive meaning to escapism, as one of the major sources for the enjoyment of cinema. She highlights the importance of looking beyond the pleasure of the text to the pleasure of the ritualized event or night out. There is also the physical pleasure of the cinema as a place, especially compared to the reality of the war years. The cinema in that sense becomes a real dream palace (Stacey 1994: 94).

Reception Studies of Contemporary Audiences

The study of the reception of contemporary films by contemporary audiences emerged in recent years, but it remains much smaller than the historical reception. The conceptual assumption is that the experience of a particular movie can best be analysed on the basis of the narratives of viewers themselves. Apart from viewers, the context of the reception is also, as in the contextual historical reception, important.

Already in the 1980s, some film reception studies were conducted, mostly in the cultural studies tradition. Bobo (1988) is one of the first film reception researchers with her study on the reception of *The Color Purple* (Spielberg, 1985). The film provoked a controversy because of the negative stereotypes about 'black man' and 'the black family', especially since the director was white. Bobo (1988: 95) situates the reception of the film in the broader public discourse that was built around the film. She uses Hall's classic 'encoding-decoding' model and focuses on oppositional readings by black women. The surprisingly positive reactions from these women were partly motivated by the recognition that they were finally represented on screen. Bobo situates the positive reception of the film in a broader cultural context of a growing black female culture. It is linked to the rise of black female writers and their readership of black women in the 1980s and, more generally, with their increasing public presence (Bobo 1988: 107).

Many current reception studies maintain the 'one film–one audience' approach. Barker and Brooks (1998), for instance, combine an analysis of the production, marketing and the actual reception of the Hollywood movie *Judge Dredd* (Cannon, 1995). They perceive a patterned array of choices that people know in advance what kind of cinematic experience they want. In another reception study, Barker, Arthurs and Harindranath (2001) examined how the public discourse in the British press constructed the movie *Crash* (Cronenberg, 1996) as a 'controversial' film, in terms of censorship, and how actual viewers deal with this discourse and with the film. Austin (2002) studies the *circulation* in Britain of three Hollywood movies, *Basic Instinct* (Verhoeven, 1992), *Bram Stoker's Dracula* (Coppola, 1992) and *Natural Born Killers* (Stone, 1994). He analyses the discourse of production and marketing (through trade journals, press, interviews) of the press (through press cuttings) and of cinema, video and television audiences of the films (through questionnaires), in a model where the (film) industry succeeds in drawing the borders of viewing strategies (Austin 2002: 94). Hill (1997) focuses on a number of films within the same genre. She starts from the question why people want to see violent movies, and the analysis focuses on the reception of extremely violent films called New Brutalism movies. Watching these films is clearly a social process, as viewers are aware of the reactions of other members in the audience (Hill 1997: 28).

Political economy perspectives have often been critical about how audiences are able to negotiate or perform an oppositional decoding of media content. This raises the question of the concept of audience resistance and freedom or the question of how audiences freely exert and organize resistance to institutional media power. One example of a study combining political economic contextualization and audience research is the large-scale Global Disney Audiences project, led by Wasko, Phillips and Meehan (2001). Covering 18 countries, the study combines audience analysis (questionnaires and interviews) with individual national profiles outlining Disney's marketing activities and the specific context for reception. One of the main conclusions of the project was that although a certain amount of negotiation takes place, it always happens 'within the intersection of the political economy of the mediated text, the national context within which that text plays economic as well as cultural roles, the cultural practices of a society and its social units (like families) and finally individual consciousness' (Wasko and Meehan 2001).

Contemporary Film Consumption as Social Practice

Studies that no longer focus their attention on the reception of a particular film but rather analyse film consumption as a social event are mainly qualitative audience studies about the role of film in the daily lives of people. Small-scale studies focus on specific groups of viewers watching in variable contexts. Film consumption is interpreted here in its broadest sense, from classic motion picture experience to movie experience in the domestic context. Corbett (1998–1999), for instance, interviews American white middle-class couples in their home context on the meaning of cinema-going and film in general. His aim is to see how film audiences use film in their daily lives and in interpersonal relationships (Corbett 1998–1999: 43–44). Watching film then is often seen as a ritual in which it is constructed as something special for the couple. Some authors focus not only on specific audiences but also on specific genres. Bolin (2000) analyses the subculture of young men 'movie swappers' who view and exchange extremely violent videos ('video nasties'). He considers this to be an alternative cultural public sphere where the subculture has an alternative production, its own distribution channels and criteria for evaluation. Their main forums are the fanzines and alternative film festivals (Bolin 2000: 62). Finally, the link between cultural identity and film consumption in a cross-cultural context is discussed in a study of diasporic film reception by Naficy (1993) on Iranian exiles in Los Angeles and their organized group viewings of videos that enable to confirm the cultural link with the homeland. Dudrah (2002) analyses the popular Indian or Bollywood cinema in Birmingham in relation to the diasporic South Asian identities of moviegoers. He shows how the concept of Bollywood as a broad cultural phenomenon (film, music, dance) is part of the construction of a British Asian identity. Bollywood films give viewers the opportunity to participate in a cultural activity that includes characters from Asianness (Dudrah 2002: 33; Gillespie 1995).

Case Study

It is impossible to illustrate this broad overview with detailed case studies for every strand. Therefore, we choose to put one major approach to practice, focusing on a recent case study of 'new cinema history' inspired research. Most oral history projects on the social experience of cinema have been conducted in the United States, the United Kingdom and some other major European countries, where film exhibition culture has already been thoroughly studied. In smaller countries or regions, however, such as Flanders, the Northern region of Belgium, film exhibition and cinema-going experiences are still widely under-researched. Therefore, we take a case study on historical cinema-going audiences in two Belgian cities (the 'Enlightened' City project).[1] Using oral histories, we argue that the social practice of cinema-going was less inspired by movies, stars and programming strategies than that it was a significant social routine, strongly inspired by community identity formation, class and social distinction. This short report focuses on the cities of Antwerp and Ghent, mainly after the World War II. Given the extremely rich and diversified responses and memories in the interviews, we report briefly on two themes: the social experience of cinema-going and the role of cinema in everyday life.

Oral History, Memory and Methods

To engage the lived experiences of ordinary audiences in their social, historical and cultural context and to investigate the role of cinema within everyday life and within leisure culture, scholars often turn to qualitative methodologies, small research designs and micro-level ethnographic approaches. These range from interviews, observations, diaries and all kinds of other written accounts to testimonies or memories. The use of oral history methods in investigating the social experience of going to the movies in a historical perspective is a much debated methodological issue. Oral history gives a voice to those memories that were seldom written down and would normally be lost. The aim of oral history research on cinema-going is not to objectively reconstruct the past based on subjective memories of our respondents but to look at the recreation of these memories about going to the cinema. In this regard, Kuhn (2002: 9–12) speaks of 'memory text'; that is, how people remember is as much a text to be deciphered as the actual memories they talk about.

On a conceptual level, the study is connected with the recent shift whereby experience and agency are re-contextualized within structures and ideology. This shift puts critical ethnography and the political economy of audiences back on the agenda (Biltereyst and Meers 2011). Thereby we tried to tackle the problem of some oral history projects on cinema, where nostalgia has become a central feature, possibly obscuring the role of social class and ideology.

The oral history part of the 'Enlightened' City project was based on a wide range of individual, in-depth interviews. The respondents were selected and found in homes for elderly people, within the social circle of acquaintances of the interviewers, or by self-selection (responding to advertisements in local newspapers). As is the case in most qualitative research, we sought as much variation as possible in terms of age, class, sex and ideological points of view to grasp a wide variety of possible routines, ideas and motives concerning cinema-going. The individual interviews were conducted in 2005 and 2006 in the respondents' home environment. A total of 389 interviews were conducted, 155 in Antwerp, 61 in Ghent and 173 in 21 smaller towns and villages. When quoting respondents in the following paragraphs, we give their first name and date of birth.

The Social Experience of Cinema-Going in the City

One of the key findings of research on the social experience of cinema is, as Kuhn claimed, that 'cinema-going appears to have been less about particular films, or even films in general, than about experiences surrounding the activity of going to the pictures'

(2002: 50). This (for some film scholars quite disturbing) result also emerged from our oral history project. Cinema-going is and has always been an utterly social experience. Reading the stories of our respondents, it became clear that cinemas were linked with different sorts of social routines, which were clearly more determining the choice of movie theatre than the actual film that was playing. First of all, both in Antwerp and Ghent, there is the obvious distinction between inner-city movie palaces and neighbourhood cinemas. The film exhibition scene is also very closely linked to the specific (cultural) geography of the city. The movie palaces in Antwerp, for instance, were all centred next to each other in the inner city, and they were remembered as luxurious, beautiful and comfortable. These cinemas were as much an object of consumption as the movies they showed. What they lacked in atmosphere, familiarity and unpredictability, they made up for by comfort, star-packed movies and status. Using respondents' mental maps, we were able to reconstruct an almost hierarchical arrangement of the city-centre movie palaces (cf. Richards 2003: 346), indicating the different status of particular movie palaces.

Antwerp neighbourhood theatres were spread across the different city districts, which mainly housed poorer blue-collar workers. Our interviews showed how neighbourhood cinemas were only visited by people actually living near these cinemas. A key issue here was the importance of a community spirit, which was still very much alive in the different city districts, resulting in a feeling among our respondents about neighbourhood cinemas as 'their' theatres. An important feature for describing various types of cinemas was accessibility and social distinction. Both in Antwerp and Ghent, respondents often talked about how audiences of neighbourhood cinemas were met with prejudice and how they were often described as being 'uncivilized, loud and vulgar', mainly by people living in the city centre attending first-run cinemas:

> Agnella (1942): We didn't go to the smaller cinemas. They were always packed and in our eyes a lesser kind of cinema. Because they would be belching, making noises, eating and smoking, and that wasn't for us.

Movie palaces, though, were not exclusively limited to higher or higher middle-class audiences. Many scholars already noticed that movie palaces can be seen as temples of classlessness that could reach as wide and heterogeneous an audience as possible (Klenotic 2007: 130) or as an alternative public sphere that was inclusive for many audiences (Hansen 1991). But the actual experience of class mixing remained limited (Klenotic 2008: 132). Even when they did come together in the same place, audiences did not simply shrug off their previous identities. In the Antwerp case, class mixing was not uncommon in city-centre theatres and most respondents from the districts claimed to have been at least once in one of the movie palaces. Going to a movie palace or to neighbourhood cinema always remained making a choice about (cultural and social) status, identity and audiences with whom one could identify.

Cinema-Going in Everyday Life

A key finding of ethnographic film audience studies is that going to the movies was a substantial part of everyday life. Although the respondents gave a wide range of reasons for 'going to the movies', these remained quite consistent throughout time. Cinema-going was most often remembered as a habit. For many, it was a weekly routine and part of the 'fabric' of daily life. It was an 'out of the home' social event as well as an extension of home life. Cinema-going often was the only (financially) available form of leisure as well as a collective and social experience:

> Achille (1919): We went to the movies because it was a habit, not really because we wanted to see a specific picture. My mom went, and I went along. We would see something new every week anyhow.

Many respondents claimed that 'there just wasn't anything else to do', by which they meant that only cinema as a key leisure activity had obtained the status of cheap and popular mass entertainment. Other forms of entertainment or leisure, like dance halls, bars or opera, were aimed at specific segments of the population, often linked to people with higher social, financial and cultural capital.

Another set of motives to go and see a movie can be classified under the broad category of escapism. Escapism, as Stacey (1994) pointed out, is mostly linked to emotions, but it also has a strong material dimension. Many went to the cinema because it offered them a level of comfort they could not afford:

> Irène (1945): That was a completely different world. I lived in a world where I did not have much. You were able to experience luxury on the screen. It provided a little bit of comfort and you wanted to have the same at home.

A final set of motives or reasons for going to the picture show deals with the sense of belonging to a community. In many interviews, cinema-going was remembered as a collective and social experience. Respondents frequented cinemas because they felt a group identity, often referred to as the 'atmosphere' of a cinema.

> Joanne (1923): Everything went on in your own neighbourhood. Those were the days.

A cinema's atmosphere was often linked to some form of social informality, security or even freedom, where in neighbourhood cinema's 'you could shout at the screen, sit on the floor, bring your own food'. Reflecting about today's cinema, many respondents expressed a sense of fear and unease about the current state of city centres, often linked to physical dangers and contemporary night-time leisure activities.

Conclusion

In this chapter, we provided an overview of the wide range of studies on film audiences over the past decades. It has become clear that this interest in the lived experiences of film audiences came about under the influence of various theoretical paradigms, methodological strands and with input from different disciplines, such as cultural studies, cognitive psychology, film history, media studies and feminist film theory. This joint interest for film audiences initiated a 'rapprochement' between different strands of film audience studies, dealing with both contemporary and historical audiences. The field also instigated a lively debate on theories, methods and research practices, and it has given rise to interesting interdisciplinary exchanges. To elaborate on the new cinema history approach, we reported on a case study dealing with historical cinema-going audiences in two Belgian cities. Using detailed analyses of oral history accounts, we detect that cinema-going was a significant social routine, strongly inspired by community identity formation, class and social distinction. The overall picture of the film audiences highlights them as social media users, historically the first social audiences for a modern mass medium, and they remain social media users in our contemporary media-saturated culture.

References

Allen, R., 1990. From exhibition to reception: Reflections on the audience in film history. *Screen*, 31(4), pp. 347–356.

——— 1999. Home alone together: Hollywood and the family film. In M. Stokes and R. Maltby, eds, *Identifying Hollywood's audiences: Cultural identity and the movies*. London: British Film Institute. pp. 109–134.

Altenloh, E., 1914. *Zur Sociologie des Kino: Die Kino-unternehmung und die sozialen Schichten ihrer besucher*. Leipzig, Germany: Spamerschen Buchdruckerei.

Austin, B.A., 1983. *The film audience: An international bibliography of research*. Metuchen & London: Scarecrow Press.

Austin, T., 2002. *Hollywood, hype and audiences*. Manchester, UK: Manchester University Press.

Barker, M., 1999. Film audience research: Making a virtue out of a necessity. *Iris*, 26, pp. 131–147.

Barker, M. and Brooks, K., 1998. *Knowing audiences: Judge Dredd, its friends, fans and foes*. Luton: John Libbey.

Barker, M., Arthurs, J. and Harindranath, R., 2001. *The Crash controversy: Censorship campaigns and film reception*. London: Wallflower Press.

Biltereyst, D. and Meers, P., 2011. The political economy of audiences. In J. Wasko, G. Murdoch and H. Sousa, eds, *The handbook of political economy of communications*. Malden: Blackwell. pp. 415–435.

Biltereyst, D., Maltby, R. and Meers, P., eds, 2012. *Cinema, audiences and modernity: New perspectives on European cinema history*. London: Routledge.

Blumer, H., 1933. *Movies and conduct*. New York: Macmillan.

Bobo, J., 1988. 'The Colour Purple': Black women as cultural readers. In E. Pribam, ed., *Female spectators: Looking at film and television*. London: Verso. pp. 90–109.

Bolin, G., 2000. Film swapping in the public sphere: Youth audiences and alternative cultural publicities. *Javnost – The Public*, 7(2), pp. 57–73.

Bordwell, D., 1985. *Narration in the fiction film*. London: Methuen.

Bordwell, D., Thompson, K. and Staiger, J., 1985. *The classical Hollywood cinema: Film style & mode of production to 1960*. London: Routledge.

Cannon, D., 1995. *Judge Dredd*. Burbank, CA: Hollywood Pictures/Santa Monica: Cinergi Pictures Entertainment.

Casetti, F., 1998. *Inside the gaze: The fiction film and its spectator*. Bloomington, IN: Indiana University Press.

Coppola, F., 1992. *Bram Stoker's Dracula*. San Francisco, CA: American Zoetrope/Culver City, CA: Columbia Pictures Corporation/Burbank, CA: Osiris Films.

Corbett, K.J., 1998–9. Empty seats: The missing history of movie-watching. *Journal of Film and Video*, 50(4), pp. 34–48.

Cronenberg, D., 1996. *Crash*. Montreal: Alliance Communications Corporation & The Movie Network/London: Recorded Picture Company (RPC)/Montreal & Toronto: Téléfilm Canada.

Davis, A.M., 2001. The fall and rise of 'fantasia'. In M. Stokes and R. Maltby, eds, *Hollywood spectatorship: Changing perceptions of cinema audiences*. London: British Film Institute. pp. 63–78.

Dudrah, R., 2002. Vilayati Bollywood: Popular Hindi cinema-going and diasporic South Asian identity in Birmingham. *Javnost – The Public*, 9, pp. 19–36.

Dyer, R., 1986. *Heavenly bodies: Film stars and society*. New York: St. Martin's Press.

Fuller-Seeley, K.H. and Potamianos, G., 2008. Introduction: Researching and writing the history of local moviegoing. In K.H. Fuller-Seeley, ed., *Hollywood in the neighborhood: Historical case studies of local moviegoing*. Berkeley, CA: University of California Press. pp. 3–19.

Gillespie, M., 1995. *Television, ethnicity and cultural change*. London: Routledge.

Gomery, D., 1992. *Shared pleasures: A history of movie presentation in the United States*. Madison, WI: University of Wisconsin Press.

Grieveson, L., 1999. Why the audience mattered in Chicago in 1907. In M. Stokes and R. Maltby, eds, *American movie audiences: From the turn of the century to the early sound era*. London: British Film Institute. pp. 79–91.

Gripsrud, J., 1998. Film audiences. In J. Hill and P. Church Gibson, eds, *The Oxford guide to film studies*. Oxford: Oxford University Press. pp. 202–211.

Hansen, M., 1991. *Babel and Babylon: Spectatorship in American silent film*. Cambridge, MA: Harvard University Press.

Hill, A., 1997. *Shocking entertainment: Viewer response to violent movies*. Luton: John Libbey.

Jancovich, M., Faire, L. and Stubbings, S., 2003. *The place of the audience: Cultural geographies of film consumption*. London: British Film Institute.

Jenkins, H., 2000. Reception theory and audience research: The mystery of the vampire's kiss. In C. Gledhill and L. Williams, eds, *Reinventing film studies*. London: Arnold. pp. 165–182.

Klenotic, J., 2008. 'Four hours of hootin' and hollerin'': Moviegoing and everyday life outside the movie palace. In R. C. Allen, R. Maltby and M. Stokes, eds, *Hollywood and the social experience of movie-going.* Exeter, UK: University of Exeter Press. pp. 130–154.

Klinger, B., 1997. Film history terminable and interminable: Recovering the past in reception studies. *Screen*, 38(2), pp. 107–128.

Kuhn, A., 1984. Women's genres. *Screen*, 25(1), pp. 18–28.

———— 2002. *An everyday magic: Cinema and cultural memory.* London: I.B. Tauris.

Lapsley, R. and Westlake, M., 2006. *Film theory: An introduction.* Manchester, UK: Manchester University Press.

Maltby, R., 2006. On the prospect of writing cinema history from below. *Tijdschrift voor Mediageschiedenis*, 9(2), pp. 74–96.

Maltby, R., Biltereyst, D. and Meers, P., eds, *Explorations in new cinema history: Approaches and case studies.* Malden, MA: Wiley-Blackwell.

Maxwell, R., 2000. Surveillance and other consuming encounters in the informational marketplace. In I. Hagen and J. Wasko, eds, *Consuming audiences? Production and reception in media research.* Cresskill, NJ: Hampton Press. pp. 95–110.

Meers, P., 2004. 'It's the language of film!' Young film audiences on Hollywood and Europe. In R. Maltby and M. Stokes, eds, *Hollywood abroad: Audiences and cultural exchange.* London: British Film Institute. pp. 158–175.

Metz, C., 1975/1984. *Le signifiant imaginaire: Psychanalyse et cinéma.* Paris: Bourgeois.

Miller, T., Govil, N., McMurria, J. and Maxwell, R., 2001. *Global Hollywood.* London: British Film Institute.

Morley, D., 1992. *Television, audiences and cultural studies.* London: Routledge.

Naficy, H., 1993. *The making of exile cultures: Iranian television in Los Angeles.* Minneapolis, MN: University of Minnesota Press.

Palmgreen, P., Cook, P., Harvill, J. and Helm, D., 1988. The motivational framework of moviegoing: Uses and avoidances of theatrical films. In B.A. Austin, ed., *Current research in film: Audiences, economics & law*, Vol. 4. Norwood, NJ: Ablex. pp. 1–23.

Pribam, D., 1988. Female spectators: Looking at film and television. In D. Pribam, ed., *Female spectators: Looking at film and television.* New York: Verso. pp. 1–11.

Prince, S., 1996. Psychoanalytic film theory and the problem of the missing spectator. In D. Bordwell and N. Carroll, eds, *Post-theory: Reconstructing film studies.* Madison, WI: University of Wisconsin Press. pp. 71–86.

Richards, H., 2003. Memory reclamation of cinema going in Bridgend, South Wales, 1930–1960. *Historical Journal of Film, Radio and Television*, 23(4), pp. 341–355.

Smythe, D.W., 2001. On the audience commodity and its work. In M.G. Durham and D. Kellner, eds, *Media and cultural studies: Keyworks.* Malden, MA: Blackwell. pp. 253–279.

Spielberg, S., 1985. *The color purple.* Universal City, CA: Amblin Entertainment/Los Angeles, CA: The Guber-Peters Company/Burbank, CA: Warner Bros. Pictures.

Stacey, J., 1994. *Star gazing: Hollywood cinema and female spectatorship in 1940s and 1950s Britain.* London: Routledge.

Staiger, J., 1986. 'The handmaiden of villainy': Methods and problems in studying the historical reception of film. *Wide Angle*, 8(1), pp. 19–27.

———— 1992. *Interpreting films: Studies in the historical reception of American cinema.* Princeton, NJ: Princeton University Press.

———— 2000. *Perverse spectators: The practices of film reception.* New York: New York University Press.

———— 2005. *Media reception studies.* New York: New York University Press.

Stokes, M., 1999. Introduction: Reconstructing American cinema's audiences. In M. Stokes and R. Maltby, eds, *American movie audiences: From the turn of the century to the early sound era.* London: British Film Institute. pp. 1–14.

Stokes, M. and Maltby, R., eds, 1999a. *American movie audiences: From the turn of the century to the early sound era.* London: British Film Institute.

———— 1999b. *Identifying Hollywood's audiences: Cultural identity and the movies.* London: British Film Institute.

———— 2001. *Hollywood spectatorship: Changing perceptions of cinema audiences.* London: British Film Institute.

Stone, O., 1994. *Natural born killers.* Burbank, CA: Warner Bros. Pictures.

Taylor, H., 1989. *Scarlett's women: 'Gone with the wind' and its female fans.* London: Virago.

Turner, G., 2002. Editor's introduction. In G. Turner, ed., *The film cultures reader.* London/ New York: Routledge. pp. 1–10.

Uricchio, W. and Pearson, R., 1999. 'The formative and impressionable stage': Discursive constructions of the nickelodeon's child audience. In M. Stokes and R. Maltby, eds, *American movie audiences: From the turn of the century to the early sound era.* London: British Film Institute. pp. 64–75.

Verhoeven, P., 1992. *Basic instinct.* Los Angeles, CA: Carolco/Issy Les Moulineaux: Le Studio Canal.

Wasko, J. and Meehan E.R., 2001. Dazzled by Disney? Ambiguity in ubiquity. In J. Wasko, M. Phillips and E.R. Meehan, eds, *Dazzled by Disney? The Global Disney Audiences project.* London/New York: Leicester University Press. pp. 329–343.

Wasko, J., Phillips, M. and Meehan, E.R., eds, 2001. *Dazzled by Disney? The Global Disney Audiences project.* London/New York: Leicester University Press.

Willis, A., 1995. Cultural studies and popular film. In J. Hollows and M. Jancovich, eds, *Approaches to popular film.* Manchester/New York: Manchester University Press. pp. 173–191.

Note

1   'The "Enlightened" City: Screen Culture between Ideology, Economics and Experience' is a study on the social role of film exhibition and film consumption in Flanders (1895–2004) in interaction with modernity and urbanization (project funded by the FWO/SRC-Flanders, promoters: Philippe Meers University of Antwerp, Daniel Biltereyst Ghent University and Marnix Beyen University of Antwerp).

Chapter 8

Talking Recipients: An Integrative Model of Socio-Emotional
Meta-Appraisal (SEMA) in Conversations about Media Content

Katrin Döveling and Denise Sommer

Introduction

Emotions play an essential role in communication processes in day-to-day interactions as well as in media exposure. Scholars are increasingly conceptualizing emotions as a relevant source of information when examining media contents (Döveling, von Scheve and Konijn 2011). However, to date, emotions have been approached mainly from the individual audience member's perspective. Yet media exposure does not end at the individual level. Mass-mediated messages are processed and discussed with peers to reassure one's subjective understanding and validate individual positions, emotions and perceptions. Consequently, this chapter elucidates the role emotions play within the communicative processing of media content and vice versa. After a review of the current literature, an integrative model of socio-emotional meta-appraisal (SEMA) in TV reception is proposed conceptualizing media reception as an ongoing emotional negotiation process (cf. Döveling and Sommer 2008). The model integrates relevant theorizing on the complex interrelations between emotions and interpersonal communication before, during and after TV use. Subsequently, a case study provides empirical illustration for the model. An experiment reveals how media users actively discuss and evaluate reality TV in their peer group. The results exemplify how emotional responses to media offerings are negotiated and may thus be changed within the process of SEMA.

The Emotional Processing of Media Messages

Psychological research on emotional aspects of media use has mostly focused on the subjective experience as well as the physiological and expressive nature of emotions. The underlying notion of such research lies in the idea that certain events elicit emotions through a complex set of evaluations, as explicated in appraisal theory (Scherer, Schorr and Johnstone 2001). Within this concept, Arnold (1960) and Lazarus (1966, 1991) advanced the groundbreaking idea that subjective interpretation and evaluation is an imperative necessity in the elicitation and differentiation of emotions. In short, we evaluate events and people in our surroundings. This assessment, or so-called 'appraisal', leads to emotion.

The stimulus-evaluation-check model (Lazarus 1991; Scherer 1984, 1992) enables us to define emotions more precisely, not only in everyday life situations but also in media use. According to Scherer, emotions fulfil an important function as 'an evolved phylogenetically continuous mechanism allowing increasingly flexible adaptation to environmental contingencies by decoupling stimulus and response and thus creating a latency time for response optimization' (Scherer 2001: 92). He thus defines emotion

> as a sequence of interrelated, synchronized changes in the states of all organismic subsystems (information processing, support, execution, action, monitoring) in response to the evaluation of an external or internal stimulus event as relevant to central concerns of the organism. (Scherer 1992: 150)

He proposes five major stimulus evaluation checks (SECs) which account for the differentiation of most emotional states. These five SECs include (1) novelty check (Have external or internal stimuli changed?), (2) intrinsic pleasantness check (Is it pleasant or unpleasant for the individual?), (3) goal/need significance check (Does it support or oppose one's own goals?), (4) coping potential check (To what extent does a person believe to control the event?) and (5) norm/self compatibility check (How does the event relate to one's internal and external standards?). In such a way, the process of appraising the stimulus 'in-relation-to-self' (Manstead and Fischer 2001: 224) is taken into account.

The original appraisal concept is a general one and explains the elicitation of emotions. Unz (2011) has applied this notion to emotions in media reception. She focuses on the appraisal component in the emotional processing of TV news and explores the role of presentation modes and editing. She notes that 'though media-induced emotions are processed in the same way as naturally occurring emotions, emotions induced by media may differ in some aspects from naturally occurring emotions' (Unz 2011: 295). Formal production attributes (e.g. editing, camera changes, cuts and movement) can influence the appraisal outcomes of novelty (orienting response), intrinsic pleasantness, causality and coping in news reception (Unz 2011).

On the one hand, the appraisal of media content in media reception leads to emotions. On the other hand, these emotions, once elicited, are appraised by recipients as well as their significant others, such as family and peers. As Rimé et al. (1992) show, most emotional experiences are shared with others shortly after they happen. Such social sharing signifies a fundamental part of emotional experiences (Christophe and Rimé 1997; Rimé et al. 1998). Moreover, research clearly demonstrates that in the hours, days and weeks following an emotional event, memories of that event tend to interfere with people's thoughts. These thoughts and appraisals are associated with an urge to talk about and to share the emotional experience with others. A number of studies have explored the 'social sharing of emotions' across cultures and have found remarkably similar social sharing rates around the world. Social sharing of emotion is thus a cross-cultural phenomenon (Rimé et al. 1992: 238–239, 1998). In such a way, we consider social sharing of emotional judgements as an integral component of emotional experiences within the different phases of TV reception.

This holds equally true for the *anticipation* of others' appraisals. We do not only consider the judgements of others with whom we socially share but we anticipate how others define the situation and how they are likely to feel about it. Expanding Lazarus' and Scherer's concept, Manstead and Fischer (2001: 224) call this phenomenon 'social appraisal'. They point out:

> What is crucial is that individuals anticipate others' definitions of the situation and how they are likely to respond to the situation and to our behaviors. This anticipation is needed in order to coordinate social activity: if we act without any consideration of the implications for how we are evaluated by others, we risk losing their esteem and ultimately our social bonds with them. (Manstead and Fischer 2001: 224)

Consequently, although a lot of fruitful research illuminates the emotions from a subjective perspective of the individual, social evaluation plays a central role in the elicitation of emotions because communicating with others is essential for one's own appraisal of media information. In this context, the exploration of recipients' discussions and elaborations on media (content) is highly beneficial. It provides further insight into the actual processing of media messages as these are embedded in a social context and into its potential consequences for subsequent media use.

Interpersonal Communication and Media Reception

Since the 'People's Choice' (Lazarsfeld, Berelson and Gaudet 1944), the importance of interpersonal communication for media effects has been acknowledged by communication scholars. Interpersonal encounters were found to have a strong influence on evaluative processes, whereas mediated communication mainly fulfilled informative functions (Lazarsfeld, Berelson and Gaudet 1944). Uses and gratifications research reveals the *conversation motive* as one core reason to turn to mass media: recipients use media to be able to talk to other people about it (Levy and Windahl 1984). Accordingly, Berelson (1949) highlights the social prestige of being able to take part in conversations about current political and societal topics. From one-third to one-half of the daily conversations examined in observation studies dealt with media topics (Greenberg 1975; Kepplinger and Martin 1986). Media contents provide important common ground for people in their conversations and thus fulfil an integrative function for society. However, it is not just media content per se but specific spectacular and emotionally moving stories from press and television which evoke the strongest need to be shared with others (Rogers and Seidel 2002). Accordingly, this social sharing of one's emotions and judgements fulfils a central gratifying emotional function, as it offers ontological security (Cohen and Metzger 1998).

Consequently, conversations about media content are crucial in appraising not only media stimuli but also our own as well as other persons' evaluations of these stimuli. Conversations give reason to turn to media before the actual exposure. They initiate media use as people anticipate later references to media content in communication (Berelson 1949;

Levy and Windahl 1984). Communicative processing accompanies media use if people watch television together and talk about the programme simultaneously (Haefner and Wartella 1987). In this context, a quite current phenomenon is the tendency to follow major television events such as the Soccer World Cup together with a group of friends or in public (Krotz 2001). In addition, media contents are repeatedly mentioned in interpersonal exchange after media use as they are helpful to initiate conversations, to teach others about certain facts, to persuade conversation partners and to validate one's own impressions and views in everyday life communication (Greenberg 1975; Kepplinger and Martin 1986).

In spite of this, there are very few systematic studies which centre on the dynamics of interpersonal communication in regard to media and explore the role of conversations within the emotional processing of media stimuli. Moreover, one must be aware of the fact that although recent communication research has started focusing on emotional reception processes and media effects, the notion of a social appraisal has rarely been applied to the emotional processing of media contents and experiences.

The Focal Point: The Interdependency of Emotional Reception and Interpersonal Communication

People have a need for social affiliation and strive for belongingness to social groups (Cohen and Metzger 1998). Because the individual is fundamentally engaged in social constellations, we claim to take into consideration that the social dimension within appraisal, as suggested by Manstead and Fischer (2001), is vital in understanding how media offers are processed.

Social appraisal involves taking the role of the other in social interaction by putting oneself into another person's position to think and reflect about oneself. Role taking fulfils the central function of being able to predict and judge the potential reactions of others and thus act in an appropriate manner in social situations. Accordingly, it is crucial for human beings to consider how the majority of reference group members assess an action and an emotion-eliciting situation (Scherer 2001: 98).

In general, there are three lines of research addressing this issue (Manstead and Fischer 2001). 'Emotional contagion' focuses on the effects of the presence of others and how their facial and other expressions may lead to imitation: 'emotional contagion is the tendency to automatically mimic and synchronize facial expressions, vocalizations, postures, and movements with those of another person and, consequently, to converge emotionally' (Hatfield, Cacioppo and Rapson 1994: 5). 'Social comparison theory' postulates the human need for social association with significant others as a relevant source of orientation within the community. Festinger (1954: 117) states that '[t]here exists, in the human organism, a drive to evaluate his opinions and his abilities'. Specifically, '[t]o the extent that objective, non-social means are not available, people evaluate their opinions and abilities by comparison respectively with the opinions and abilities of others' (Festinger 1954: 118). These comparisons are mainly drawn with close and similar persons because of the attractiveness of reference groups: the more we feel attracted to a group, the more we want to be similar to its members and be liked by them. A third line of research deals with 'the shared construction of social reality', which can be described as an ongoing long-term process of our manifold everyday communicative actions resulting in shared reflections, images and evaluations of and within our social community. Based on symbolic interactionism, meaning is not fixed by an objective reality (Mead 1934). Instead, it is constructed and permanently adjusted in human interaction. Through socialization processes and role taking, we learn to understand shared symbols, knowledge, rules and norms within specific communities as well as within society. These experiences all shape and influence our perceptions of reality (Keppler 1994; Krotz 2001).

By taking these different processes into account, it becomes obvious that they all are intertwined and connected to interpersonal communication. Whereas the first type is a very spontaneous, perhaps often non-verbal, interpersonal communication, the second and third type most probably encompass series of interpersonal encounters over longer periods of time. The underlying focal point here is that interpersonal communication is to be seen as the basic process in connecting with others and thus an essential component within social appraisal. Following this argument, we postulate that emotions are subject of ongoing negotiation processes, which are elaborated in the model of SEMA.

'Dynamic Transaction' in Media Use

The SEMA model is built on the notion of dynamic transaction in media use (Früh and Schönbach 1982; Schönbach and Früh 1984). According to Wenner (1985), the concept of transaction has a long tradition in psychological and sociological approaches to human communication. He characterizes these approaches as follows: '[b]asic to these concepts is an ontological view of man as actively creating meaning within the context of a system, and a related epistemological view of scientific inquiry that stresses holism and process' (Wenner 1985: 76). Furthermore, he specifies that 'the concept of transaction [...] is the clear focus on dynamic change, not only within the individual, but within and among individuals, media, and society' (Wenner 1985: 92–93).

Transaction thus takes into account that every communicative act has an effect on its environment as well as a reflexive impact on oneself. Therefore, the concept widens the scope of causal effects as it takes into account the diverse interrelations of self and media on the micro-, meso- and macro-level. Its process-oriented conceptualization of communication includes (a) the cultural and societal context of the shared construction of reality as well as (b) the specific individual and situational contexts of social comparison processes and emotional contagion. Moreover, this concept can be used to integrate social appraisal mechanisms before, during and after media exposure.

Pertaining to the process of media use, two distinctive ways of dynamic transaction are taken into account. The first, 'intra-transactions', arise as feedback processes within the recipient. They refer to the interplay of long-term structures such as knowledge and beliefs, and short-term reactions like activation and evaluations of the current situation (Schönbach and Früh 1984: 315). It is here that individual appraisal processes take place, which result in emotions. 'Inter-transactions', in contrast, connect recipients with media offerings in specific ways. Recipients select and interpret media stimuli according to their general dispositions and current cognitive as well as emotional states. In this manner, the media text becomes 'their' subjective stimulus. During media exposure, the communicator cannot influence the individual reception process. However, this subjective understanding is by no means independent from media form and content (cf. Döveling and Sommer 2008) and can be regarded as a reciprocal exchange on both sides.

These two types of processes are closely intertwined with each other in an ongoing dynamic interplay. Compared to direct interaction processes, the idea of transaction enables an analysis which posits an integrative view on processes that are related to each other within a larger context without being directly connected – as we typically find them in mass communication (Wenner 1985). Such a complex and dynamic view of media reception is essential for the model of SEMA as it considers the discrete dynamics of media use; the individual, cultural and situational context; as well as the manifold interdependencies between recipient, media offers and its environment over time.

The Model of SEMA in Media Reception

Based on the dynamic-transactional perspective on communication, the model of SEMA (see Figure 1) integrates the concept of social appraisal and interpersonal communication so as to depict and elucidate the complex process of socio-emotional processing of television messages.

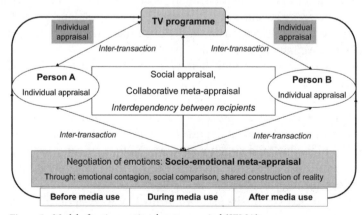

Figure 1: Model of socio-emotional meta-appraisal (SEMA).

The upper and outer part of the model illustrates individual appraisal processes accompanying the dynamic-transactional process of television use. It is here that inter-transaction comes into play. On the one hand, this inter-transaction entails individual appraisal mechanisms from the recipients' subjective interpretations of the mediated situation. On the other hand, media messages expose their specific facets in form as well as in content, which disclose a set of shared social notions that are intertwined with the recipients' own worlds. That is, in inter-transaction, media recipients actively interpret and decipher mediated messages based on their subjective appraisals and social experiences.

The lower part of the model illustrates the distinctive time perspectives which converge in the sphere of SEMA. The processing of media information does not only take place during exposure: it entails different phases of social interaction before, during and after TV use. At the same time, in all three phases, not only individual appraisal mechanisms take place. Socially shared appraisals directly influence one's own individual appraisal mechanisms at all phases of media use. These may lead to direct effects in expressing one's emotions (Manstead and Fischer 2001: 227), involving emotional (re)appraisal and change. This point of view equally takes into account that social appraisal appears to be more salient in the phases of media use when the other person is a friend rather than a stranger (Manstead and Fischer 2001: 229).

Individual appraisals, however, may have been subject to preceding interpersonal communication, highlighted as social appraisal not only in the centre but also in the lower part of the model. In a coviewing situation, individuals often instantaneously initiate a discussion about their appraisals and subsequent feelings. However, this consideration of others is not limited to the phase of exposure with others. Even when watching TV alone, recipients anticipate the reactions of and later interactions with significant others (like peers and family) to be able to integrate and later validate their own feelings in a social context. In such a manner, the social sphere impacts individual appraisal processes even when others are not physically present during media reception.

As revealed above, in social interaction, a collaborative meta-appraisal of the recipients' different individual appraisals takes place. In contrast to individual appraisal processes, the collaborative evaluation checks do not only relate to the assessments of novelty, pleasantness and so forth. At the same time, emotions themselves are appraised in such a way that recipients check how well their emotional reactions towards the TV programme correspond to the feelings of their peers. This meta-appraisal can either result in consonance or dissonance with one's own appraisal. The complexity of social interactions, whether they occur parallel to media use or afterwards, affects individual appraisals through (a) a reinforcement and enhancement of one's individual appraisal, strengthening and supporting one's own emotional assessment, or in contrast, (b) an attenuation of one's individual appraisal, weakening one's own emotional assessment.

The interdependency between recipients is to be considered a central link in the analysis of emotional reception processes. As Manstead and Fischer note, 'physical or symbolic presence of another person may induce social appraisals and affect secondary appraisal processes, if the presence of other persons is in some way functional' (Manstead and Fischer 2001: 227). Through interpersonal communication about media content, a meta-/reappraisal is undertaken which subsequently and reciprocally affects and changes the emotional dispositions and assessments of the individual in all phases of media exposure.

Empirical Evidence: A Case Study of SEMA in Popular Reality TV Reception

The SEMA model is a theoretical framework that explains the role of emotions and interpersonal communication for processing and appraising media stimuli, specifically focusing on social appraisal mechanisms. Following this idea, an explorative empirical support for the model is presented. The negotiation of emotions is examined in an experiment comparing the emotional processing of a reality TV show under the conditions of solo versus group viewing.

Undoubtedly, reality TV appeals to large audiences around the world. Nabi et al. (2003: 304) defined reality TV as

> programs that film real people as they live out events (contrived or otherwise) in their lives, as these events occur. Such programming is characterized by several elements: (a) people portraying themselves (i.e., not actors or public figures performing the roles), (b) filmed at least in part in their living or working environment rather than on a set, (c) without a script, (d) with events placed in a narrative context, (e) for the primary role of viewer entertainment. (Nabi et al. 2003: 304)

This analysis is built on literature suggesting that reality TV viewers are highly sociable and enjoy interacting with others (Nabi et al. 2003). As 'real'-life characters and stories are presented, reality TV allows for a discussion about real incidents. This holds especially true for so-called casting shows, where candidates are presented who compete against each other to reach 'fame and fortune'. Individual and collective narration animates the formation of social consensus. Through this social consideration of media content in interpersonal communication, an exchange is engendered about moral assessment, principles and belief systems. This transforms individual experiences into collective ones and acts as an important influence on one's own emotional experience, which in turn stimulates further media reception.

Furthermore, as found by Haefner and Wartella (1987) and McDonald (1986), peer coviewing is one of the most common viewing styles in our everyday life. Viewing television with others may give individuals the opportunity to reduce uncertainty and increase accurate predictions about media personae by sharing judgements and evaluations with others (Southwell and Yzer 2009). Peer coviewing may have a number of consequences:

(a) group norms may serve to reinforce both positive and negative views of media characters and their experiences; (b) at the same time, in interpersonal communication, individuals can reflect on their emotional assessments and negotiate on individual appraisal; (c) thus, groups supply a helpful resource for individual appraisals in the formation of opinions and emotional judgements about media texts.

Consequently, it is hypothesized that peer coviewing has a direct influence on individual appraisal mechanisms in dynamic-transactional processes as proposed by the SEMA model. Discussions with others, before and after being exposed to reality TV, influence individual appraisals through either readjustment or reinforcement.

Method

A laboratory experiment investigating the emotional processing of a reality TV show was conducted in 2008 at a large German university.[1] Participants were recruited in classes and randomly assigned to either group or solo viewing conditions. All participants were asked to watch a clip (approx. 25 minutes) of a popular German reality TV casting show, *Deutschland sucht den Superstar (DSDS)/German Idol* showing four successful and four unsuccessful auditions. Eleven groups, comprised of three members each, watched the show together and were allowed to talk to each other freely while watching. The control group consisted of nine solo viewers. The average age of the viewers was 24. In total, 30 per cent of the viewers were male.

The co-viewing situations were videotaped to capture the distinctive verbal and non-verbal interactions. These videotapes were transliterated by keeping track of every verbal and facial expression observed for each person in a group. As the participants had been observed while watching the show, any response was matched to the timeline of the TV stimulus, thus allowing a process measure of individual and group appraisals in the reception situation itself. A qualitative analysis investigated the particular individual and group reactions to the TV show. Each response was studied and related to (a) the TV stimulus as well as (b) the potential responses of the conversation partners.

By matching the timelines of the television clip and conversations, we could identify the situations within the show to which recipients responded emotionally. The timelines also suggested how participants responded to each other and interacted. All their responses were interpreted against the background of the SEMA model.

Additionally, all participants filled in a post-task questionnaire individually. Emotional responses to the show were assessed by ten adjectives describing the stimulus (*amusing, shocking, enjoyable, disgusting, exciting, offensive, inspiring, annoying, true to life and unrealistic*). Participants' emotional judgments about the candidates of the show were measured by statements about the most successful contestant, i.e. "*I hope this contestant achieves his/her goals*", "*I can imagine being friends with this contestant*", "*I admire this contestant*", etc. All items were measured on 5-point Likert scales ranging from (1) "*strongly disagree*" to (5) "*strongly agree*".

Results

Following our assumption that interpersonal communication elicits reappraisals, we compared the experimental conditions with regard to their emotional responses. Significant differences between the group viewing situation and the solo viewing situation were disclosed for the emotions 'excitement' (group: $M = 2.66$, $SD = 1.32$; solo: $M = 3.89$, $SD = 0.33$; $t = -2.94$, $p < .001$) and 'inspiration' (group: $M = 1.53$, $SD = 0.98$; solo: $M = 2.78$, $SD = 0.83$; $t = -3.46$, $p < .001$). In both instances, participants in the group viewing condition reported lower emotional reactions than those in the solo viewing condition. Similarly, emotional judgements about the most successful contestant of the show were significantly lower in the group viewing condition than in the solo viewing condition (see Table 1).

Interestingly, we do not find evidence for an enhancement or intensification of certain emotions after social interaction in a group viewing situation but an attenuation leading to a more moderate appraisal of the show. Obviously, the social comparison processes in the group seem to result in a rationalization and a more distanced view of the format. Subsequently, the videotaped group conversations were analysed to identify the processes behind these effects.

SEMA in Dynamic Transaction

First, we observe individual appraisals of the show (Table 2, time: 9:50–9:55 and Table 3, time: 20:40–20:45): Recipients are quite concentrated on what is happening in the show, trying to evaluate subjectively what they see. They express their individual reactions to the show by grinning or looking sceptical. Interestingly, subjective reactions to the show differed

Table 1: Appraisals of most successful candidates after TV use

Appraisal of most successful candidates	Group (*n* = 32)		Solo viewers (*n* = 9)		t test		
	M	*SD*	*M*	*SD*	*df*	*t*	*sig*
Hope they achieve their goals	3.47	1.270	4.89	0.333	39	−3.296	.002
Admire them	2.09	0.963	4.11	1.269	39	−5.176	.000
Like their attitude	3.34	1.066	4.78	0.667	39	−3.812	.000
Like their personality	3.56	1.014	4.89	0.333	39	−3.835	.000

Table 2: Example of individual appraisals and emotional contagion

Time	Stimulus	Verbal expression (A)	Facial expression/gesture (A)	Verbal expression (B)	Facial expression/gesture (B)	Verbal expression (C)	Facial expression/gesture (C)
09:50	Candidate: 'Sure, I got something.'			'It is so cool when he tries to convince them, you know? Like …' (to A and C)	Grins		Looks sceptical (towards TV)
09:55	Candidate: 'Tell me, who was the biggest flop in DSDS history?'		Looks concentrated (towards TV), open mouth, stiff posture		Looks concentrated (towards TV), open mouth (partly covered by her hand), eyes wide open, stiff posture		Looks concentrated (towards TV), stiff posture
10:00	Dieter Bohlen (jury member): 'You!'	Laughs			Grins, covers mouth with sheet of paper		
10:05						'Pretty mean, eh?' (to A and B)	

153

Table 3: Illustration of social comparison and interaction

Time	Stimulus	Verbal expression (A)	Facial expression/ gesture (A)	Verbal expression (B)	Facial expression/ gesture (B)	Verbal expression (C)	Facial expression/ gesture (C)
20:40	Candidate talks about Dieter Bohlen: 'he always speaks extremely critical'	'Oahh'			Looks (towards TV), eyes and mouth wide open, bites nails, stiff posture		Looks (towards TV), arms crossed, stiff posture
20:45		'Well, that wasn't too bad'	Grins	'Ssh! wait' (to A)	Puts finger on lips, nudges (A)		Looks (towards TV)
20:50	Candidate: 'I know exactly what Dieter Bohlen is like: tough like a pig!'	Laughs		Laughs	Looks (towards C)	'Dumb', laughs	Looks (towards B)
20:55		'Yeah', laughs		Laughs	Nods, looks (towards C)	'So a pig is tough? I see.'	

between group members but equally revealed similar responses. Thus inter-transactions oscillating back and forth between TV stimulus and recipients become observable. Individual interpretations and influences of the specific show interrelate at a time during media exposure.

Moreover, in parallel, recipients also observe their co-viewers and react to them by looking at them (Table 3, time: 20:50–20:55), prompting them to be silent (Table 3, time: 20:45) or agreeing with them (Table 4, time: 17:20 and Table 5, time: 19:10). In addition, they display the same or similar behaviours, expressions or responses at a time (Table 2, time: 9:55–10:00 and Table 3, time: 20:50), indicating processes of social comparison.

As postulated in the SEMA model, not only verbal but also non-verbal cues prompt communicative processes. These revealed processes of emotional contagion. In the first example (Table 2), all three recipients remain in the same stiff posture while experiencing the suspense of the scenery. Participants A and B in Table 4 both show the same non-verbal reaction to the embarrassing behaviour of the TV character (putting their hands on their heads). Later on, participants B and C follow the show by displaying the same gestures and posture (crossing their arms).

Obviously, in this group viewing situation, recipients follow the media offering and their co-viewers' reactions concurrently, appraising both in an ongoing dynamic inter-transactional process. This process illustrates the need for social orientation as part of the SEMA. Compatibility not only with one's own internal standards but equally with social consensus among co-viewers appears to be a vital factor that affects emotional evaluation and processing.

Finally, as revealed in Table 5, participants engage in a conversation by commenting on the show, and within this communicative behaviour directly reacting to each other. Thus, they negotiate their specific shared constructions of reality. These shared assessments refer to their individual perceptions and appraisals of the TV offering as well as the viewing situation.

However, this conversation might as well have taken place outside the direct reception situation. It could also have occurred after the show as recipients talk about their general experiences with the format, which could also stem from former episodes of media use. This fact demonstrates the dynamics of SEMA reaching beyond the moment of media use and exposure, expanding directly into people's everyday lives.

Consequently, in a group viewing situation, the dynamic complexity of transactional reception processes becomes apparent as viewers express their appraisals verbally and non-verbally. The examples given above provide a first illustration of the complex mechanisms involved in social media use, when co-viewers' and individual emotional responses to the whole situation occur in parallel. Appraisals are expressed and reflected, both verbally and non-verbally. Eventually, they merge and lead to a dynamic and complex SEMA process (as postulated in the SEMA model). As a result, emotional responses to the media offering may change in the course of action within SEMA as illustrated by the differences in emotional responses between the experimental conditions.

Table 4: Examples of non-verbal cues: emotional contagion and group adjustment

Time	Stimulus	Verbal expression (A)	Facial expression/ gesture (A)	Verbal expression (B)	Facial expression/ gesture (B)	Verbal expression (C)	Facial expression/ gesture (C)
17:15	New candidate introduces herself	'Oh no …'	Puts hands on her head	'Oah, this is bad, oah, I feel so sorry for that' (to TV)	Points (towards TV), puts hands on her head		Looks (towards TV), arms crossed
17:20	Ringing bells are edited in	'I love how they imitate the bells', laughs		'Yeah' (to A), laughs	Arms crossed		Looks (towards TV), arms crossed
17:25		'Oah this is always so cool'		Laughs, 'Man, this is so mean' (towards TV)	Arms crossed	'What kind of voice is that?' (towards TV)	Arms crossed
17:30			Looks (towards TV)	'But somehow she's cute … I don't know …'	Covers mouth with her hand		Looks (towards TV)

Table 5: Illustration of verbal interaction and emotional negotiation

Time	Stimulus	Verbal expression (A)	Facial expression/ gesture (A)	Verbal expression (B)	Facial expression/ gesture (B)	Verbal expression (C)	Facial expression/ gesture (C)
19:05	Candidate's conversation with jury is altered with sound and video effects		Looks (towards B and C)	'I somehow always feel sorry for something like that ... that's weird, I don't know' (to C)	Gesticulates with her hands	'Well, because they are shamelessly put on display'	
19:10		'Do they let anybody in or what?'		Yes (to C)	Nods	'Those who don't experience it can laugh about it' (to B)	

Conclusion and Outlook

Concluding from the SEMA model and the explorative study, emotional media consumption and interpersonal communication are intertwined within a larger context of dynamic-transactional communicative action. Apparently, recipients influence each other in coviewing and co-assessing, and adjust their emotional appraisals verbally and non-verbally. Hence, appraisal of TV programmes is not just to be regarded as an individual evaluation check process that leads to certain emotions. In SEMA processes, individual appraisals are also re-evaluated with reference to the emotional assessment of relevant others. This reveals direct consequences in the effects that media offers may have.

Consequently, media stimuli and their emotional appraisals are subject to continuous processes of social validation and negotiation which influence our feelings and even have the power to modify them. Negotiation processes may lead to an emotional polarization if people have consonant feelings and reinforce emotions in conversation. Communicative processing of emotions, however, may also result in an attenuation of affective reactions, if people perceive that their peers feel different from themselves. In this case, normative pressure is induced and the need for affiliation may prompt a modification of individual appraisal processes.

Based on the concept of appraisal, we conclude that emotions are generated by diverse evaluation checks which need to be integrated into a larger social context. Although media effects may occur on the individual as well as the group level, the concept of transaction takes into account the interdependencies between media stimuli, the individual assessments of these stimuli and the diverse feedback loops. These involve interrelated dynamics between media offerings and recipients as well as between and within recipients in the different phases of media use.

Media offerings do not only 'affect' individual appraisal. In a dynamic transaction, recipients integrate media stimuli into their own lives. They talk about and evaluate it with or by considering relevant others. Thus, social appraisal becomes a central theme in media reception processes.

In this framework of SEMA, social appraisal and the diverse transactional interdependencies involved are to be seen as key variables not only within emotional processing of TV content but also within motivational reception regarding further media exposure. Hence, interpersonal communication can be considered a central component of emotional experiences which directly influences the recipients' appraisal and reappraisal not only of media-related information but also of their own as well as others' emotional assessments related to mass-mediated messages in all phases of media reception.

References

Arnold, M.B., 1960. *Emotion and personality*. New York: Columbia University Press.
Berelson, B., 1949. What 'missing the newspaper' means. In P.F. Lazarsfeld and F.N. Stanton, eds, *Communications research, 1948–1949*. New York: Arno Press. pp. 111–129.

Christophe, V. and Rimé, B., 1997. Exposure to the social sharing of emotion: Emotional impact, listener responses and secondary social sharing. *European Journal of Social Psychology*, 27, pp. 37–54.

Cohen, J. and Metzger, M., 1998. Social affiliation and the achievement of ontological security through interpersonal and mass communication. *Critical Studies in Mass Communication*, 15, pp. 41–60.

Döveling, K. and Sommer, D., 2008. Social Appraisal in der dynamischen Transaktion: Emotionale Aushandlungsprozesse und ihre komplexe Dynamik. In C. Wünsch, W. Früh and V. Gehrau, eds, *Integrative Modelle in der Rezeptions- und Wirkungsforschung: Dynamische und transaktionale Perspektiven*. Munich, Germany: Fischer. pp. 173–196.

Döveling, K., von Scheve, C. and Konijn, E.A., eds, 2011. *Handbook of emotions and the mass media*. Oxfordshire, NY: Routledge/Taylor & Francis.

Festinger, L., 1954. A theory of social comparison processes. *Human Relations*, 7, pp. 117–140.

Früh, W. and Schönbach, K., 1982. Der dynamisch-transaktionale Ansatz. Ein neues Paradigma der Medienwirkungen. *Publizistik*, 27, pp. 74–88.

Greenberg, S.R., 1975. Conversations as units of analysis in the study of personal influence. *Journalism Quarterly*, 52, pp. 128–31.

Haefner, M.J. and Wartella, E.A., 1987. Effects of sibling coviewing on children's interpretations of television programs. *Journal of Broadcasting & Electronic Media*, 31(2), pp. 153–68.

Hatfield, E., Cacioppo, J.T. and Rapson, R.L., 1994. *Emotional contagion*. Cambridge, UK: Cambridge University Press.

Keppler, A., 1994. *Tischgespräche. Über Formen kommunikativer Vergesellschaftung am Beispiel der Konversation in Familien*. Frankfurt, Germany: Suhrkamp.

Kepplinger, H.M. and Martin, V., 1986. Die Funktion von Massenmedien in der Alltagskommunikation. *Publizistik*, 31, pp. 118–128.

Krotz, F., 2001. *Die Mediatisierung des kommunikativen Handelns*. Wiesbaden, Germany: Westdeutscher Verlag.

Lazarsfeld, P.F., Berelson, B. and Gaudet, H., 1944. *The People's Choice – How the voter makes up his mind in a presidential campaign*. New York: Columbia Press.

Lazarus, R.S., 1966. *Psychological stress and the coping process*. New York: McGraw.

———— 1991. *Emotion and adaption*. Oxford, NY: Oxford University Press.

Levy, M. and Windahl, S., 1984. Audience activity and gratifications. A conceptual clarification and exploration. *Communication Research*, 11, pp. 51–78.

Manstead, A.S.R. and Fischer, A.H., 2001. Social appraisal: The social world as object of and influence on appraisal processes. In K.R. Scherer, A. Schorr and T. Johnstone, eds, *Appraisal processes in emotion. Theory, methods, research*. Oxford, UK: Oxford University Press. pp. 221–232.

McDonald, D.G., 1986. Generational aspects of television coviewing. *Journal of Broadcasting & Electronic Media*, 30, pp. 75–85.

Mead, G.H. (1934). *Mind, Self, and Society*. Chicago, IL: University of Chicago Press.

Nabi, R.L., Biely, E.N., Morgan, S.J. and Stitt, C.R., 2003. Reality-based television programming and the psychology of its appeal. *Media Psychology*, 5(4), pp. 303–330.

Rimé, B., Finkenauer, C., Luminet, O., Zech, E. and Philippot, P., 1998. Social sharing of emotion: New evidence and new questions. In W. Stroebe and M. Hewstone, eds, *European Review of Social Psychology*, 9, Chichester, UK: Wiley. pp. 145–189.

Rimé, B., Philippot, P., Boca, S. and Mesquita, B., 1992. Long-lasting cognitive and social consequences of emotion: Social sharing and rumination. In W. Stroebe and M. Hewstone, eds, *European Review of Social Psychology*, 3. Chichester, UK: Wiley. pp. 225–258.

Rogers, E.M. and Seidel, N., 2002. Diffusion of news of the terrorist attacks of September 11, 2001. *Prometheus*, 20, pp. 209–219.

Scherer, K.R., 1984. On the nature and function of emotion: A component process approach. In K.R. Scherer and P. Ekman, eds, *Approaches to emotion*. Hillsdale, NJ: Lawrence Erlbaum. pp. 293–318.

——— 1992. What does facial expression express? In K.T. Strongman, ed. 1992. *International Review of Studies on Emotion*, 2, Chichester: Wiley. pp. 139–165.

——— 2001. Appraisal considered as a process of multilevel sequential checking. In K.R. Scherer, A. Schorr and T. Johnstone, eds, *Appraisal processes in emotion. Theory, methods, research*. Oxford, NY: Oxford University Press. pp. 92–129.

Scherer, K.R., Schorr, A. and Johnstone, T., eds, 2001. *Appraisal processes in emotion. Theory, methods, research*. Oxford, NY: Oxford University Press.

Schönbach, K. and Früh, W., 1984. Der dynamisch-transaktionale Ansatz II: Konsequenzen. *Rundfunk und Fernsehen*, 32, pp. 314–29.

Southwell, B.G. and Yzer, M.C., 2009. When (and why) interpersonal talk matters for campaigns. *Communication Theory*, 19, pp. 1–8.

Unz, D., 2011. Effects of presentation and editing on emotional responses of viewers: The example of TV news. In K. Döveling, C.V. Scheve and E.A. Konijn, eds, *Handbook of emotions and the mass media*. Oxfordshire, NY: Routledge/Taylor & Francis. pp. 294–309.

Wenner, L.A., 1985. Transaction and media gratifications research. In K.E. Rosengren, L.A. Wenner and P. Palmgreen. Eds, *Media gratifications research. Current perspectives*. Beverly Hills, CA: Sage. pp. 73–94.

Note

1   The study was conducted by Katrin Döveling at the Freie Universität Berlin. We thank Ludwig Issing for the kind supply of the laboratory.

Chapter 9

Parasocial Relationships: Current Directions in Theory and Method

David Giles

Introduction: Relationships between Audiences and Media

With what aspects of media do audiences develop relationships? It very much depends on disciplinary perspective. Cultural scholars have examined text–audience relationships; others have explored engagement with specific TV series or other media phenomena. Psychologists have traditionally treated audiences as passive recipients of media stimuli, whether visual images or concepts (violence, typically), but this research has often worked from the topic backwards – for instance, media as one factor that predicts aggression, or disordered eating, or behaviour change (e.g. giving up smoking).

What much of this work tends to overlook is the fact that media are populated with people, or fictional characters, and so from a psychological perspective it makes sense to cast audience–media relationships as those between two sets of people – those using media (watching TV, logging on to the Web) and those producing it or, more commonly, featuring in it. The emergence of the uses-and-gratifications tradition in the 1970s placed the media user at the centre of the communication process, selecting media and favouring certain media over alternatives, and parasocial theory has attempted to explain how basic human responses to other human beings (or simulated humans) have played an integral part in that process.

What Are Parasocial Relationships (PSR)?

Origins of Research on Parasocial Phenomena

From infancy, humans are bound into a relationship with media that is fundamentally social. Human faces, voices and bodies appear on TV screens, and children engage with a multitude of fictional characters with clearly defined identities and personalities. Throughout the lifespan, these media figures are experienced as meaningful others with whom we interact. If real, we may try to meet them or at least write to or e-mail them. We may fall in love with them. They may influence the course our life takes. Although this does not sound very much like interaction in the traditional social sense, it is safe to say that an individual develops relationships with media figures or at least the cognitive representations of relationships. Not social, then, but *para*social.

The concept of parasocial interaction (PSI) was first suggested in a 1950s psychiatric journal article (Horton and Wohl 1956) and became firmly established during the 1970s and 1980s by communication researchers seeking a concept that could explain motivations for television dependence (to local newsreaders, soaps, cartoons, even shopping channels). However, the concept has taken some time to really take root in the communication literature, and it is only in the past decade that it has been picked up beyond multivariate uses-and-gratifications studies where it has tended to be one of several predictors in studies of topics such as motivation and hours of viewing.

PSI, then, has spent much of its life as a concept tightly bound to a psychometric scale, the Parasocial Interaction Scale (PIS) developed initially by Mark Levy in the 1970s (Levy 1979) and refined by Alan Rubin, Elisabeth Perse and others in the 1980s (Perse and Rubin 1989; Rubin, Perse and Powell 1985). Prior to this, it had put in a few brief cameos in Scandinavia and the United Kingdom (e.g. Nordlund 1978). The PIS is a typical Likert-type attitude instrument that presents respondents with a series of statements and asks them to what extent (typically on a scale of 1 to 7) they agree or disagree with each statement. The resulting score gives the researcher a value that can be interpreted as the strength of PSI with that figure.

PIS items include statements like 'If my favorite [media figure] appeared on another television program, I would watch that program', and 'I would like to meet my favorite [media figure] in person.' The scale was originally constructed by Levy (1979) on the basis of a series of focus groups he conducted with viewers of local TV news about their favourite newscasters (newsreaders). It has since been adapted for use with all kinds of media figures, from TV shopping hosts (Grant, Guthrie and Ball-Rokeach 1991) to soap characters (Rubin and Perse 1987), and an oral version was used to investigate PSI with children's favourite cartoon characters (Hoffner 1996). Given the nature of the original study, some of the items have been easier to adapt than others. Clearly a statement such as 'When the newscasters joke around with one another it makes the news easier to watch' has limited use for studies of other figures, and the suitability of the PIS for studies involving other television figures, and figures from other media, has been questioned by other authors (Schramm and Hartmann 2008).

More recently, European and North American researchers alike have made serious attempts to advance research on PSI and relationships, and I will begin by giving a brief overview of the literature from the current century.

Parasocial Research in the Twenty-First Century

Advances in Research on PSI and PSRs

The first authors to undertake a critical review of PIS as a measuring tool were Philip Auter and Philip Palmgreen, who set out to create a measure that could be used to study PSRs with sitcom characters, the Audience-Persona Interaction Scale (Auter and Palmgreen 2000). The authors were critical of the limitations of the PIS to do this, arguing that it failed to capture the aspects of the parasocial phenomenon first mentioned by Horton and Wohl. Subsequently, their own scale has been critiqued for effectively doing the same thing – limiting its application to one specific type of media figure, sitcom characters (Schramm and Hartmann 2008).

My own contribution to the field was a review of the existing literature and a model for future research on PSI (Giles 2002). I argued in this paper that a more qualitative approach might be required to satisfy Horton and Wohl's original demand that social psychologists 'learn in detail how these parasocial interactions are integrated into the matrix of usual social activity' (1956: 225). That challenge has not really been taken up by researchers since the publication of the paper, partly, I suspect, because of the tendency for psychometric measures to constrain thinking around psychological constructs (I have had papers rejected by journals for 'not measuring parasocial interaction' simply because I failed to use the PIS).

One other issue that I touched on in my 2002 paper was the fine-grained but important distinction between PSI and PSRs. PSI would seem to best describe the moment-by-moment process of media consumption – typically watching a TV show – and therefore proceeds in an episodic fashion. A relationship requires time to build up, and a PSR may involve interaction with the same figure across different media.

Nevertheless, many studies have now been conducted on PSRs using the PIS, and in a meta-analysis across 30 different studies, attractiveness/likeability, perceived realism and perceived similarity emerged as the three most important determinants of strong PSI (Schiappa, Allen and Gregg 2007). The authors of this analysis presented their own definition of PSRs as 'the perception of the television viewer of a relationship with someone known through the media' (Schiappa, Allen and Gregg 2007: 302). This (working) definition is inevitably limited to the studies that the authors included in their analysis, thereby excluding PSRs formed through interaction with figures via media other than television.

Elsewhere, researchers have begun to problematize the interaction/relationship distinction, notably Holger Schramm, Tilo Hartmann and colleagues, who have developed a set of measures to research the 'intensity and breadth' of PSI processes (Schramm and Hartmann 2008). They argue that the distinction between established PSRs and moment-to-moment PSI makes existing measures difficult to use, particularly those including items specifically tailored to one type of media figure (i.e. newscasters). Focusing exclusively on PSI, they identified three core aspects of the PSI process: cognitive (thoughts about the media figure), affective (emotional responses) and behavioural (such as commenting out loud). On this basis, they generated 14 separate subscales with acceptable reliabilities, although again these are restricted solely to the act of watching television.

Hartmann, Stuke and Daschmann (2008) used the newly created PSI Process Scales in a study of Formula 1 motor racing fans. Participants were asked a series of questions about their 'favourite' and 'most disliked' Formula 1 drivers to establish existing positive and negative PSRs, and then asked questions about specific viewing episodes (hoped-for positive and negative outcomes for the drivers, and the degree of suspense experienced by participants). For drivers with whom participants enjoyed positive PSRs, positive outcomes were hoped for during viewing of actual races, and suspense was high. For negative PSRs, negative outcomes were hoped for, although there was no association with suspense level.

The authors argued that the distinction between established PSRs, and the viewing episode during which PSI takes place, can be likened to the trait/state distinction in psychology. Media use episodes elicit affective dispositions, which can potentially modify the long-held schematic mental model of the figure (the PSR). Therefore, if our favourite driver is caught cheating in a race, we may experience negative affect during the broadcast, but if the PSR is sufficiently robust, we could perhaps re-evaluate the incident (by trivializing or excusing the cheating); alternatively, we might experience a decrease in liking over time, which could be later reinforced (or countered) by subsequent PSI episodes. Thus, PSRs evolve similarly to actual relationships in their continued monitoring and evaluation of others' behaviour.

Psychological Dimensions of Parasocial Phenomena

Although the concept of PSI has developed largely outside the field of psychology, a few recent studies suggest that at last psychologists have started to consider the topic important. Jaye Derrick has explored social cognitive aspects of PSRs and their impact on health behaviour. Using a novel methodology for parasocial research, in one study participants were asked to write for 6 minutes about what they liked about their favourite celebrity (Derrick, Gabriel and Tippin 2008). It was found that by 'priming' the PSR in this way, the discrepancy between participants' actual and ideal selves was significantly reduced compared with groups that wrote either about a close partner or about a random US TV presenter. The authors found that this had particular benefits for low self-esteem individuals, whose ideal selves were more similar to their favourite celebrities than those of participants with high self-esteem.

In a related study (Derrick, Gabriel and Hugenberg 2009), writing about a favourite television show was found to buffer against threats to a close relationship (generated by writing about a fight with a close friend or partner). They called this the 'social surrogacy hypothesis'. In other words, they regard television and the PSRs it offers as an alternative for actual social interaction based on the finding that, when feeling lonely, their participants were more likely to report watching a favourite television show than anything other than listening to music (and watching television in general).

These findings relate back to some of the earlier concerns of PSI research; specifically, that PSRs act as substitutes for social relationships and that lonely or isolated individuals are more likely to develop them. Although studies from that period did not record significant correlations between PSI and loneliness (e.g. Rubin, Perse and Powell 1985), these more recent findings may reflect more sophisticated methodologies (such as Derrick's cognitive priming manipulation). Likewise, a recent study directly testing the hypothesis that PSI is related to loneliness (Greenwood and Long 2009) explored several dimensions of loneliness and found that stronger PSI was related to some but not others. Notably, PSI was not just associated with negative experiences of loneliness (i.e. an unrequited need for human company) but with positive aspects of spending time alone, such as creativity and 'self-expansion'.

Another psychological perspective on PSRs is that they reflect anthropomorphic tendencies to some degree. In an ingenious study (Gardner and Knowles 2008), experimental participants were asked to complete an unrelated cognitive task while, in one condition, an image of their favourite TV character remained on a computer screen in the background. The sense of presence of their favourite character actually enhanced performance on the task in the same way as the presence of a human friend in previous research (as compared with participants who had either a random character on screen or no figure at all). The authors also found that participants regarded their favourite characters as more 'real' than less favoured characters, arguing that the experimental manipulation was successful because it generated anthropomorphism (i.e. the belief that the screen image represented an actual person). However, they did not measure individual differences in anthropomorphism in relation to the experiment.

Within communication research, further concepts have been developed with relation to parasocial phenomena in recent years. I will mention here just two examples, namely Schiappa's parasocial contact hypothesis and Cohen's work on parasocial break-up.

Schiappa, Gregg and Hewes's (2005) parasocial contact hypothesis is based on a long-standing phenomenon in social psychology known as the contact hypothesis (Allport 1954), which argues that prejudice is reduced through greater contact with different ethnic or minority groups, which results in greater differentiation. The more members of those groups we encounter, the less powerful the stereotypes become, resulting in less prejudicial attitudes. Schiappa, Gregg and Hewes demonstrated how the same process works through parasocial contact by exposing three sets of college students to TV series featuring members of minority groups and comparing 'before' and 'after' measures of attitudes to those groups.

Cohen's (2004) parasocial break-up research is similar in the way it explores parallels between social and parasocial relationships. He found that reactions to the prospect of favourite television characters being taken off air resembled those of people facing relationship break-ups, and these were related to both PIS scores and general attachment styles. Appropriately enough, he replicated findings from previous research (Cole and Leets 1999) that the strongest PIS scores were associated with individuals who have anxious attachment styles, suggesting that the same psychological processes are involved in forming social and parasocial relationships.

One of the reasons that parasocial concepts have been slow to influence research in communication and media studies generally is that many scholars regard the basic concept of PSRs as potentially 'pathologizing' – at least the assumption that they are regarded as false (or 'faux'; Derrick, Gabriel and Tippin 2008), imaginary or 'pseudo' relationships. The idea that they might function as substitute relationships is particularly sensitive given the amount of time and effort invested in fandoms and media enthusiasms of various kinds and the assumption that these represent a psychological need (and by implication a corresponding lack, or want, of social gratifications). Research demonstrating precisely this finding may indicate that the parasocial concept eventually drifts away from communication towards psychology. However, as media psychology as a discipline gathers strength, it may yet act as a cross-disciplinary home for this type of research.

Concepts Related to Parasocial Phenomena

Elsewhere in the literature, a number of concepts have been developed over recent decades that are closely related to, though not necessarily synonymous with, PSI. I will review a handful of these concepts here briefly.

First, there has been a gradual trend in communication research to explore media phenomena in terms of their 'realism', or the extent to which they function as equivalent to real experiences, much the same way as the research described earlier on anthropomorphic aspects of PSI. Reeves and Nass (1996) described this tendency as 'the media equation' – in other words, the tendency to equate media with the real objects represented in those media. So saying 'good night' to a TV newsreader is functionally equivalent to saying 'good night' to an actual person in the same room. Reeves and Nass stretch the media equation to all representative systems so that they cite people yelling at malfunctioning computers and thanking cash dispensers as examples of the same phenomenon. Likewise, research on 'presence' and transportation makes much the same set of assumptions about the power of media to fool us into accepting artificial, or fictional, environments as equivalent to real ones. Despite the clear parallels, there has been no explicit attempt to relate these concepts to PSI.

Another concept related to PSI is identification. As Cohen (2001) points out, identification is, like PSI, conceptually ill-defined and is used by different authors to mean different things. In film theory the concept has been taken largely from either the Freudian or Lacanian versions of psychoanalysis, with the absorption of the viewer into the persona of the protagonist and the resulting merging of self and character (Fuss 1995). However, in communication research, the concept has been used more loosely, and most authors tend to distinguish 'similarity identification' (perceiving yourself as similar to a media figure) from 'wishful identification' (desire to become like a media figure). As Hoffner and Buchanan (2005) have argued, the latter concept extends beyond the viewing process itself, in the same way that PSRs persist beyond specific episodes of media use. Researchers generally agree that identification signifies a more intense relationship between audience members and media figures than PSI, but more importantly it is restricted to positive audience–media relationships alone. It is possible to have a PSR with a figure we hate, but identification implies positive evaluation.

Because PSI and identification can be seen as separate, though complementary, processes, William Brown and Mike Basil have developed the concept of 'celebrity involvement' to describe close attachments to celebrities (Brown, Basil and Bocarnea 2003). They argue that both processes are essential for understanding how celebrities exert social influence: to raise awareness of and change attitudes towards various social issues (not to mention endorsing products). They have applied the concept of involvement to a number of celebrities – dead and alive – including Princess Diana, Magic Johnson and Elvis Presley.

Similarly, the concept of 'celebrity worship' has been developed over the past decade to explain specific attachments to celebrities (as opposed to media figures in general). Like PSI, the field of celebrity worship has been defined through the use of a psychometric scale – the Celebrity Worship Scale (McCutcheon, Lange and Houran 2002) that measures the degree of 'worship' exhibited by respondents towards their favourite celebrity. Subsequent research has explored the factor structure of the scale, arguing that two dominant factors explain most of the scale variance – one representing an 'entertainment-social' dimension of celebrity worship and the other an 'intense-personal' dimension (Maltby and Giles 2008).

Finally, a more complex theoretical model (PEFiC – Perceiving and Experiencing Fictional Characters) has been developed by Konijn (Konijn and Hoorn 2005) to explain engagement with fictional characters or, more specifically, movie characters, where aesthetic judgements play a role. A particularly important feature of the first application of the model was the deliberate tactic of not asking research participants to nominate 'favourite' characters, as is typical in most parasocial studies. Instead they argued that 'most [fictional characters] stir mixed emotions and ambivalence' (Konijn and Hoorn 2005: 110) and presented participants with movie characters who represented moral and physical extremes (such as Count Dracula vs. Gandhi). They found that ethical, aesthetic (whether characters are ugly or beautiful, as defined by the researchers) and epistemic (real vs. unreal) factors predicted engagement and appreciation with the characters.

Empirical Test of Realism Hypothesis with Regard to Media Figures

The remainder of this chapter is devoted to an empirical study that explored the extent to which the perceived reality status of media figures influences their relationship with media users. If we can describe a PSR as a cognitive representation of a relationship (i.e. it contains all the elements – evaluative, emotional and so on – that are present in thinking about our relationships with figures in our social network), then the possibility of actually meeting a media figure should intensify that representation relative to those involving imaginary figures. This is effectively the 'reality hypothesis' with regard to parasocial phenomena.

An alternative hypothesis, following the 'media equation' of Reeves and Nass (1996), is that human brain has not evolved quickly enough to counteract the perceived similarity between media and the objects they represent – by which we would expect no differences between PSRs with real figures and those with fictional figures, as all are represented by the same category. Given the 'unreality hypothesis', then, all PSRs have equal validity for a media user irrespective of the figures' reality status, and may be rejected entirely (that is to say, discerning individuals have no PSRs as such, dismissing all such representations as meaningless).

Background to the Empirical Study

The present study is based on a realist typology that I developed in Giles (2002) in which PSRs were conceptualized as encounters between an individual and another figure (either human or fictional) that can be ranked on a continuum ranging from fully reciprocated, intimate social encounters (such as a romantic couple in face-to-face conversation) to fully parasocial encounters, in which no reciprocation could ever be possible by the other figure, such as an encounter with a cartoon figure.

Three types of media figures can be located at positions on this continuum. First-order figures (MF1s) are human figures whose real existence is unambiguous, such as celebrities and other people in the news and entertainment media; second-order figures (MF2s) are fictional characters who nonetheless possess a visible human form, typically a character in a film or TV series. Third-order figures (MF3s) are fictional figures who do not possess a visible human form, such as a cartoon character or a fantasy character.

The theorized distinction between each of these three types is related to the potential relationship resulting from an encounter. Even if an individual only encounters an MF1 through television use, it is possible, either through deliberate pursuit or by accident, to have a subsequent social encounter with that figure. A passionate fan of a television presenter could, in theory, end up having an intimate social relationship with that television presenter (see Giles 2000 for several examples of fans who have ended up marrying their idols). With an MF3, such an eventual outcome is impossible. MF2s occupy a middle position because, although it is impossible to have a social relationship with the persona as such, it is nonetheless possible to have a social relationship with the physical form that the character inhabits. Indeed, when actors are encountered by media users 'in the flesh', they are sometimes responded to as if they are still in character (Tal-Or and Pepirman 2007).

We could describe this typology as the reality theory of PSRs and hypothesise that MF1s should invite more elaborated and richer PSRs than MF3s because, should they wish to develop the relationship further, the media user can hold out some theoretical prospect of an actual social encounter. This is in line with Hartmann, Stuke and Daschmann's (2008) relational schema theory of PSRs, a knowledge structure consisting of, among other things, a script for a potential meeting with the media figure (e.g. would he or she like me?). We could also hypothesise that PSRs with MF2s would be richer and more elaborate than those with MF3s because of the findings that realism is related to greater engagement with narrative (Busselle and Bilandzic 2008) and character (Konijn and Hoorn 2005).

Following from this, we can also hypothesize that media users should identify more strongly with the more realistic figures, and most of all with real figures, as perceived factuality has been found to enhance identification with protagonists in films (Pouliot and Cowen 2007). We would also expect media users to feel closer, or more intimate, with MF1s than fictional characters (Eyal and Cohen 2006). Following Cohen (2004), it can be hypothesized that parasocial break-up (which is operationalized in the present study as the imagined death of the MF) would be more unpleasant a prospect for more realistic figures.

Participants

Participants were 164 students from a sixth-form college and a university in southern England, of which 130 were female. The mean age of the sample was 19 years 10 months, and although there were a few older participants among the university sub-sample, the analyses were rerun omitting the outliers at the top end of the age range without any noticeable effect on the results.

Measures

Questionnaires were divided into six sections relating to the six different types of hypothesized media figure. For MF1s, respondents were asked to identify their favourite celebrity. For MF2s, respondents were asked to identify their favourite fictional character. For MF3s, respondents were asked to identify their favourite fictional nonhuman, cartoon or animated character.

MF Elaboration and Richness. This was measured by three separate open-ended items in which respondents were asked to describe their favourite and least favourite media figures with regard to their appearance and personality, and to explain why they liked each figure. The cumulative totals of adjectives for each of the first two items were entered into the analysis, along with the number of identifiable reasons given for liking the figure.

Desire to Meet the Figure. For MF2s and MF3s, respondents were asked to indicate on a 7-point scale how much they would like to meet the character 'in real life'. For MF1s, they were asked simply how much they would like to meet 'this person' (i.e. the celebrity they had selected). Two additional items were provided for respondents who had actually met their selected celebrities; anyone falling into this category would have to be eliminated from the MF1 analysis. Only two participants were excluded on this basis.

Intimacy with the Figure. Respondents were asked to indicate, on a 4-point scale how close they felt to the person/character.

Identification with the Figure. Following Feilitzen and Linne (1975), two items were included to differentiate between similarity identification and wishful identification. Similarity identification was measured on a 6-point scale on which respondents were asked to indicate how similar 'in character' the person or character is to them. Wishful identification was measured on a 4-point scale on which respondents were asked to indicate 'how much you would like to be like this person/character'.

Response to Figure Death. For MF1s, respondents were asked to indicate, on a 7-point scale, how they would feel if they 'heard that this person had been killed in an accident'. For MF2s and MF3s, they were first asked if their selected character *had* been killed off in the film or series, then to indicate, on variants of the above scale, either how they had felt about the figure's death or how they would react if they 'found that the character was about to be killed off'.

Results

Figure Elaboration and Richness. MF2s elicited more complex descriptions (combined $M = 6.53$, $SD = 1.96$) than MF3s ($M = 5.98$, $SD = 2.10$) and MF1s ($M = 5.81$, $SD = 1.88$). A separate one-way analysis of variance (ANOVA) found the difference between MF2s and the other groups to be significant ($F (2,138) = 8.2$, $p < .001$, $\eta^2 = .11$). One-way analyses found that there were no significant differences between the number of reasons given for liking figures ($F (1,138) = 2.3$, $p = .10$).

Desire to Meet the Figure. For the main effect of figure type, there was a significant linear trend in the direction predicted by the hypothesis, $F (1,124) = 9.9$, $p = .002$, $\eta^2 = .07$. Overall, respondents' desire to meet MF1s was highest (combined $M = 7.96$, $SD = 1.35$), followed by MF2s ($M = 7.76$, $SD = 1.76$) and then MF3s ($M = 7.38$, $SD = 1.95$).

Intimacy. There was a marginally significant main effect of figure type ($F (2,266) = 3.4$, $p = .034$, $\eta^2 = .03$), whereby respondents felt slightly closer to MF2s than to other figures.

Similarity Identification. There was no main effect of figure type ($F (2,266) = 1.36$, $p = .26$).

Wishful Identification. A significant linear trend was observed for figure type in the direction predicted by the hypothesis, whereby respondents would rather be like MF1s ($M = 5.93$, $SD = 1.04$) than MF2s ($M = 6.00$, $SD = 1.03$) and MF3s ($M = 6.28$, $SD = 1.04$) ($F (1,133) = 10.22$, $p = .002$, $\eta^2 = .07$).

Response to Figure Death. There was a significant main effect of figure type ($F (2,154) = 4.74$, $p = .01$, $\eta^2 = .06$), whereby respondents were more upset at the prospect of an MF1's death ($M = 6.41$, $SD = 1.28$) than either those of MF3s ($M = 7.19$, $SD = 1.62$) or MF2s ($M = 7.81$, $SD = 4.74$).

Discussion

The main purpose of the present study was to explore the usefulness of the Giles (2002) typology of media figures by comparing different aspects of PSRs between favourite figures from each category. It was one of the first studies to compare PSRs with real people (specifically celebrities) and with fictional figures. The findings suggest that there are several features of PSRs for which the typology is useful, but some characteristics of PSRs for real people may differ little from those for fictional figures, lending some support to the alternative unreality hypothesis.

First of all, participants found the activity meaningful: the large majority were able to generate favourite figures for each category. It was hypothesized that celebrities (MF1s) would elicit more complex descriptions than fictional figures, although this was not supported. Indeed, for personality, fictional humans (MF2s) elicited more complex descriptions. Respondents felt no closer to favourite celebrities; overall, again, fictional humans produced the highest intimacy ratings and were more likely to be compared to actual friends than were favourite celebrities.

Similarity identification (being like your selected figure) did not differentiate real from fictional figures. Most surprisingly of all, perhaps, the idea of respondents' favourite celebrities dying did not seem to trouble them any more than the idea of their favourite fictional characters dying. However, several measures supported the typology and the realism hypothesis (i.e. that we should have more positive PSRs with humans than fictional characters). Respondents wished to meet their favourite celebrities significantly more than their favourite human fictional characters, who they desired to meet significantly more than their favourite nonhuman fictional characters. Also, respondents wished to resemble their favourite celebrities more than fictional characters (wishful identification), and again they preferred to resemble their favourite fictional humans than their favourite fictional nonhumans.

Overall, these findings suggest that the PSRs that media users develop have several characteristics that are not related to the reality status of the media figures and are therefore purely symbolic in nature. Intimacy, similarity identification with the figure and attachment (as measured by the imagined death item) are seemingly unrelated to the figure's reality. However, we are more likely to wish to resemble our favourite celebrities than our favourite fictional characters, and we are more likely to want to meet them (perhaps not surprisingly as it was the concept of the potential encounter between user and figure that provided the rationale for the typology in the first place).

The symbolic function of PSRs is even more important when we consider the lack of differences between human and nonhuman figures. On very few measures were these figure types differentiated. The little research currently existing on these different figures has suggested that, for identification and idealization, PSRs with cartoon characters are no different to those with fictional humans (Greenwood, Pietromonaco and Long 2008). In the present study, even the imagined death of cartoon characters produced no greater upset than that of human characters from film and TV.

The many interesting findings of the present study need to be balanced against certain study and methodological limitations. First of all, the samples involved, apart from their limited age range, are overwhelmingly drawn from a white middle-class population, with a sizeable female majority. Therefore, the results cannot be regarded as representative of the UK population as a whole. The use of single items to cover a range of measures may be seen as restrictive, as might the crude method for measuring complexity (simply counting number of adjectives). It could be argued that fictional characters elicited more personality adjectives simply because their scripted nature makes it easier to identify salient characteristics than real, more complicated human personalities.

Future research on parasocial phenomena might consider modifications that could be made to the three-part typology. The MF1 category, represented by the broad term 'celebrity' in this study, could be differentiated according to whether real human figures are still alive. Only one respondent selected a dead celebrity (Marilyn Monroe), but clearly the attribute of 'real' does not preclude the importance of PSRs with historical humans (see Fraser and Brown 2002, on identification with Elvis Presley).

Another modification that is necessary relates to the MF2/MF3 distinction. Presently the MF2 category is presumed to be higher in reality status because TV and film characters are represented by human actors, whose visual features become familiar to viewers and thereby generate a different sort of attachment from that to a cartoon character that is represented only by an animation. However, where does that leave fictional human characters from radio or, perhaps more importantly, from novels?

Given the rationale for MF2s, one might imagine PSRs with characters from books to be closer to those with MF3s (who have no visual human form). It is possible, therefore, that film and TV characters are a category by themselves and that 'fictional human characters' is potentially a broader category. Furthermore, most cartoon characters are represented by a human voice (cartoon dogs do not just bark, and even aliens from outer space are fluent in viewers' native language), which means that their nonhuman-ness is perhaps not as salient as the present typology supposes.

These issues notwithstanding, I believe that the present study makes a substantial contribution to our understanding of the complexity and diversity of PSRs, and I hope that my attempts to open up the psychological black box of media–audience relationships will inspire much more research on the phenomena within.

References

Allport, G.W., 1954. *The nature of prejudice*. Cambridge, MA: Perseus Books.

Auter, P.J., and Palmgreen, P., 2000. Development and validation of a new parasocial interaction measure: The Audience-Persona Interaction Scale. *Communication Research Reports*, 17, pp. 79–89.

Brown, W.J., Basil, M.D. and Bocarnea, M.C., 2003. Social influence of an international celebrity: Responses to the death of Princess Diana. *Journal of Communication*, 53, pp. 587–605.

Busselle, R. and Bilandzic, H., 2008. Fictionality and perceived realism in experiencing stories: A model of narrative comprehension and engagement. *Communication Theory*, 18, pp. 255–280.

Cohen, J., 2001. Defining identification: A theoretical look at the identification of audiences with media characters. *Mass Communication and Society*, 4, pp. 245–264.

——— 2004. Parasocial break-up from favorite television characters: The role of attachment styles and relationship intensity. *Journal of Social and Personal Relationships*, 21, pp. 187–202.

Cole, T. and Leets, L., 1999. Attachment styles and intimate television viewing: Insecurely forming relationships in a parasocial way. *Journal of Social and Personal Relationships*, 16, pp. 495–511.

Derrick, J.L., Gabriel, S. and Hugenberg, K.J., 2009. Social surrogacy: How favored television programs provide the experience of belonging. *Journal of Experimental Social Psychology*, 45, pp. 352–362.

Derrick, J.L., Gabriel, S. and Tippin, B., 2008. Parasocial relationships and self-discrepancies: Faux relationships have benefits for low self-esteem individuals. *Personal Relationships*, 15, pp. 261–280.

Eyal, K. and Cohen, J., 2006. When good *Friends* say goodbye: A parasocial breakup study. *Journal of Broadcasting and Electronic Media*, 50, pp. 502–523.

Feilitzen, C. and Linne, O., 1975. Identifying with television characters. *Journal of Communication*, 25, pp. 51–55.

Fraser, B.P. and Brown, W.J., 2002. Media, celebrities, and social influence: Identification with Elvis Presley. *Mass Communication & Society*, 5, pp. 183–206.

Fuss, D., 1995. *Identification papers: Readings on psychoanalysis, sexuality, and culture.* New York: Routledge.

Gardner, W.L. and Knowles, M.L., 2008. Love makes you real: Favorite television characters are perceived as "real" in a social facilitation paradigm. *Social Cognition*, 26, pp. 156–168.

Giles, D.C., 2000. *Illusions of immortality: A psychology of fame and celebrity.* Basingstoke, UK: Macmillan.

——— 2002. Parasocial interaction: A review of the literature and a model for future research. *Media Psychology*, 4, pp. 279–305.

Grant, A.E., Guthrie, K.K. and Ball-Rokeach, S.J., 1991. Television shopping: A media dependency perspective. *Communication Research*, 18, pp. 773–798.

Greenwood, D.N. and Long, C.R., 2009. Psychological predictors of media involvement: Solitude experiences and the need to belong. *Communication Research*, 36, pp. 637–654.

Greenwood, D.N., Pietromonaco, P.R. and Long, C.R., 2008. Young women's attachment style and interpersonal engagement with female TV stars. *Journal of Social and Personal Relationships*, 25, pp. 387–407.

Hartmann, D., Stuke, D. and Daschmann, G., 2008. Positive parasocial relationships with drivers affect suspense in racing sport spectators. *Journal of Media Psychology*, 20, pp. 24–34.

Hoffner, C., 1996. Children's wishful identification and parasocial interaction with favourite television characters. *Journal of Broadcasting and Electronic Media*, 40, pp. 389–402.

Hoffner, C. and Buchanan, M., 2005. Young adults' wishful identification with television characters: The role of perceived similarity and character attributes. *Media Psychology*, 7, pp. 325–351.

Horton, D. and Wohl, R.R., 1956. Mass communication and para-social interaction: Observation on intimacy at a distance. *Psychiatry*, 19, pp. 215–229.

Konijn, E.A. and Hoorn, J.F., 2005. Some like it bad: Testing a model for perceiving and experiencing fictional characters. *Media Psychology*, 7, pp. 107–144.

Levy, M.R., 1979. Watching TV news as para-social interaction. *Journal of Broadcasting*, 23, pp. 69–80.

Maltby, J. and Giles, D.C., 2008. Toward the measurement and profiling of celebrity worship. In J.R. Meloy, L. Sheridan and J. Hoffman, eds, *Stalking, threatening, and attacking public figures*. New York: Oxford University Press. pp. 271–286.

McCutcheon, L.E., Lange, R. and Houran, J., 2002. Conceptualization and measurement of celebrity worship. *British Journal of Psychology*, 93, pp. 67–87.

Nordlund, J., 1978. Media interaction. *Communication Research*, 5, pp. 150–175.

Perse, E.M. and Rubin, R.B., 1989. Attribution in social and parasocial relationships. *Communication Research*, 16, pp. 59–77.

Pouliot, L. and Cowen, P.S., 2007. Does perceived realism really matter in media effects? *Media Psychology*, 9, pp. 241–259.

Reeves, B. and Nass, R., 1996. *The media equation: How people treat computers, television, and new media like real people and places*. Chicago, IL: University of Chicago Press.

Rubin, A.M. and Perse, E.M., 1987. Audience activity and soap opera involvement: A uses and effects investigation. *Human Communication Research*, 14, pp. 246–268.

Rubin, A.M., Perse, E.M. and Powell, R.A., 1985. Loneliness, parasocial interaction, and local television news viewing. *Human Communication Research*, 12, pp. 155–180.

Schiappa, E., Allen, M. and Gregg, P., 2007. Parasocial relationships and television: A meta-analysis of the effects. In R. Preiss, B. Gayle, N. Burrell, M. Allen and J. Bryant, eds, *Mass media effects: Advances through meta-analysis*. Mahwah, NJ: Lawrence Erlbaum. pp. 301–314.

Schiappa, E., Gregg, P.B. and Hewes, D.E., 2005. The parasocial contact hypothesis. *Communication Monographs*, 72, pp. 92–115.

Schramm, H. and Hartmann, T., 2008. The PSI-Process Scales. A new measure to assess the intensity and breadth of parasocial processes. *Communications: The European Journal of Communication Research*, 33, pp. 385–401.

Tal-Or, N. and Papirman, Y., 2007. The fundamental attribution error in attributing fictional figures' characteristics to the actors. *Media Psychology*, 9, pp. 331–345.

PART III

Cultural, Political and Technological Participation

Chapter 10

From Semiotic Resistance to Civic Agency: Viewing Citizenship through the Lens of Reception Research 1973-2010

Kim Christian Schrøder

Introduction

How would we be able to determine from the perspective of media audience studies whether the population of a given European country deserves the label of 'competent citizens'? Presumably the first prerequisite would be to theoretically define what to understand by citizenship. Second, we would ideally have to familiarize ourselves with the cornucopia of existing research which historically has thrown light on the citizenship/media nexus as defined by researchers across scholarly disciplines. Third, we could launch new research designed to map the phenomenon in light of recent theories of mediated citizenship, thereby contributing a contemporary snapshot of the health of the democratic system, diagnosed under conditions of increasing mediatization of societies across the globe.

While necessarily drawing to some extent on notions of citizenship as theorized and analysed by political science and other social and cultural sciences, this chapter will focus on the mapping and evaluation of competent citizenship which has been accomplished within media studies and more particularly within the research tradition of 'reception research' since its inception in the early 1970s.

The chapter offers a historical model that distinguishes five successive, but not exclusionary, reception perspectives on citizenship since 1973, labelled 'hegemonic', 'monitorial', 'popular', 'participatory' and 'ubiquitous'. Due to limitations of space, the model is presented fairly briefly here (for a more detailed analysis, see Schrøder, in press), followed by a presentation of a case study which illustrates an innovative empirical approach to the study of some aspects of the last stage of 'ubiquitous' mediated citizenship.

Citizenship and the Media: A Common-Denominator Perspective

As pointed out by scholars who have theorized the media/democracy nexus (e.g. Dahlgren 2001, 2006; Keane 1991; Thompson 1995), it is possible to distinguish a range of different notions of democracy and citizenship, including liberal, communitarian and republican. These distinctions depend among other things on the relative emphasis given to the fact, in itself, that citizenship is anchored in the existence of constitutional political rights and freedoms, vis-à-vis the importance attached to richness of the actual participatory and deliberative practices of citizens in the exercise of those rights.

Here, while leaning towards an acceptance of the view that participation in deliberative processes is constitutive of sound citizenship, I shall adopt a common-denominator perspective on citizenship, which cuts across the different notions of democracy. Such a perspective has also characterized the analyses of audiences as citizens conducted by reception researchers during the four decades singled out for scrutiny. This perspective, then, which is fundamentally indebted to Habermas's theory of the public sphere (Habermas 1962, 2006), perceives citizenship to be crucially related to processes of political power, seeing a democratic system to be functionally designed to channel the exercise of societal power, which resides in popular sovereignty, through deliberative processes inside and outside parliamentary institutions, resulting in majority decisions to be implemented by the political executive institutions of government.

Citizenship, in addition to the possession and exercise of formal political rights, also crucially involves the subjective dimension of political and cultural identity (Hall 1996; Hermes and Stello 2000; Turner 2001), being and feeling like a member of a specific national community (Anderson 1983) and of various sub-communities constituted along class, ethnic, generational, gender and other differences (Fraser 1992). This subjective dimension is necessary to understand how citizens are motivated to exercise their formal rights by participating (through voting and deliberation) and thereby influencing the life of the national entity as well as one's own social groups and one's personal future. As a final delimitation of the realm of the political in this context, it must also be emphasized that over the last couple of decades the scope of politics has been extended, as grassroots organizational practices (for instance, in non-governmental organizations) and everyday political action (for instance, in the form of consumers' political consumption) have become increasingly recognized as legitimate and valuable forms of political action, under the labels of, respectively, 'sub-politics' and 'life politics' (Beck 1997; Giddens 1994).

The importance of the mass media for the formation and exercise of citizenship has been growing since the emergence of local and national print media centuries ago, and has increased further through the effects of first the broadcasting media and more recently the Internet and digital, converging media with global reach and implications (Habermas 1962; Jenkins 2006; Jensen 1998; Negrine 1996; Rantanen 2005; Thompson 1995). The media as vehicles of and resources for citizenship have become the key guarantors for ensuring that the democratically vital public sphere may function as a transparent informative and deliberative forum to which all citizens must have equal access.

McNair (2003) lists five democratic functions of the media for the public sphere: the media must inform the citizens reliably about what is going on in the political entity; they must educate people about the significance of social events and discourses; they must provide platforms of deliberation with equal access for all citizens; they must be available for political institutions (e.g. governments) to disseminate, in the form of publicity, reports on their activities and plans; and they must serve as channels through which citizens and institutions can advance their political viewpoints. These functions, though not always distinguished sharply, have been central points of investigation when reception researchers have designed empirical research with the objective of illuminating the democratic provision of the media for their audiences.

Reception Research – Focus on Sense-Making Citizens

It is rarely possible to date the birth of scientific schools precisely because they tend to emerge gradually and imperceptibly out of previous traditions. However, with reception research it is possible to point to the founding text which, so to speak, constitutes the genesis of reception research, namely Stuart Hall's short article 'Encoding and Decoding in the Television Discourse' (Hall 1973) about the formation of audiences' political ideologies through televised content. The article argues that any claims about the 'effects', 'uses' and 'gratifications' of a mediated message are secondary to the illumination of the semiotic sense-making aspects of such a message. In laying the conceptual foundations of audience sense-making research, Hall proclaimed in modest fashion, that 'there seems some ground for thinking that a new and exciting phase in so-called audience research, of a quite new kind, may be opening up' (Hall 1973: 5). There had been an earlier qualitative tradition of research into audience sense-making processes (e.g. Herzog 1944; Warner and Henry 1948), but it had become delegitimized by the dominant quantitative paradigm in American communication research after World War II (Gitlin 1978).

As he set about the empirical operationalization of his mentor Hall's theory, David Morley in his reception study of the British current affairs programme *Nationwide* defined reception as the semiotic process through which 'audiences differentially read and make sense of messages which have been transmitted, and act on those meanings within the context of the rest of their situation and experience' (Morley 1980: 11). Reception research is thus concerned with audiences' 'reading' of media messages, regarded as complex verbal and visual signs, and with how they act on these readings, in the situational and social context of their daily lives.

Reception research is fundamentally interdisciplinary, a cross-fertilization project which in its early years, with a helpful overstatement by Jensen, 'draws its theory from the humanities and its methodology from the social sciences' (Jensen 1991: 135). At the time, this portrayal of reception research was due to the fact that it tended to draw theoretically principally on hermeneutic theories borrowed from semiotics, literary studies and discourse analysis, while its analytical toolbox was largely indebted to the various fieldwork methods used by the social sciences (Jensen and Rosengren 1990). Today, however, this characterization is misleadingly reductionist, as the theoretical inventory of reception research is heavily indebted to the rich theoretical landscape of social science (e.g. Bourdieu 1984; Castells 1996; Giddens 1984; Habermas 1962) and as the use of multimethod research, including qualitative interviews, ethnographic fieldwork and statistical surveys, has become the order of the day also in the humanities (for further definition of the field, see Schrøder et al. 2003: 121–142).

Nowadays the landscape of reception research is still dominated by qualitative methods, although this dominance has become less dogmatic than during the pioneering years. It is only natural that a scholarly discipline oriented to the elucidation of meaning is biased towards qualitative methods because these have the 'thick' description of cultural meanings, with all their complexities and ambivalences, as their main deliverable. But it is equally clear that the mapping of the landscapes of media audiences and users may benefit from methods with the inherent capability of calculating and generalizing findings across larger populations (Lewis 1997). Today, therefore, there is consensus that methodological pluralism is often the best way to obtain explanatory power (Schrøder et al. 2003: 349–365).

This chapter limits itself to empirical research which has focused on news rather than entertainment media and to research that has adopted a qualitative rather than a quantitative approach. The account will consider the 'political' and largely exclude insights about cultural and subcultural identities, and about the gendered and ethnic dimensions of citizenship (Ang 1985; Hermes 1995; Jhally and Lewis 1992; Liebes and Katz 1990; Radway 1984). Readers who are particularly interested in political science-anchored discussions of citizenship in the context of media studies are referred to the extensive discussions in the work of scholars like Livingstone and Lunt (1994), Dahlgren (2001, 2006) and Couldry, Livingstone and Markham (2007).

Audiences as Citizens: Five Historical Stages

Before embarking on the short profiles of the five historical stages of reception research on citizenship, a few words about the notion of 'stage' itself. A stage should be understood as a phenomenon derived from the Kuhnian notion of a scientific paradigm (Kuhn 1962), which denotes the framework of understanding that governs the practices of a scholarly community (Gitlin 1978). This framework of understanding encapsulates the consensus within the community about what counts as a relevant object of study as well as what the appropriate methods for studying it are. It also covers a certain horizon of expectations with respect to the probable findings of empirical work and sometimes assumptions about how scholars may intervene in the observed practices.

The proposed succession of stages may induce speculation about the driving forces behind the shifting lenses for investigating mediated citizenship. One reason for the historical developments of reception 'paradigms' is to be found in the changing agendas of the political landscape itself from the 1970s to the 2000s, from a political climate characterized by ideological polarization (the youth revolts of the 1960s and 1970s; the Cold War) to a tendency towards consensual centrism in Europe and North America. Another reason for investigating mediated citizenship in a new perspective may lie in genre and programme innovations, for instance, the blurring of boundaries between fact and fiction, and news and entertainment, manifesting itself in talk shows and reality programming (Hill 2007). Finally, the rapid development of digital, interactive communication technologies has increased the opportunities for participating in net-based conversational and potentially deliberative processes (Graham 2009).

It must be stressed, of course, that the boundaries between the five stages should be seen as porous, that previous stages (except for Stage 1) continue to coexist with emerging ones, and that the dating of the stages to specific time intervals should be taken not in absolute terms but as an indication of the approximate emergence of a spirit of enquiry.

Stage 1: Hegemonic Citizenship (1973–1990)

The reception research of Stage 1 can be dated to Stuart Hall's seminal (1973) article mentioned above. It seeks to theoretically explain the formation of citizens' political consciousness in a class-divided society. Understanding the mindset governing this research may be quite a challenge for contemporary individuals, as the empirical work is based on the then more fashionable Marxist theory of capitalist society, as developed by the Italian Marxist Antonio Gramsci (1971). According to this mindset, which is quite crudely outlined here, the media are ideological state apparatuses (Althusser 1971), which disseminate false consciousness about the social order by making present social arrangements appear to guarantee freedom and equality for all, while the truth is that the social structures privilege the wealthy ruling classes and oppress the working classes. The challenging issue for politically committed reception researchers is to explain the absence of popular resistance: why this oppressive situation is condoned by working people, so that no coercive mechanisms are necessary for the ruling classes to maintain their hegemony (hence the label 'hegemonic citizenship').

Operationalizing this scenario into an empirical fieldwork design, reception researchers of Stage 1 analyse the ways in which citizens make sense of the hegemonic ideological meanings disseminated by the news media (for instance when reporting on legislation in the areas of the economy and labour relations), dividing the range of responses elicited from group interviews into three categories of readings: 'dominant', 'negotiated' and 'oppositional' (Hall 1973; Morley 1980).

In Morley's study, some citizens were found to simply accept the version of reality offered by the hegemonic media fare (the so-called 'preferred meaning') as something that cannot be questioned ('dominant readings') and to end up supporting conservative political forces. Others adopted a stance where they did not just swallow media meanings but adapted them in light of their own divergent experiences of inequality in the workplace and in everyday life ('negotiated readings') so as to partially accept the media's depiction of reality, partially question it, with the political outcome of supporting political parties with a reformist agenda. Finally, a few groups – composed, for instance, of labour activists – resisted and completely rejected the 'rosy' media depictions of labour market reforms ('oppositional readings'), calling for more radical political solutions that would topple the established balance of power.

This reception research thus tries to explain the micro-mechanics of social class domination in terms of semiotic domination and resistance. Within the same theoretical framework, the reception research of John Fiske (1987) proposed that people's pleasures from the consumption of much fictional drama on film and TV derive from their identification with protagonists who are somehow in opposition to 'the system'. At the subjective, emotional level, therefore, subordinated viewers may experience a satisfying semiotic, symbolic resistance to representatives of the system. Fiske thus labels them the citizens of a 'semiotic democracy', in the absence of a genuinely democratic social order.

The tripartite division of the dominant, negotiated and oppositional reading positions invented by Hall and Morley has lived on long after the demise of the Marxist mindset of Stage 1 in the late 1980s. This is due to the fact that this set of terms lends itself, without the political implications, with intuitive plausibility to many different mediated semiotic scenarios in which media users can logically adopt stances of acceptance and rejection towards media texts or a neither/nor position between these two opposites. Schrøder (1997) thus translates these labels to his informants' 'sympathetic', 'cynical' and 'sceptical' readings of corporate social responsibility advertisements.

Stage 2: Monitorial Citizenship (Approx 1985–)

The aim of reception research in Stage 2 is to examine, first, whether the news media can be seen to enable citizens to adequately monitor what goes on in their society and, second, whether they thereby empower citizens and serve as a launching pad for political activity.

In terms of grand theory, Stage 2 builds on the same Marxist theoretical platform as Stage 1, but when it operationalizes this theory, the research agenda becomes more pragmatic. Jensen (1986, 1990) draws a descriptive map based on individual qualitative interviews with 24 male American informants, in which he screened yesterday's mainstream news programme. The map, which is indebted to Lull's pioneering ethnographic study of 'the social uses of television' (1980) distinguishes four social uses of TV news: (1) 'contextual uses' have to do with the way news programmes are watched as a flow and 'punctuate daily life', often in the family environment; (2) 'informational uses' occur when viewers watch the news for the Habermassian purpose of acquiring the 'factual knowledge of political issues and events' which they need 'in their roles as consumer, employee, and, above all, as citizen and voter' (Jensen 1990: 66); (3) 'legitimating uses' occur when citizens use the news to maintain their political self-image of being enlightened citizens; and (4) 'diversional uses' have to do with using the news as a kind of parasocial political entertainment.

Jensen agrees with Fiske that the polysemic potential of the news text may lead to differentiated readings, which can be seen as semiotically 'oppositional' in the sense of diverging from the ideologically dominant 'preferred' reading inscribed into the news message. But Jensen disputes Fiske's assertion that oppositional readings are in themselves politically significant. For Jensen, semiotic resistance is not political resistance. He concludes that TV news serves as a public forum (Newcomb and Hirsch 1983) that enables citizens to monitor their society on a routine daily basis, but in a hegemonic manner that has few or no consequences for what happens on the nation's political scene, as conceptualized in Habermas's theory of the public sphere.

Stage 3: Popular Citizenship (Approx 1990–)

In Stage 3, empirical attention is directed towards the then newly emerged TV programme formats of studio debates, which give access to popular voices, as lay citizens are invited into an amphitheatre TV studio to discuss socially and politically controversial issues with system representatives like politicians and experts.

In a pioneering reception study of studio debate programmes, Livingstone and Lunt (1994) investigated whether such programmes have any democratic value. An affirmative answer would depend on whether domestic audiences actually acquired the prerequisites of citizenship by watching the on-screen deliberations of lay and expert debaters.

One of the innovative properties of their research was the use of complementary qualitative and quantitative methods, which was considered almost heretical by the overwhelmingly qualitative congregation of reception researchers. Livingstone and Lunt found in the qualitative focus group study that domestic audiences were broadly appreciative of the multi-vocal lay participants in the studio debates and that domestic audiences possessed critical repertoires which they applied to their personal evaluation of the televisual debates. Moreover, audiences felt that the lay participants entered the debate on equal terms with experts and politicians. Consequently, they concluded that these programmes represented a genuine extension of the national public sphere, as a channel for the voices of popular citizenship (see also Johansson's 2009 reception study of tabloid newspapers).

The quantitative survey findings, based on a nationally representative sample of citizens, on the whole corroborated the qualitative findings almost universally across demographic groups, with older viewers being more critical of the chaotic nature of the debates and more respectful of the experts (Livingstone, Wober and Lunt 1994: 355).

Reflecting on their findings, Livingstone and Lunt (1994: 179) propose that the traditional division between informative and entertaining genres, and between the corresponding audience gratifications of 'critical insight' versus 'mindless pleasure', is not applicable to audience discussion programmes. This proposal has since been taken up by other scholars, whose reception studies on the political implications of Hollywood fan cultures and reality TV shows have confirmed the need for 'an agenda to think about entertaining politics, instead of simply discarding it as irrelevant and dangerous to citizenship and the democratic project' (van Zoonen 2005:viii; see also Curran 2010; Graham 2009; Graham and Hajru 2011).

Stage 4: Participatory Citizenship (Approx 2000–)

The analytical focus of Stage 4 of reception research on participatory citizenship is mainly a consequence of innovative developments in communication technologies with revolutionizing interactive affordances. These technological developments coincided with a changing political culture in which 'life political' participatory practices, such as political consumption, were gaining ground.

Greeted by shifting waves of utopian enthusiasm and dystopian pessimism, the digital culture of convergence (Jenkins 2006) with its incessant launching of revolutionizing digital and mobile communication technologies has offered humans new possibilities for interaction along different dimensions: one-to-one, one-to-many and many-to-many, and all of these both in synchronous and asynchronous forms (Jensen 2010: 71). As a consequence, the relationship of citizens to mediated politics need no longer be restricted to sedentary interpretive sense making of media fare produced by professionals. It may, for growing numbers of digital immigrants and digital natives alike, take the form of interventionist participation in communicative processes characterized by collective intelligence and collective creativity (Jenkins 2006), not all of which can be categorized as deliberative or even participatory in the full political sense of the words (Carpentier 2011).

Sometimes such interventions voice alternative and critical points of view which are more radical than those of consensual mainstream politics (Ross and Nightingale 2003: 153).

In light of such developments, the empirical scope of reception research must be extended. It must encompass, as before, interview-based studies of the often domestic processes of media use in which consumers and citizens make sense of and interact with mediated content: But it must also turn towards observational 'netnographic' studies (Hine 2000) of the practices where citizens participate in the creation of such content, for mainstream and niche platforms, in the form of user-generated content (UGC) in social arenas spanning education, journalism, the workplace, leisure and lifestyle (Kozinets 2002). And irrespective of whether the content was generated by professional or lay agents, and their purposes in doing so, it may enter into hierarchical or viral circuits of dissemination, meeting the eyes of sense-making majority audiences of 'lurkers'.

Wahl-Jørgensen, Williams and Wardel (2010), in a conventional qualitative reception study of British audiences' perception of UGC in news stories, found that audience appreciation of different types of UGC was remarkably different. Across 12 focus groups representing the key demographics of class, age, gender and levels of activism, it was found that audiences really valued 'content UGC' in the form of eyewitness accounts and visual material of dramatic events, which gave a freshness to news narratives by providing content based on immediacy and authenticity.

In contrast, there was widespread resentment over 'comment UGC', in which ordinary citizens contributed to the discussion of public issues. Such argumentative and postulatory comments, which are supposedly the heart blood of public sphere deliberation, were dismissed as the self-important effusions of the usual exhibitionist suspects. From a democratic perspective, this study appears to show that the more UGC is offered by active citizens seeking to make a contribution to democratic deliberation, the less it is valued by the news consuming audiences.

Stage 5: Ubiquitous Citizenship (Approx 2005–)

The notion of 'ubiquitous citizenship' owes its existence to the recent retheorizations of the Habermassian theory of the public sphere, which challenge the confinement of legitimate political action to a particular domain labelled 'the political public sphere'. Instead, scholars observing human interaction in the digital mediascape propose that citizenship is everywhere. They make a distinction between, on the one hand, a broad 'public sphere' in which all kind of inconspicuous everyday behaviours may have political implications and, on the other hand, a strictly 'policy sphere' in which political interests and sentiments are channelled directly into the parliamentary institutions invested with constitutional powers (Bennett and Entman 2001; see also Barnhurst 2003).

There is thus a new strand of political thinking about media and citizenship which wishes to map and assess mediated citizenship in practices which are firmly lodged in the realm of the everyday and often not subjectively perceived by individuals as political: 'we engage politics everywhere, all the time, and the media are central to that engagement' (Jones 2006: 379). Peter Dahlgren, perhaps echoing one of Habermas's more inclusive definitions of the public sphere that 'a portion of the public sphere is constituted in every conversation in which private persons come together to form a public' (Habermas 1989: 398), suggests that we may find citizenship, also labelled 'civic agency', even in the dormant political potential of people's informal conversations in daily life. It also follows from this retheorization that rational deliberative argument and emotional, embodied engagement are regarded as equally indispensable for the vitality of a democratic society (van Zoonen 2005).

Reception research has played an important parenting role in redefining citizenship, as its empirical explorations of how 'ordinary people' make sense of the media (e.g. Meijer 2007) have provided eye-opening insights about the interpretive, aesthetic and critical capabilities that people bring to bear on mediated representations of social reality in factual and fictional forms.

A study of viewers' discussions of reality TV shows in online fora (Graham 2009) may serve here as an example of the new netnographic form of reception research, which analyses people's spontaneous, unsolicited participation in everyday conversations on the net about communicative phenomena, identifying and evaluating their democratic implications and potentials. Calling for a more 'porous' approach to politics, which extends its boundaries to include sub-, life-, and lifestyle politics, Graham finds that conversations among fans of reality TV programmes, which lack any overt political purpose, nevertheless often turn to serious political issues, as topics 'from the role of bullying among British youth to the Iraq war' are hotly discussed among the participants, in 'a public sphere where free, equal, and open deliberation among citizens can flourish' (Graham 2009: 2; see also Sandvoss's 2009 analysis of the Internet discussions of German soccer fans as an alternative public sphere).

Ubiquitous Citizenship from Latency to Agency – Challenges for Reception Research

We may tentatively and perhaps radically conclude from this historical journey through five stages of reception research that, as a consequence of the mediatization of society (Hjarvard 2008; Livingstone 2009; Lundby 2009), today's media as digital communicative fora spanning the continuum from mass to interpersonal communication *are* the public sphere or a substantial and indispensible part of it. Consequently, in virtue of being a member of the media audience, the individual *is* a politically inscribed citizen everywhere. For media and reception studies, this means that, programmatically and conceptually, media experiences with democratic implications must be explored intertextually across the total ensemble of media.

Second, it becomes a challenge for reception research to understand how mediated dormant citizenship may transform into mediated, engaged, or even interventionist, citizenship: in short, how latency becomes agency.

Some scholars have started to address this daunting task empirically in a way that must necessarily take a microscopic starting point. Mascheroni (2010), for instance, has analysed the ways in which social network sites may serve as platforms of mobilization for political action online and in real life. Others have devoted their energies towards the exploration of the landscapes of media use from a higher altitude, as they try to map people's life with the media in the perspective of political engagement. This may involve an investigation of the 'media repertoires' (Hasebrink and Popp 2006) or 'constellations of media' (Couldry, Livingstone and Markham 2007), which people assemble for their everyday consumption, and of the political and other functionalities served by the elements of such individually and socially composed media packages (Linaa Jensen 2009; Pew Research Center 2008, 2010).

In the remainder of this chapter, I shall present a reception study of the latter kind, which tries to map citizen-consumers' constellations of news media, which they assemble from the landscape of traditional and new media, a landscape which collectively provides the affordances of ubiquitous citizenship. The resulting map of the news media available to citizen-consumers will enable us to calibrate the civic and other roles played by the individual news media and formats, serving as the interrelated nodes of the news media network as a whole.

Worthwhileness of News Media

The case study was firmly lodged in a radical user's perspective on news consumption – as we premised our theoretical conceptualization of individuals' motivations for using some news media and not others on the subjectively *perceived worthwhileness* of the offers available on the shelves of 'the supermarket of news'. Naturally an individual's news media portfolio is not a static thing: as new technologies and new content formats become available, people will be tempted to try some of them. Similarly, if their daily schedule changes, they may substitute the free newspaper read on the commuter train for the radio news in the cocoon of their car or another option as the case may be.

'Perceived worthwhileness' is defined as the meeting point of seven dimensions that together influence an individual's choice of news media (for a more detailed account, see Schrøder and Kobbernagel 2010). 'Temporality' plays a key role. One must have the necessary time to consume a particular news medium in a particular time slot in one's daily schedule. For some people some news media can be so worthwhile that they will *make time* for, say, the daily newspaper. 'Spatiality' also matters (i.e. the situational circumstances and social relations to other people may be decisive for not turning on the TV news in spite of time being available), just as the need to concentrate on driving will prevent one from checking the news on the mobile phone.

A third dimension of worthwhileness is 'materiality', which crucially involves the technological affordances of news media. The sensory pleasure of touching the pages of a glossy magazine may make one discard the possibility of reading it on a digital reading device. The technological (and situational) ease of using the remote control may induce one to consult the text TV news.

Perhaps the most decisive dimension of worthwhileness is a news medium's affordance of the social quality of 'public connection', a concept invented by Couldry, Livingstone and Markham (2007: 3) to conceptualize the fact that 'as citizens, we share an orientation to a public world where matters of shared concern are, or at least should be, addressed'. We extend the scope of the concept to also cover an individual's need for belonging and connecting to daily networks of significant and not so significant others. We thus distinguish between *civic* public connection and *everyday* public connection. This is the content dimension of worthwhileness: whether people find the verbal and visual content of a news medium relevant and interesting depends on the ability of this content to satisfy their need for mediatized public connection, encompassing both their need to equip themselves with mediated information about public affairs and to belong as a community member in the broadest possible sense.

Fifth, related to public connection, worthwhileness depends on the 'normative constraints' surrounding a given news medium in the form of the encouragement and support versus the discouragement and condescension in the feedback coming from one's social networks. Such tacit or explicit taste judgements surround, for instance, the reading of tabloid newspapers. A sixth dimension is provided by the 'participatory affordances' offered by a news medium. For some individuals, the possibility of giving spontaneous comment or producing UGC in digital news formats will enhance the worthwhileness of these media. Finally, 'economy' matters, as people's relative affluence affects which newspaper they read (if any) or which mobile phone subscription they can afford.

Importantly, worthwhileness (a concept we never used with informants) should not be confused with importance. Sometimes a news medium is used simply because it happens to be around, as in the case of free newspapers on a commuter train. In such cases, we would talk about 'worthwhileness by default'.

Multimethod Research Design

With perceived worthwhileness as our theoretical mindset, our fieldwork, conducted in Denmark in 2008 and 2009, applied a dual, sequential research design. First, we explored, through an online survey with a representative sample of individuals aged 18+, which news media were most and least worthwhile across the whole population. Second, we carried out a qualitative study based on interviews with 35 individuals, in which we wanted to construct a typology of cross-media news consumption. This qualitative study was methodologically innovative in complementing the qualitative core with a quantitative generalization capability.

The Danes' Top 10 of Worthwhile News Media

In the online survey (fully reported in Schrøder and Larsen 2010), we asked respondents to report, from a list of 16 news media and genres, which news media and genres they had used during the past week. Although the findings (which do not encompass 'time spent' on the different media) provide an interesting indicator of the extent to which news on Danish Internet sites had soared to almost equal the role of TV news, the most surprising finding was that text TV news, which had been neglected in previous research, actually held fourth place on the list of worthwhile news media and, by this finding, is a highly important news medium. In eighth place, free newspapers had established themselves as an important news source for many people. Mobile news at this point (2008) had not gained wide currency. When we asked people which news medium was 'most worthwhile' (in the questionnaire phrased as 'most indispensable'), predictably news on Danish TV channels came out far ahead of the other news media, with Internet news trailing far behind. Again, text TV news manifested itself surprisingly high on the list, with 5 per cent of respondents finding it 'the most indispensable'. The role of free newspapers as merely worthwhile by default was evident in a score of 1 per cent on this question.

Rather than seeing all news media as competing for attention on one parameter, we wanted to explore an idea generated by previous qualitative research (Schrøder and Phillips 2007) that people distinguish between two functionalities of news media: overview and depth. We therefore asked people to choose the three news media that they deemed most important for each of these functions.

Table 1: News functionalities in Denmark: Most important overview and depth news media, October 2008. Each respondent listed 3 news media

	Overview Ranking	%	Depth Ranking	%
Prime-time Danish TV news	1	55	1	45
News on Danish Internet news sites	2	50	4	24
Radio news programmes	3	41	6	13
Text TV news	4	36	—	—
National broadsheet newspapers	5	15	2	36
Free dailies	6	13	—	—
Current affairs Danish TV	—	—	3	35
Professional journals	—	—	5	13
Local/regional dailies	7	10	7	11
Radio current affairs	—	—	8	10
Local free weekly newspapers	8	9	9	7

Table 1 shows that one news medium (prime-time Danish TV news) presides as the all-round news medium in Denmark, with top rankings in both functionalities. Internet news appears to be on its way to challenge this role, with second place for overview and fourth place for depth. For overview, text TV is on the heels of radio news. National dailies, being close to negligible for overview, reassert themselves with a clear second place for background, ahead of both Internet news and TV current affairs. All news media except TV news and Internet news display a clear functional differentiation, with radio news, text TV and free dailies being 'mono-functional overview' media, and national dailies, TV current affairs and professional magazines being 'mono-functional background' media.

Packages of Worthwhile News Media

Seeing people metaphorically as shoppers in 'the supermarket of news media', we wanted next to explore the ways in which it might be possible to discern patterns in the ways different shoppers selected 'their' news media from the shelves. At the same time, we wanted people to tell us in what ways they perceive the news media they regularly consume as worthwhile.

We therefore adopted, first, a qualitative fieldwork design, based on 35 informants' narration about 'A day in the life' with the news media. The informants were diverse with respect to age, gender and geography. Although researchers have often distilled patterns, or typologies, from such purely qualitative research designs (Halkier 2003), we, second, wanted to explore a way to compute, more reliably than through the human brainpower of the researchers, how news consumption could be said to be patterned. We therefore added a quantitative generalization mechanism to the qualitative design, which enabled us to apply a typology-generating factor-analytical calculation. The raw material of this computation was produced by asking informants to playfully place 25 cards, each carrying the name of a news medium or genre, on a pyramidal grid with numbered squares ranging from 'important in my life' to 'not important in my life'. We asked them to accompany this puzzle game by thinking aloud, thus informing us about the reasoning underlying the placing of each card/ medium on the grid. The merit of this method is that informants so to speak self-analyse their individual worthwhileness-of-news universe. Moreover, this universe as represented on the grid is a relational network because their consumption of the 25 news media comes out as a personal constellation, not atomized verdicts about 25 separate news media. For further methodological details, see Schrøder and Kobbernagel (2010).

Here we shall merely summarize the typological findings in the form of presenting the top five of each of the seven types of news consumer generated by the factor analysis, leaving the qualitative amplification for future publications to interpret.[1]

Table 2 shows how the informants can be grouped into seven different types of news user (5 of the 35 informants did not fit into these types). We have tentatively supplied each type with a label that sums up the particular news profile of its members. In some cases, some of the features which contribute to distinguishing one type from another are located outside the top five. Most remarkably, not least in comparison with other countries (Pew Research Center 2008), is the fact that irrespective of clear differences between the seven types, they display equally clear cross-type homogeneity. All groups have prime-time Danish TV news and news on Danish Internet news sites in their top five. This homogeneity can be used as a basis for addressing the issue of democratic adequacy of these Danish news consumption profiles.

Coming Full Circle: Assessing Competent Mediated Citizenship?

In the very first sentence of this chapter, the question was asked how we may determine from the perspective of media reception studies whether the population of a given European country deserve the label of 'competent citizen'?

Granting that the typology presented here is based on a qualitative study of 35 informants, and is thus not representative of the whole population of Denmark, we may nevertheless legitimately ask whether we should be concerned about the mediated civic prerequisites of these seven kinds of citizens, who surely represent a substantial portion of the country's adult population. So do these Danes' constellations of news media appear to qualify them as well-informed, competent citizens?

The answer, naturally, depends on how we wish to define such a democratic animal. If we require a well-informed citizen to read a daily newspaper, these Danes fall short, as only three of the groups rank a quality newspaper in the top five. However, all seven groups have a public service TV news provider in the top five, and previous research has

Table 2: Typology of cross-media news users in Denmark (based on top five rankings from 25 news media), June–September 2009

	The traditional, versatile news user (no. of participants: 9)	The 'popular' digital news user (no. of participants: 4)	The depth digital news user (no. of participants: 3)	The light newspaper reader (No. of participants: 4)	The heavy newspaper reader (no. of participants: 3)	The news update addict (no. of participants: 4)	The regional omnivore (no. of participants: 3)
1	Prime-time Danish TV news	Social net media	Danish Internet news sites	Prime-time Danish TV news	National mainstream newspapers	24-hour TV news	Prime-time Danish TV news
2	National mainstream newspapers	Danish Internet news sites	Social net media	Tabloid newspapers	Prime-time Danish TV news	Prime-time Danish TV news	Local/regional dailies
3	Radio news (before 9 a.m.)	Prime-time Danish TV news	Prime-time Danish TV news	Free daily newspapers	Text TV	Text TV	'Serious' current affairs TV
4	'Serious' current affairs TV	'Entertaining' current affairs TV	Internet: culture sites	Danish Internet news sites	Danish Internet news sites	Danish Internet news sites	Family and women's magazines
5	Danish Internet news sites	Free daily newspapers	Free daily newspapers	'Entertaining' current affairs TV	National niche newspapers	Social net media	Danish Internet news sites

demonstrated that people who live in strong public service media systems have more public knowledge than people in countries with no, or a weak, public service tradition (Curran et al. 2009).

Pulling in the same direction is the fact that all seven groups have Danish Internet news sites in their top five. This news is provided by large established news institutions (i.e. newspapers and public service broadcasting houses) and should therefore count as equal to the quality news provision of newspapers and public service TV news. Finally, five of the groups have a high ranking of social media, showing that in spite of the often trivial (but often subjectively vital) purposes of using Facebook and similar sites, a large proportion of the Danes have considerable digital literacies which will be crucial prerequisites of citizenship in the future. Although the present study thus ends on an optimistic note, in the mediatized future only the continuous monitoring by reception and other kinds of audience research of people's social uses of news will be able to answer our continued curiosity, and perhaps concern, whether the media fulfil their role as vital resources for democratic citizenship.

References

Althusser, L., 1971. Ideology and ideological state apparatuses. In L. Althusser, ed., *Lenin and philosophy and other essays*. London: Monthly Review Press. pp. 121–176.

Anderson, B., 1983. *Imagined communities: Reflections on the origin and spread of nationalism*. London: Verso.

Ang, I., 1985. *Watching Dallas*. London: Methuen.

Barnhurst, K., 2003. Subjective states: Narratives of citizenship among young Europeans. *Multilingua*, 22, pp. 133–168.

Beck, U., 1997. *The reinvention of politics*. London: Routledge.

Bennett, L.W. and Entman, R.M., 2001. Mediated politics: An introduction. In L.W. Bennett and R.M. Entman, eds, *Mediated politics: Communication in the future of democracy*. Cambridge, UK: Cambridge University Press. pp. 1–32.

Bourdieu, P., 1984. *Distinction*. Cambridge, MA: Polity Press. (Originally published in French 1979.)

Carpentier, N., 2011. *Media and participation. A site of ideological-democratic struggle*. Bristol, UK: Intellect.

Castells, M., 1996. *The rise of the network society. The information age: Economy, society and culture*, Vol. 1. Oxford, UK: Blackwell.

Couldry, N., Livingstone, S. and Markham, T., 2007. *Media consumption and public engagement. Beyond the presumption of attention*. Basingstoke, UK: Palgrave Macmillan.

Curran, J., 2010. Entertaining democracy. In J. Curran, ed., *Media and society*. London: Bloomsbury. pp. 38–62.

Curran, J., Lund, A.B., Iyengar, S. and Salovaara-Moring, I., 2009. Media system, public knowledge and democracy: A comparative study. *European Journal of Communication*, 24(5), pp. 5–26.

Dahlgren, P., 2001. The public sphere and the net: Structure, space, and communication. In L.W. Bennett and R.M. Entman, eds, *Mediated politics: Communication in the future of democracy*. Cambridge, UK: Cambridge University Press. pp. 33–55.

—— 2006. Doing citizenship: The cultural origins of civic agency in the public sphere. *European Journal of Cultural Studies*, 9(3), pp. 267–286.

Fiske, J., 1987. *Television culture*. London: Methuen.

Fraser, N., 1992. Rethinking the public sphere. A contribution to the critique of actually existing democracy. In C. Calhoun, ed., *Habermas and the public sphere*. Cambridge, MA: MIT Press. pp. 109–142.

Giddens, A., 1984. *The constitution of society*. Cambridge, UK: Polity Press.

—— 1994. Living in a post-traditional Society. In U. Beck, A. Giddens and S. Lash, eds, *Reflexive modernization. Politics, tradition and aesthetics in the modern social order*. Cambridge, UK: Polity Press. pp. 56–108.

Gitlin, T., 1978. Media sociology: The dominant paradigm. *Theory and Society*, 6, pp. 205–253.

Graham, T.S., 2009. *What's wife swap got to do with it? Talking politics in the net-based public sphere*. Doctoral dissertation, Faculty of Social and Behavioural Sciences, University of Amsterdam.

Graham, T.S. and Hajru, A., 2011. Reality TV as a trigger of everyday political talk in the net-based public sphere. *European Journal of Communication*, 26(1), pp. 18–32.

Gramsci, A., 1971. *Selections from the prison notebooks*. New York: International Publishers.

Habermas, J., 1962. *Strukturwandel der Öffentlichkeit*. Darmstadt & Neuwied, Germany: Hermann Luchterhand Verlag.

—— 1989. The public sphere. In S. Seidman, ed., *Jürgen Habermas on society and politics: A reader*. Boston, MA: Beacon Press. pp. 398–404.

—— 2006. Political communication in the media society: Does democracy still enjoy an epistemic dimension? The impact of normative theory on empirical research. *Communication Theory*, 16, pp. 411–426.

Halkier, B., 2003. The challenge of qualitative generalizations in communication research. *Nordicom Review*, 24(1), pp. 115–124.

Hall, S., 1973. Encoding and decoding in the television discourse. Stenciled occasional paper, Media Series No. 7, Centre for Contemporary Cultural Studies, University of Birmingham. Abridged version, in S. Hall, D. Hobson, A. Lowe and P. Willis, eds, 1980. *Culture, media, language*. London: Hutchinson. pp. 128–138.

—— 1996. Introduction: Who needs 'identity'? In S. Hall and P. du Gay, eds, *Questions of cultural identity*. London: Sage. pp. 1–17.

Hasebrink, U. and Popp, J., 2006. Media repertoires as a result of selective media use. A conceptual approach to the analysis of patterns of exposure. *Communications*, 31, pp. 369–387.

Hermes, J., 1995. *Reading women's magazines: An analysis of everyday media use*. Oxford, UK: Polity Press.

Hermes, J. and Stello, C., 2000. Cultural citizenship and crime fiction: Politics and the interpretive Community. *Cultural Studies*, 3(2), pp. 215–232.

Herzog, H., 1944. What do we really know about daytime serial listeners? In P.F. Lazarsfeld and F. Stanton, eds, *Radio Research 1942–1943*. New York: Duell, Sloan & Pearce. pp. 2–23.

Hill, A., 2007. *Restyling factual TV. Audiences and news, documentary and reality genres*. London: Routledge.

Hine, C., 2000. *Virtual ethnography*. London: Sage.

Hjarvard, S., 2008. The mediatization of religion: A theory of the media as agents of religious change. *Northern lights 2008. Yearbook of film and media studies*. Bristol, UK: Intellect Press. pp. 9–26.

Jenkins, H., 2006. *Convergence culture. Where old and new media collide*. New York: New York University Press.

Jensen, K.B., 1986. *Making sense of the news*. Aarhus, Denmark: Aarhus University Press.

———— 1990. The politics of polysemy: Television news, everyday consciousness and political action. *Media, Culture and Society*, 12, pp. 57–77.

———— 1991. Reception analysis: Mass communication as the social production of meaning. In K.B. Jensen and N.W. Jankowski, eds, *A handbook of qualitative methodologies for mass communication research*. London: Routledge. pp. 135–148.

———— 1998. *News of the world. World cultures look at television news*. London: Routledge.

———— 2010. *Media convergence. The three degrees of network, mass, and interpersonal communication*. London: Routledge.

Jensen, K.B. and Rosengren, K.E., 1990. Five traditions in search of the audience. *European Journal of Communication*, 5, pp. 207–238.

Jhally, S. and Lewis, J., 1992. *Enlightened racism: The 'Cosby Show', audiences and the myth of the American dream*. Boulder, CO: Westview Press.

Johansson, S., 2009. 'They just make sense': Tabloid newspapers as an alternative public sphere. In R. Butsch, ed., *Media and public spheres*. Basingstoke, UK: Palgrave Macmillan. pp. 83–95.

Jones, J.P., 2006. A cultural approach to the study of mediated citizenship. *Social Semiotics*, 16(2), pp. 365–383.

Keane, J., 1991. *The media and democracy*. Cambridge, MA: Polity Press.

Kozinets, R.V., 2002. The field behind the screen: Using netnography for marketing research in online communities. *Journal of Marketing Research*, 39, pp. 61–72.

Kuhn, T., 1962. *The structure of scientific revolutions*. Chicago, IL: University of Chicago Press.

Lewis, J., 1997. What counts in cultural studies. *Media, Culture & Society*, 19(1), pp. 83–97.

Liebes, T., and Katz, E., 1990. *The export of meaning*. New York: Oxford University Press.

Linaa Jensen, J., 2009. New convergences of political participation? The Internet and other media. Paper presented at Nordmedia 2009, Karlstad, Sweden, 13–15 August.

Livingstone, S., 2009. On the mediation of everything. *Journal of Communication*, 59(1), pp. 1–18.

Livingstone, S. and Lunt, P., 1994. *Talk on television*. London: Routledge.

Livingstone, S., Wober, M. and Lunt, P., 1994. Studio audience discussion programmes: An analysis of viewers' preferences and involvement. *European Journal of Communication*, 9, pp. 355–379.

Lull, J., 1980. The social uses of television. *Human Communication Research*, 6, pp. 197–209.

Lundby, K., 2009. *Mediatization: Concept, changes, consequences*. New York: Peter Lang.

Mascheroni, G., 2010. Remediating participation and citizenship practices on social network sites. *Medien Journal*, 3, pp. 22–35.

McNair, B., 2003. *An introduction to political communication*. 3rd ed. London: Routledge.

Meijer, I.C., 2007. Checking, snacking and bodysnatching. How young people use the news and implications for public service media journalism. In G.F. Lowe and J. Bardoel, eds, *From Public Service Broadcasting to Public Service Media*. Gothenburg, Sweden: Nordicom. pp. 167–187.

Morley, D., 1980. *The 'nationwide' audience: Structure and decoding*. London: BFI.

Negrine, R., 1996. *The communication of politics*. London: Sage.

Newcomb, H. and Hirsch, P., 1983. Television as a cultural forum: Implications for research. *Quarterly Review of Film Studies*, 8(3), pp. 45–55.

Pew Research Center, 2008. *Audience segments in a changing news environment: Key news audiences now blend online and traditional sources*. Washington, DC: Pew Research Center for the People and the Press.

——— 2010. *Understanding the participatory news consumer*. Washington, DC: Pew Internet and American Life Project.

Radway, J., 1984. *Reading the romance: Women, patriarchy and popular literature*. Chapel Hill, NC: University of North Carolina Press.

Rantanen, T., 2005. *The media and globalization*. London: Sage.

Ross, K. and Nightingale, V., 2003. *Media and audiences. New perspectives*. Maidenhead, UK: Open University Press.

Sandvoss, C., 2009. Public sphere and publicness: Sport audiences and political discourse. In E. Butsch, ed., *Media and public spheres*. Basingstoke, UK: Palgrave Macmillan. pp. 58–70.

Schrøder, K.C., 1997. Cynicism and ambiguity: British corporate responsibility advertisements and their readers in the 1990s. In M. Nava, A. Blake, I. MacRury and B. Richards, eds, *Buy this book: Studies in advertising and consumption*. London: Routledge. pp. 276–290.

Schrøder, K.C., in press. Audiences as citizens: Insights from three decades of reception research. In R. Parameswaran, ed., *The Blackwell companion to audience research*. Boston, MA: Blackwell.

Schrøder, K.C. and Kobbernagel, C., 2010. Towards a typology of cross-media news consumption: A qualitative-quantitative synthesis. *Northern Lights. Yearbook of Film and Media Studies*, 11, pp. 115–137.

Schrøder, K.C. and Larsen, B.S., 2010. The shifting cross-media news landscape: Challenges for news producers. *Journalism Studies*, 11(4), pp. 524–534.

Schrøder, K.C. and Phillips, L., 2007. Complexifying media power: A study of the interplay between media and audience discourses on politics. *Media, Culture & Society*, 29(6), pp. 890–915.

Schrøder, K.C., Drotner, K., Kline, S. and Murray, C., 2003. *Researching audiences*. London: Edward Arnold.

Thompson, J.P., 1995. *The media and modernity. A social theory of the media*. Cambridge, UK: Polity Press.

Turner, B.S., 2001. Outline of a general theory of cultural citizenship. In N. Stevenson, ed., *Culture & Citizenship*. London: Sage. pp. 13–32.

van Zoonen, L., 2005. *Entertaining the citizen. When politics and popular culture converge*. Lanham, MD: Rowman & Littlefield.

Wahl-Jørgensen, K., Williams, A. and Wardle, C., 2010. Audience views on user-generated content: Exploring the value of news from the bottom up. *Northern Lights. Yearbook of Film and Media Studies*, 11, pp. 177–194.

Warner, W.L. and Henry, W.E., 1948. The radio daytime serial: A symbolic analysis. *Genetic Psychology Monographs*, 37, pp. 3–71.

Note

1   While we await the results of the qualitative analysis, which will illuminate aspects of people's civic engagement, the notion of 'ubiquitous citizenship' in this study is mainly a feature of the research design, that is the way we explore news consumption as an empirical phenomenon that is unlimited in spatio-temporal terms, not confined to particular, privileged domains of citizenship. The realization of potentially democratic practices in these domains must be studied with methods designed to illuminate the way people make sense of specific media content, such as the netnographic studies of Sandvoss (2009) and Graham and Hajru (2011).

Chapter 11

For and against Participation: A Hermeneutical Approach to Participation in the Media

Lars Nyre and Brian O'Neill

Introduction

Media use is a social activity, and nowhere is it more social than during participatory acts where the user is personally engaged in the public sphere and can lose face or have success in the eyes of others. This chapter deals with ordinary people's reasons for and against participating in modern media like television, radio and the Internet. This topic is also important in a research perspective, as 'participation' has been one of the most popular trends in audience and reception studies for the past 20 years (Carpentier 2009; Dahlberg 2001; Dahlgren 2005).

The chapter presents the hermeneutic paradigm in social studies and demonstrates its relevance for participation in the media. The chapter goes on to present a study of opinions among media participants in Norway and Ireland in 2005–2006, and as such it is intended to show an empirical application of the hermeneutical paradigm. We particularly focus on motivations for and against participation, as formulated by our informants during qualitative interviews. Informants claim that private enjoyment is the main reason for taking part in the media, whereas unsuitable formats for political debate are the main reason for not taking part. People are entertained by their own participation in quiz shows or talk shows because these formats are relatively harmless, and you do not lose face by participating. At the same time, they do not trust the political debate formats to secure their integrity and equality with others during participation. You do not lose face by giving the wrong answer to a quiz, but you lose face if you are cut off by a moderator in mid-sentence. In political formats, the participants' integrity is constantly at stake, not because of their opinions but because of the strategies of the station. This tension between positive and negative motivation comes across as well-informed and serves as a paradigmatic example of how empirical hermeneutics works.

Hermeneutics and Participation

Before we describe our approach to participation, the hermeneutical tradition must be introduced. Hermeneutics traditionally refers to systematic text readings, for example, exegeses of the Bible, consultations of law texts or interpretations of dramatic literature. We are concerned with philosophical hermeneutics, a theory of understanding that emerged with Wilhelm Dilthey (1833–1911). He established an important epistemological difference between 'explanation' in the natural sciences and 'understanding' in the social sciences and humanist fields. Explanation is factual and finite, whereas understanding is intelligent and infinite. In the social sciences and humanities, language became the primary research object during the twentieth century, and along with it the act of understanding became a central topic in philosophy. The main hermeneutical writers are Hans-Georg Gadamer (1989), Jürgen Habermas (1987), Paul Ricoeur (1991) and Wolfgang Iser (1991).

The object of understanding in hermeneutic approaches is texts and actions in situations where you as a 'reader' revise your prejudices all of the time because you have learnt more, and if you relate to the same phenomenon a second time, you know something about it from before and can penetrate it further. This process is called the hermeneutical circle, and it has become a famous metaphor for the process of human understanding. After Gadamer it could have been renamed the hermeneutical spiral, as the faculty of understanding is in constant development.

'Double hermeneutics' is another key notion in the hermeneutical tradition, and it indeed serves as the methodological core of our approach. Hans Skjervheim (1959) considers the relationship between researcher and research object in social sciences to be communicative. The people who are studied and their researchers are potential conversation partners. The natural scientists, however, cannot communicate with their research objects in this way. Anthony Giddens calls this communicative phenomenon 'double hermeneutic' in that it consists of a connection between two provinces of meaning: the meaningful social world of lay actors and the metalanguages invented by social scientists to describe the world. There is 'a constant "slippage" from one to the other involved in the practice of the social sciences', Giddens (1991: 374) states.

In this chapter, we will apply the hermeneutical approach to the study of participation in the media. Media participation must be considered an act by non-professionals, where the aim is to contribute content to the otherwise professional 'text' of a programme. By singing, speaking or delivering information by short message system (SMS), e-mail and so on, the participant contributes a prepared text to a programme genre that is recognizable to him or her. This strongly communicative and public character makes it possible to distinguish participation from reception (lying on the sofa), programme interactivity (using menus, time-shifting), bureaucratic service requests (upgrading your cable service) and peer-to-peer contact (calling your mother on the phone). For other conceptualizations of media participation, see Carpentier (2007), Jensen (2008), Kiousis (2002) and Siapera (2004).

'Participation' should not be confused with 'interactivity'. The latter is restricted to describing the situation where a human interacts with a technology, as when a person uses the mouse and keyboard of the computer to write a message and post it somewhere. Such interactivity presumes an interface between a skilled user and a technological set-up where the apparatus and its programmes continuously change the data output according to changes in the input. Furthermore, if the interface is changed the content of the interaction is also changed. In the computer world, this implies that the user is frequently forced to acquire new skills because the functionality of the apparatus has been changed in the updated version. This is a conception where the patterns of interaction are ultimately technologically determined. This is not an accurate description of the hermeneutic act of participating.

To define participation as something more complex and fulfilling, we turn to the American sociological tradition called symbolic interactionism. Here, the important connection is that between human and human. Beyond the handling of instruments, contact takes the form of persons interpreting each other, a process of making judgements and taking action in the face of the constant actions and judgements of others. Herbert Blumer sketches the playing field of human interaction like this:

> [People] are caught up in a vast process of interaction in which they have to fit their developing actions to one another. This process of interaction consists in making indications to others of what to do and in interpreting the indications as made by others. (As cited in Collins 1994: 320)

He equally presumes that we live in worlds of objects and are guided in our orientation and action by the meaning of these objects. These objects, including media technologies and content, are formed, sustained, weakened and transformed in our interaction with one another (Collins 1994: 320). In this model of participation, the entities that act on each other are equally sensitive, equally responsible for their actions and equally able to display initiative. The purpose in any case goes far beyond the activity of pushing buttons or navigating through pages. It is a form of technology-mediated participation that Andrew Feenberg refers to as 'the most fundamental relation to reality' (Feenberg 1999: 196).

What kind of interpretational behaviour is required? Ideally, citizens engage in a public dialogue that acknowledges every participant as a responsible fellow citizen. To participate in a dialogue, according to the philosopher Hans Skjervheim, is to recognize the subject matter of the other's speech, to listen carefully and evaluate its claim to truthfulness or trustworthiness, and to move further along its interpretative trajectory when speaking yourself. 'This means that I am participating or engaging in this problem', Skjervheim says in his 1957 essay called 'Participant and Onlooker' (1996: 71). The words take part in an ongoing discourse of cooperation which could not exist without such base human bonds like trust, respect and acceptance, and their opposites during conflict and enmity. Your career, your self-esteem, your identity are all related to others through this reciprocal dimension of communication and its social repercussions. If you promise to participate, you have committed in a way that has consequences for your future communication – not with computers, but with humans.

If you want to participate in the media, you must have language-oriented skills so that you can handle the interfaces for text, sound and video in a communicative way. Media use involves knowledge about genres, formats and topics, and this knowledge is absolutely necessary to be able to play along with the programmes' communicative style or be critical towards it. Participation also requires integrity, at least in the minimum sense of being able to tackle the pressures of public attention in a coherent way and avoid embarrassing yourself in front of everybody. The content-producing function of participation is interesting because it inspires a high level of self-reflexivity. The person in question necessarily sees himself or herself in the eyes of others. In comparison with watching a film or reading a book, the activity of participating involves nervousness, self-consciousness and the ambition to do good and save face.

Participatory behaviour can be graded according to the public exposure of skills, personality and character during participation. People who make broadcast content for example at a community radio station or a student newspaper have relatively high exposure. People who appear as contestants in talent and reality shows, or guests in talk shows, also have high exposure. Examples of moderate exposure are postings in blogs, commentary fields and chat rooms as well as voting for videos on a music TV channel and voting for the football player of the week by sending an SMS message. Since 2005, it has become quite common for people to maintain a personal profile in social media. This is a permanent low exposure that comes alongside the traditional forms of participation.

Case: Motivation for Participation

Our project is to construct a meta-language to describe people's motivation to participate or their lack thereof. Motivation implies enthusiasm for doing something or the need or reason for doing something. Motivation may be rooted in a basic need to minimizing physical pain, eating, drinking and maximizing pleasure (Morris 1967), or it may be attributed to more hermeneutical reasons such as a state of being, an ideal, an ethical norm and so on. We distinguish between three types of hermeneutical objectives: private enjoyment, social attraction and political purpose. Below we will define this triad of reasons more carefully and quote from our empirical material from Bergen and Dublin.

Qualitative research projects often challenge people to formulate quite precisely thoughts and experiences that they may never have formulated before. Some researchers are sceptical about this slightly confrontational method (Gentikow 2005), but we consider it a fruitful approach. There are many topics that people do not really think carefully about until they are asked about it. When questioned by a small child, the adult may suddenly be required to explain what 'gravity' is, and during a heated discussion you are challenged to state your opinion about Islam. Such communicative confrontations can lead to new ideals and opinion, and it would be too strict a restriction on qualitative studies if it could only deal with issues that the informant is comfortable with and knowledgeable about. Most of the justifications quoted below were provoked during the interview phase, with informants routinely saying things like 'I've never really thought about that before, but …'.

Our study focuses on people in Norway and Ireland. They live in a cultural and historical context that influences the forms of communication, both in private and public life. Norway is a Protestant, social democratic welfare state with a long history of independence or lenient colonization from Danes or Swedes. Ireland is known as a Catholic-conservative welfare state with an equally strong culture of political awareness as in Norway but with a much more fractious past, including a long period of British colonization, a war of independence, followed by a civil war and later civil strife over partition. Norway did not have the same traumatic liberation from Sweden in 1905 as the Republic of Ireland did from the United Kingdom in 1921. The media industries in the two countries are approximately of the same size, with relatively homogenous audiences where regional differences are more pronounced (and less harmful) than national division. Both countries have a healthy number of local and regional independent media (Day 2009).

As our empirical material represents two national audience research cultures, we will give a brief review of each. In Norway, several studies are influenced by hermeneutics and/or cultural studies and look, for example, at participation in television formats (Gentikow 2010), dating programmes on television (Syvertsen and Bakøy 2001) and general media use by children and youngsters (Hagen and Wold 2009; Tønnessen 2007). There is also a study of opinions about participating in broadcast programmes based on the original research reported in this chapter (Bøe 2006). When it comes to Ireland, participation in broadcast programming and citizen engagement in public service broadcasting has been a long-standing theme of communications research. Kelly and O'Connor (1997) examined a wide range of audience practices in mainstream media (radio, television, print) focusing on the complex interplay of power and cultural identity. The potential of communication technologies for facilitating democratic participation for media consumers was first studied by Trench and O'Donnell (1997), with further studies of their domestication in Ward (2003), Kerr (2000) and Komito (2007). Participatory media in Ireland, in particular the case of community radio, has been the subject of ongoing research (Day 2009; Mitchell 2002), reflecting its importance in the Irish media landscape, whereas more recently media literacy policy has been examined from the point of view of enabling greater civic engagement (O'Neill and Barnes 2008). O'Sullivan (2005) has made an interesting qualitative study of talk radio, and Ross (2004) has studied the political dimension of participation in radio and television.

For this research project, we interviewed a total of 64 people, 32 in Norway and 32 in Ireland, during 2005 and 2006. We wanted to interview a cross-section of citizens in Bergen and Dublin. When selecting informants we created a systematic mixed population group, with gender balance, four age groups from 15+ and equal inclusion of people with basic and higher education.

Among our informants, there was a clear tendency for Internet users to be younger and radio users to be older, which conforms to the presumption that young people will adopt new media habits quite easily, whereas older people rely on their established diet of paper newspapers and public service broadcasting. However, TV dominated in the evening among all age groups (see Figure 1).

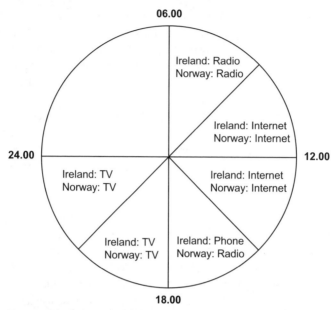

Figure 1: The dominance of different media during the day among our informants (*n* = 64).

In both Norway and Ireland 29 of 32 informants used the Internet regularly, with similar numbers regularly using SMS messaging. It may be that Ireland and Norway are in reality quite different, but both share in media and communications technology trends characteristic of western industrialized countries.

Informants completed the same questionnaire, and researchers followed the same interview guide in both countries. We used semi-structured interviews to research the diverse forms of participation in contemporary media. Based on their statements, we accumulated a list of 31 unique reasons for and against participation, and we categorized them as three types of motivation: private enjoyment, social attractions and political change.

Motivation can be studied in terms of language. Alfred Schutz distinguishes between 'in-order-to motives', which have a clear purpose that will presumably be reached in the future, and 'because motives', which are rooted in the past experiences and habits of the person (Schutz 1970: 126–127). For example, you can participate to win money, or you can participate because you are sure you know the right answer. Our material requires us to introduce 'if motives', which have a clear purpose in the future but will only be accomplished under certain limited conditions. For example, you will participate if a friend joins you in the endeavour. These three types of motives – 'in order to', 'because' and 'if' – are used to identify reasons and categorize the empirical material.

The hermeneutic object of study can in this case be defined as a 'reason' or 'justification' formulated orally by informants and transcribed by researchers. To justify an action means to explain that the motivation for it is just, right or reasonable and to show awareness of other people's perspectives from which the justification may not seem as reasonable as it does for the participant. Justifications typically relate to things in a situated way, where the speaker starts from his or her own life experiences and branches out into generality if he or she manages. Sociologists call this field of experience 'the common sense province of meaning' (Schutz 1970) or 'the lifeworld' (Habermas 1987). Grown-ups are in general able to describe their personal experiences and perspectives in varying detail and truthfulness, and make rationalizations and justifications of their own behaviour and that of others. This type of rational speech is the raw material of our investigations.

We asked simple yes/no questions and the most important was the following: 'Have you ever felt that you should have participated more in public debate?' We always prompted a follow-up from the informants, and the statements made during this dialogue were the really interesting ones, as this is where justifications were formulated. Using Schutz's distinction between motives, we identified justifications, for example, by the words 'since', 'because', 'if' and through a plethora of contracted formulations that explain the motivation, interest or gain from a certain action (or non-action). For example, 'It's stupid' can be completed as 'I will not participate because I consider it a stupid activity.'

Categories are always disputable. We made an interpretation scheme where we listed all the formulations of reasons our informants made, and they were more and more carefully categorized as the list grew. There are two dimensions in the organization of our findings: Dimension 1 relates to a rather theory-driven distinction between ways of formulating motivations ('in order to', 'because' and 'if'), whereas Dimension 2 relates to a more inductive or grounded distinction between different topical fields of justification ('personal enjoyment', 'social attraction' and 'political purpose').

Personal Enjoyment

As stated earlier, motivation may be rooted in a basic need to minimize physical pain and maximize pleasure. It could be called egotism rather than altruism, and it is marked by the wish for monetary gain, self-promotion and personal enjoyment. The list of reasons will help to explain it better:

Yes, because it is fun.
Yes, if I don't have to spend money on it.
Yes, in order to win prizes.
Yes, in order to compete with others and display knowledge.
Yes, if I become agitated and want to voice my opinion.
Yes, because it is easier to participate now than it was before.
No, because I would be too shy.
No, in order not to be bothered.

No, because I don't want to spend my time like this.
No, because it's too expensive.
No, because it wouldn't give me a valuable enough experience.

Yes, Because It Is Fun

A typical statement was made by Arne (15): 'As long as it is based on competition, it is great fun.' Nina (37) says,

> The last time I was interactive was in *Easter Quiz* where you can send in an SMS and join an SMS competition. The questions are damned difficult, and you are supposed to give answers until the time runs out, or you answer incorrectly. It was incredible fun, but you must have Internet because it's so difficult.

Yes, In Order To Win Prizes

Bjarte (25) would like to call into a show on the Norwegian station Radio 1 called *Hunted*. 'There was 40,000–50,000 kroner in the jackpot, so I guess that's what made me interested.' Kine (27) has long wanted to call a radio show where you are supposed to shout 'stop' at the right moment, and you can win anything from 200 to 4200 kroner. When asked why she wanted to, she answered, 'Cash is king. No-no! But it is a good way of getting some money quickly, so that's really the reason.'

Yes, If I Become Agitated

Participation may happen more or less spontaneously, for example, when people get annoyed with a statement they hear or read. Harald (47) wrote to the local newspaper to speak up against an unfair review of a theatre play.

> **Interviewee:** 'It was annoyance that made me write to the editor, you know.'
> **Interviewer:** 'Did you feel that it helped in any way?'
> **Interviewee:** 'It didn't help in relation to the theatre play, but it helped me that I got to let off some steam.'

The result was therapeutic only, but still it contains an acknowledgement that the public is a thoroughly real space, where you can fight back on the same turf even though no one may notice.

No, Because of Stressful Self-Awareness

Carla (23) is asked whether she would like to appear on television, and she answers, 'I would hate to be on TV actually. I would be too shy.' Her temperament is such that she would rather write than speak. 'It's easier for me', she says. This is a because-motive in Schutz's sense; her non-participation is the result of her personal circumstances and qualities, and does not reside in any future gain like the in-order-to motive presumes. Referring to political debate shows, Carla says, 'I think it is hard to find the confidence to participate. It is very daunting and the people who are on these shows often seem very confident and very educated and political. You know it is hard to match that.'

It is a core concern for people how they will be exposed if they go on air. The social reflexivity contained in this concern is well studied in the micro-sociology of Erving Goffman and others (see Goffman 1986; O'Sullivan 2005). Frida (23) is sensitive about her skills as a public speaker, especially about her ability to handle the complexity of public issues. She refers to a debate about gas-fuelled electricity plants. 'Most of those who have learnt something about the topic realize that there is more than one side to it. So I would perhaps get confused if I were to talk about it [she laughs].' Hans (28) says the same thing.

> Although I have clear opinions about gas power plants, I don't feel that I can give very good reasons for why I mean what I do. And that's why I wouldn't call. I think it is important to answer well and give reasons for what you mean if you are to express your opinions in public. You can't 'just say 'It's because I mean it.'

We interpret this as motivation to save face rather than a protest against formats, and as such it is a private and not political motivation (more about the latter below).

Social Attractions

The motivation for social encounters is rooted in emotional sentiments like altruism, morality or wish for consensus. People want to be together with others, or share time with others, and this activity can be almost entirely without instrumental motives while still be very fulfilling for those involved. Scannell (1996) reminds us that before anything else, radio and television are social phenomena. 'Sociability is the most fundamental characteristic of broadcasting's communicative ethos. The relationship between the broadcasters and audiences is a purely social one, that lacks any specific content, aim or purpose' (Scannell 1996: 23).

Yes, in order to contribute with information.
Yes, if somebody I know is already participating.
Yes, because I like a person, group or team.
Yes, in order to allow amateurs too and not only professionals.

Yes, if media participation were a more common and respected activity.
No, in order to shield my job role from embarrassment.
No, because people who do it are stupid.
No, because so many are doing it that there's no need for me to take part.

Yes, In Order To Contribute with Information

Clive (16) regularly contributes with information on the Web. Finn (41):

> Yeah, because often people discuss things in general terms. If you are involved in something and have a lot of experience of it, and you hear somebody really misinforming or not understanding the issue, you could ring up and maybe clarify a few things.

This kind of statement could also belong to the category 'political purpose', but there is a decidedly social character to this motivation. It is altruistic to stop in your tracks to provide information to the public; at least this is how informants felt about it. With blogs and social media, the social satisfaction of contributing with information is greater than ever.

Yes, If Somebody I Know Is Already Participating

For example, it is important to support friends and family who appear on air in a contest where SMS voting is part of the entertainment, as your votes are likely to make a real difference for them. In principle, Viktor (23) is fed up with SMS participation. He voted for all kinds of reality shows, especially during the first seasons of *Big Brother*, but in the future he will only make one exception: 'I will never vote in the future, unless close family members and relatives are in it.' In these, the act of voting becomes more like a duty or an act of loyalty. 'If it is family you are bound to vote a few times.'

Yes, Because I Like a Person, Group or Team

Voting programmes thrive on the allure of beautiful, talented and innocent contestants. Audience members often get hooked on a 'favourite' and proceed to vote incessantly to support them, all based on a quite vague impression of their talents. Trine (56) voted for a female favourite in the 2005 season of *Norwegian Pop Idol*. 'I thought she deserved it because she was a good singer and a very cute and very, very nice girl.' People are charmed by such behaviour and react in highly emotional ways that are basically unforeseeable.

No, In Order To Shield My Job Role from Embarrassment

People are able to acknowledge quite pragmatically that something happens to your social role distribution if you participate in public. For example, interests in your work life can collide with media participation. Stine (27) works as an information consultant in Bergen, and she wanted to contact the local newspaper about an issue.

Interviewer: 'Why didn't you, after all?'

Interviewee: 'I don't know. I should have done so, but as time goes by I feel it has become more difficult because of the job I have. There is a confusion of roles in that I'm suddenly expressing opinions as a private individual when I'm a professional information worker and am supposed to be neutral. I will be connected with that job in any case, so now it is difficult.'

No, Because People Who Do It Are Stupid

The refusal relates to negative personal identification. In particular, it comes about towards people who seem socially incompetent. Victor (23) is full of contempt for unintelligent participants.

If you are sitting watching for example *Tabloid* [current debate on TV], and listen to the comments that are sent afterwards [he sighs and laughs], you notice that there are many idiots among us. It's strange that they exist, really. It's the politicians who are really good at presenting their case, and callers often hurt their cause when they present things the way they do.

Victor seems to be a person of strong negative and positive attachments to people.

No, Because I Won't Be Treated with Civility

Lise (47) thinks the SMS fortune-telling programme contains a fruitless social coercion.

I think it is unstructured, chaotic and disrespectful for both parties. As a listener I also felt offended by this form. This form makes the callers appear as idiots, and it lies in the format itself – although the people who call in are not exactly the world's brightest.

Political Purpose

Political motivation is rooted in recognition of society's collective need to minimize physical harm and maximize material gain, and to promote a certain political system and more or less contested values for the development of society. We focus on the degree to which our informants think that political purpose can be channelled through participation in the media.

The final list of justifications deals with political debate. Joshua Cohen argues that democracy requires the citizens not only to be free and equal but also to behave in a 'reasonable' way. This means that everybody must defend and criticize the issues at stake in ways that other citizens, as free and equal individuals, have reason to accept (as cited in Mouffe 2000: 90). Amateur participants in the media cannot be exempted from this requirement. They too are required to be prepared to explain their position on any given public matter, and our informants are very much aware of this requirement – although they may not therefore feel that they satisfy it. John Dewey (1960) calls the successful performance of public reasoning a type of 'well-considered' or 'intelligent' behaviour. Dewey's anthropology generously presumes that citizens are aware of the complexity of the society in which they live, in our case the media society with a largely digitalized public sphere. The more awareness there is about editorial and communicative strategies among citizens who participate in public, the better the public sphere will become.

In a political sense, the purpose of public speaking is to create concrete change in some province of reality, for example, by persuading somebody to change their opinion or to cause action to be taken by one or more people in a specific case. C. Wright Mills requires that 'opinion formed by [public] discussion readily finds an outlet in effective action, even against – if necessary – the prevailing system of authority' (quoted in Habermas 1990: 358). Informants have a quite realistic assessment of their opportunities in this regard. In real life, laypersons do not have much influence on the media, and they know it well.

Yes, if I have a well-informed opinion.
Yes, in order to become more well informed and resourceful.
Yes, because I'm engaged in my local surroundings.
Yes, because it is every citizen's right to participate.
Yes, because it is every citizen's duty.
Yes, because it would have worked well.
No, because it is every citizen's right not to participate.
No, in order to keep the public sphere as professional as possible.
No, because I'm not sufficiently competent.
No, because it wouldn't change things anyway.
No, because I don't trust the formats/genres.

Yes, because It Is Every Citizen's Right to Participate

Kai (25) considers public speaking a desirable and valuable political right. 'After all, we're talking about the people who walk the streets and live in this country, and when an issue is relevant for more than one person the others must also have their say.' Kristin (51) considers it a human right to express oneself in public. 'Well, yes, it's a human right. Those who are preoccupied with something must be allowed to express themselves about it. I express myself about everything I'm concerned with!' George (63) was a young man of 16 years when the Troubles in Northern Ireland started in 1969.

> At the time of the Troubles, I had a lot to say and I said it to my friends, but we should have said it out loud. There was a lot of anger and a lot of stupidity, and then a lot of violence and condemnation and everything else. There wasn't much reflection on 'putting this into context' or 'could we say this in a calmer way'. So I am sorry I didn't write to the papers or ring in to the radio.

No, Because It Is Every Citizen's Right Not to Participate

Interestingly, this is just another version of the justification discussed above. A widespread sentiment among the informants is that they have the political freedom not to act publicly. Fred (15) is a believer in extensive liberal rights. 'Do you think the audience should be more active in the public?' 'No', Fred says.

> They must be allowed to do as they please about that. I don't think they ought to do anything at all. I have no wish that people should participate if they don't want to participate or participate more than they do now. It's all up to themselves.

Yes, Because It Is Every Citizen's Duty

Alongside the consciousness about the right to speak in public (and the right not to do so), there are sentiments about a collective obligation or duty to participate, and these could be labelled 'social democratic'. Several informants focus quite adamantly on the individual's responsibility to improve the public. Dan (64) says,

> I am of the opinion that you can't just criticize without letting others speak up. It's like you can't criticize the politicians and then not vote afterwards, that's just bullshit. If you are part of the community and you are a voter, then you can also criticize things. It's the same with the media. You can't criticize them without bringing in another suggestion yourself.

Dan's justification for public participation is explicitly normative and requires active and resourceful behaviour on the part of the citizens. A democracy needs participation from all its citizens to work properly, and therefore it is a duty to participate.

No, Because I Don't Trust the Formats/Genres

Informants are critical of what they conceive of as the lack of common courtesy in the way hosts treat callers to radio and television. Indeed, these criticisms were often eloquent and rich in detail. Stine (27) feels uncomfortable with the typical social setting of participation programmes:

> There are so many debates where private persons, or the man on the street, is supposed to talk about this and that. But they are not allowed to speak for very long, or they are interrupted all the time. There is a pattern here that makes me turn it off; I get more and more annoyed and cannot listen any more. On *Tabloid* and programmes like that, the debate moves so quickly; there are so many opinions, but nobody is discussing things. They just throw out arguments, and it's not the good arguments that come across; what counts is to scream loudest.

Kari (20) comments more specifically on the screaming and shouting:

> In those discussion programmes, almost nobody gets their opinion across; everybody just [baaaauu] screams in each other's face, and then there's a politician who speaks a little once in a while. Often when an ordinary person opens his mouth it takes 2 seconds before they are told that what they're saying is wrong.

Conclusion

We believe hermeneutics is a well-suited paradigm for studies of the conscious level of media activities, where justifications and explanations are prompted by researchers and the double hermeneutics is at work. People who reflect on their own behaviour make statements that are interpreted by social researchers.

Our case study of motivation was meant to demonstrate the fruitfulness of the hermeneutical approach, with people in Bergen and Dublin making up our interview panel. To sum up the analysis, there is an interesting tension between wanting to participate in entertaining and competitive contexts, and not wanting to participate in political debate.

Polat (2005) asks why people do not participate in the context of political Internet use:

> It may be the case that people do not participate simply because of matters of convenience such as lack of time or proximity. However, if the lack of political participation stems from a lack of resources of motivation, the potential of the Internet will become less significant. (Polat 2005: 454–455)

This position suggests that there may be insufficient energy or political willpower among people, and that this can hamper the development of participatory practices on the Internet.

Our suggestion is that people want a proper discourse ethics in the media. Ordinary people are media savvy, and they know a lot about genres, formats, programmes and presenters. Their criticism can be read as a wish for discourse ethics in the sense that Stanley Deetz defines it. He says, 'Every communicative act should have as its ethical condition the attempt to keep the conversation – the open development of experience – going' (Deetz 1999: 151). Informants do not consider the media debates to be open but closed and prejudiced. As seen in the analysis above, informants frown upon *ad hominem* argumentation, where the person is targeted instead of the arguments, and they are frustrated by the inability of hosts and participants to really listen to each other. Their discourse ethics means that everybody must discern and respect the rights of others. They must listen as well as speak and be able to follow up the ideas and problems of others instead of taking turns presenting monologues to each other (Skjervheim 1996). It is interesting, but not surprising, that the age-old desire for dialogue is so prominent in our material.

References

Bøe, T., 2006. *Hva synes publikum om å delta i medier? En kvalitativ analyse.* Bergen, Norway: University of Bergen.

Carpentier, N., 2007. Participation and interactivity: Changing perspectives. The construction of an integrated model on access, interaction and participation. In V. Nightingale and T. Dwyer, eds, *New media worlds. Challenges for convergence.* Melbourne: Oxford University Press. pp. 214–230.

——— 2009. Participation is not enough. The conditions of possibility of mediated participatory practices. *European Journal of Communication*, 24(4), pp. 407–420.

Collins, R., 1994. *Four sociological traditions. Selected readings.* New York: Oxford University Press.

Dahlberg, L., 2001. Democracy via cyberspace. Mapping the rhetorics and practices of three prominent camps. *New Media & Society*, 3(2), pp. 157–177.

Dahlgren, P., 2005. The Internet, public spheres, and political communication: Dispersion and deliberation. *Political Communication*, 22, pp. 147–162.

Day, R., 2009. *Community radio in Ireland: Participation and multiflows of communication.* Cresskill, NJ: Hampton Press.

Deetz, S., 1999. *Theoretical approaches to participatory communication.* Cresskill, NJ: Hampton Press.

Dewey, J., 1960. *Theory of the moral life.* New York: Holt, Rinehart and Winston. (Originally published 1908.)

Feenberg, A., 1999. *Questioning technology.* New York: Routledge.

Gadamer, H.G., 1989. *Truth and method.* New York: Crossroad. (Originally published 1960.)

Gentikow, B., 2005. *Hvordan utforsker man medieerfaringer?* Kristiansand, Norway: IJ-forlaget.

——— 2010. *Nye fjernsynserfaringer. Teknologi, bruksteknikker, hverdagsliv.* Kristiansand, Norway: Høyskoleforlaget.

Giddens, A., 1991. *Modernity and self-identity. Self and society in the late modern age.* Cambridge, UK: Polity Press.

Goffman, E., 1986. *Frame analysis. An essay on the organization of experience.* Boston, MA: Northeastern University Press. (Originally published 1974.)

Habermas, J., 1987. *The theory of communicative action.* London: Heinemann.

——— 1990. *Strukturwandel der Öffentlichkeit. Untersuchungen zu einer Kategorie der bürgerlichen Gesellschaft.* Frankfurt, Germany: Suhrkamp.

Hagen, I. and Wold, T., 2009. *Mediegenerasjonen. Barn og unge i det nye medielandskapet.* Oslo, Norway: Samlaget.

Iser, W., 1991. *The act of reading.* Baltimore, MD: Johns Hopkins University Press. (Originally published 1978.)

Jensen, J.F., 2008. The concept of interactivity revisited: Four new typologies for a new media landscape. In M. Darnell et al., eds, *UXTV '08 proceedings of the 1st international conference on designing interactive user experiences for TV and video.* New York: ACM. pp. 129–132.

Kelly, M. and O'Connor, B., 1997. *Media audiences in Ireland: Power and cultural identity.* Dublin, Ireland: UCD Academic Press.

Kerr, A., 2000. Media diversity and cultural identity: The development of multimedia content in Ireland. *New Media and Society,* 2(3), pp. 286–312.

Kiousis, S., 2002. Interactivity: A concept explication. *New Media & Society,* 4(3), pp. 355–383.

Komito, L., 2007. *E-governance in Ireland: New technologies, local government and civic participation.* Dublin, Ireland: Geary Institute at the University College Dublin.

Mitchell, C., 2002. On air/off air: Defining women's radio space in European women's community radio. In N. Jankowski and O. Prehn, eds, *Community media in the information age: Perspectives and prospects.* New York: Hampton Press. pp. 85–105.

Morris, D., 1967. *The naked ape. A zoologist's study of the human animal.* London: Cape.

Mouffe, C., 2000. *The democratic paradox.* London: Verso.

O'Neill, B. and Barnes, C., 2008. *Media literacy and the public sphere: A contextual study for public media literacy promotion in Ireland.* Dublin, Ireland: Broadcasting Commission of Ireland.

O'Sullivan, S., 2005. 'The whole nation is listening to you': The presentation of the self on a tabloid talk radio show. *Media, Culture and Society,* 27(5), pp. 719–738.

Polat, R.K., 2005. The Internet and political participation. Exploring the explanatory links. *European Journal of Communication,* 20(4), pp. 435–459.

Ricoeur, P., 1991. *From text to action.* Evanston, Il: Northwestern University Press.

Ross, K., 2004. Political talk radio and democratic participation: Caller perspectives on Election Call. *Media, Culture and Society,* 26(6), pp. 785–801.

Scannell, P., 1996. *Radio, television and modern life.* Oxford, UK: Blackwell.

Schutz, A., 1970. *On phenomenology and social relations. Selected writings.* Chicago, IL: University of Chicago Press.

Siapera, E., 2004. From couch potatoes to cybernauts? The expanding notion of the audience on TV channels' websites. *New Media & Society*, 6(2), pp. 155–172.

Skjervheim, H., 1959. *Objectivism and the study of man*. Oslo, Norway: University of Oslo.

———— 1996. *Deltakar og tilskodar og andre essays*. Oslo, Norway: Aschehoug.

Syvertsen, T. and Bakøy, E., eds, 2001. *Sjekking på TV: Offentlig ydmykelse eller bare lek?* Oslo, Norway: Unipub.

Tønnessen, E.S., 2007. *Generasjon.com. Mediekultur blant barn og unge*. Oslo, Norway: Universitetsforlaget.

Trench, B. and O'Donnell, S., 1997. The Internet and democratic participation: Uses of ICTs by voluntary and community organisations in Ireland. *Economic and Social Review*, 28, pp. 213–234.

Ward, K., 2003. An ethnographic study of Internet consumption in Ireland: Between domesticity and the public participation. Key Deliverable to the European Media and Technology in Everyday Life Network. Dublin, Ireland: ComTech Centre, Dublin City University.

Chapter 12

Using the Domestication Approach for the Analysis of Diffusion and Participation Processes of New Media

Corinna Peil and Jutta Röser

Introduction

This chapter centres on the domestication approach that describes and analyses the process in which new media technologies move into the household and become part of everyday life (Berker et al. 2006; Haddon 2006; Hynes and Richardson 2009; Röser 2007a, 2007b; Röser and Peil 2010a, 2010b; Silverstone 2006; Silverstone and Haddon 1996). Essentially, domestication is about allocating technologies a physical and symbolic place within the domestic sphere by integrating them into the daily routines, social interactions and spatiotemporal structures of the household. The concept regards the social arrangements and activities of the users as crucial factors for the implementation and appropriation of new technologies. In domestication theory, media technologies are not thought of as developing to an inner logic; they are considered as 'something social' (Hynes and Richardson 2009: 483) – as something that is defined by social actions and negotiations rather than by mere technical properties as technologically deterministic approaches suggest.

Domestication theory is rooted in British and European cultural media studies and has been strongly influenced by ethnographically oriented television research of the 1980s. With its keen interest in the mundane, it now has more analytical power than ever, given the ongoing processes of digitization and mediatization (e.g. Hepp, Hjarvard and Lundby 2010; Krotz 2007; Lundby 2009) that underpin the idea of the complex interwovenness of media use and everyday life. So far, domestication theory has been drawn on primarily to strengthen the analytical focus on the everyday within the study of media. Our aim, however, is to show a further dimension of the domestication approach: its potential to analyse the diffusion process of new media technologies and to gain a deeper understanding of their implementation and appropriation following adoption. By giving evidence of the relevance of domestic uses regarding Internet diffusion, we argue that domestication theory can be linked to the question of how participation in new digital technologies is stimulated or hindered. Besides the micro-dimension of the approach, this analytical perspective of domestication also accentuates the macro-level by asking how participation arises and accordingly how inequality regarding access and use of new media is reduced. Domestication, with its process orientation, can thus be used to compensate the shortcomings of the digital divide concept which is mainly concerned with aspects of exclusion, while neglecting the social negotiations and participatory dynamics that come into play after the purchase of a device. Our theoretical perspective is supported by empirical findings based on a German Research Foundation (GRF) funded research project about Internet diffusion in Germany between 1997 and 2007.

The Domestication of New Media Technologies and Everyday Life at Home

The domestication concept filled a gap both in media and communication studies and in the sociology of technology. It represents a step away from the belief in the one-sided transformative power of technology (Berker et al. 2006; Haddon 2006; Hynes and Richardson 2009). Basically, it helps one to understand and analyse the dynamic process of media appropriation from the perspective of the users. Domestication takes into account the complexity of everyday life when it comes to the use or non-use of new media technologies other than approaches assuming the adoption of an innovation as predetermined by its technological capacities. Domestication calls for the consideration of the situations, places and social constellations of media appropriation and underlines the significance of the household as meaningful sphere of media-related activities. The claim of domestication is thus to illuminate the intertwining of different domestic practices and to analyse in more detail the interactions of media use, social relations and personal communication as well as their connection to related discourses and societal structures (Röser 2007b; Röser and Peil 2010a, 2010b).

Media Ethnography and Cultural Studies as Origins of the Domestication Approach

The domestication concept was originally developed within the Household Uses of Information and Communication Technologies (HICT) project carried out by Silverstone, Hirsch and Morley (1992), and Livingstone (1992) at the end of the 1980s. The authors not only intended to elaborate on a conceptual model for exploring the role of information and communication technologies in home life but also wanted to challenge the idea of a technological determinism by accentuating the active role of users in the process of media adoption. Other than mainstream television reception research at that time, the project shifted the analytical attention towards the whole set of information and communication technologies inside the home. It aimed at understanding media use with regard to the household and to family, generation and gender constellations. One of the key objectives was the recontextualization of media studies in a broader socio-technical and cultural setting (Berker et al. 2006; Morley 1992; Morley and Silverstone 1990; Silverstone and Hirsch 1992). The project started at a very early stage of home computing and became a pioneering study on the early phase of household digitization. Even though the results of the project need to be updated and adjusted to the media environments that are characteristic of today's households, the theoretical implications of the domestication approach emphasizing the interplay between media use and everyday life are effective as ever (Röser 2007b, 2007c).

Grasping media appropriation as social action that is deeply rooted in everyday life, the domestication approach follows the ethnographic research tradition in media studies. Ethnographically oriented approaches in media research have emerged from the 1980s onwards, particularly within the framework of British cultural media studies. Instead of creating artificial research settings, they seek to analyse media reception within the 'natural' contexts of everyday life (Bausinger 1984; Morley 1992). What these ethnographically oriented studies in media reception research have in common is that they share awareness of the processes, activities and interactions that are taking place during media consumption. Consequently, the social practice of television viewing or Internet use is analysed in the actual homes of people. Being questioned about their media behaviour, the users provide insights of how media are integrated into their daily routines and of how they are used to manage family relationships. To meet the demands of 'radical contextualism' (Ang 1996), detailed accounts of specific aspects of media use are favoured over generalized interpretations. As Ang (1996: 70 et seq.) states,

> What ethnographic work entails is a form of 'methodological situationalism', underscoring the thoroughly situated, always context-bound ways in which people encounter, use, interpret, enjoy, think and talk about television and other media in everyday life. The understanding emerging from this kind of inquiry favours interpretive particularization over explanatory generalization, historical and local concreteness rather than formal abstraction, 'thick' description of details rather than extensive but 'thin' survey.

Accordingly, ethnographically oriented studies[1] analyse media use at the micro-level and take into consideration not only individual needs and expectations but also the situations, contexts and social constellations of media activities. At the same time, this research perspective is committed to the discussion of cultural practices and situations in a broader sociopolitical context (Röser 2007b). Analogically, the domestication approach looks at how media and non-media activities interact in everyday life and how they are connected to society in a broader sense. In this manner, domestication theory is expanded to an 'overlapping between research on audiences and wider studies of cultural consumption, technology and everyday life' (Moores 1993: 54).

Domestication theory is not only rooted in ethnographic research traditions but also more generally in the cultural studies paradigm because of its interest in the attribution of meanings and significance. The localization within cultural studies is supported by the critical impetus of domestication theory, which becomes manifest in its aspiration to criticize structural inequalities within society. As Hynes and Richardson (2009: 489) state, 'It involves a critical stance against "taken-for-granted" assumptions and a dialectical analysis to reveal the historical and ideological contradictions within social practices.' According to domestication theory, meanings are assigned on two different levels which are expressed in the assumption of the 'double articulation' of media technologies. On the one hand, the symbolic level of media content is brought into view; on the other hand, it is of interest how the technical artefact becomes the object of meaning attributions (e.g. when it is perceived as modern or male) – the latter is about the appropriation of the material side of media technologies. Meanings are subject to negotiations and alterations. Therefore, the signifying activities of the users have to be seen as a continuous process rather than a one-off activity that pins down a fixed meaning of media technologies. In theory, the domestication concept claims to take into account both dimensions of media technologies – media content and technical artefact – when analysing the appropriation process (Livingstone 2007; Silverstone and Haddon 1996). The empirical experience, however, is proof of a concentration on the level of the artefact and its integration into everyday life while neglecting the symbolic level of media content (Hartmann 2006).

Given the interest in reconstructing the meaning of media use from the users' perspective, it seems comprehensible that domestication research relies mostly on qualitative methodology. In-depth interviews, time-use diaries or home-site inspections are just some of the methods that are part of the ethnographic orientation. With the emergence of online technologies, new and more diverse methodological approaches have been applied that are partly quantitative in nature, such as log-file documentation, online surveys or Web-based content analysis (Haddon 2006). For a broader contextualization of media usage patterns, a complement of both quantitative and qualitative methods can be considered as particularly fruitful.

The Meaning of Home

The focus on the household in ethnographically oriented studies of the 1980s is not surprising given their interest in the situational embeddedness of media use. The domestication approach has also always been interested in the household's transformative relationship to the public sphere. Households are seen as 'part of a transactional system, dynamically involved in the public world of the production and exchange of commodities and meanings' (Silverstone, Hirsch and Morely 1992: 19). It is assumed that there are economic and social forces at work expressed in the incorporated values, power relations and lifestyles of the household members. This is what Silverstone, Hirsch and Morley (1992: 16 et seq.) call the 'moral economy of the household'.

They identified four different phases or 'non-discrete elements' that constitute the dynamics of integrating new media technology into the domestic sphere (Silverstone, Hirsch and Morley 1992: 20 et seq.): (1) appropriation, (2) objectification, (3) incorporation and (4) conversion. In the 'appropriation' phase – or rather 'commodification' phase, as Silverstone (2006: 233) later suggested – a new medium is purchased and becomes the acquired property of the household. It moves into the home and crosses the threshold between the public and private sphere. It is thereby transformed from a commodity into an object that is given relevance by being integrated into the structures of the household. 'Objectification' is about the physical and symbolic arrangement of objects in the spatial and social environment of the home. The domestic sphere becomes subject to change as it makes room for the new medium. The 'incorporation' phase is concerned with the temporal aspects of the household. It emphasizes how the technology finds its way into the everyday routines and the social community of the household members. Eventually, the 'conversion' phase tries to capture the alteration of the relationship between the household and its surroundings – 'the boundary across which artefacts and meanings, texts and technologies, pass as the household defines and claims for itself and its members a status in neighbourhood, work and peer groups in the "wider society"' (Silverstone, Hirsch and Morley 1992: 25). The four phases can be further classified: objectification and incorporation especially concern the internal processes of the household as they relate to the implementation of the technology into the given structures of the household, the micro-politics of gender and generation relationships, and the rearrangement of rooms, routines and interactions due to impulse set by the new medium. Appropriation and conversion deal with the relationship between the home and the outside world as the household is connected to the policies of production and consumption, and marketing and development through the purchase of a device. Contrariwise, the media-related changes within the household affect the macro-level because the discussions, negotiations and arguments concerning the role of a media technology refer back to society (Bakardjieva 2005; Röser 2005, 2007c; Silverstone 2006).

As Haddon (2001: 4) points out, domestication is an ongoing rather than a 'once off process'. It is never entirely 'successful'; neither do the four phases occur in the described order. Instead of representing fixed appropriation patterns, they dynamically interact and mutually shape and affect each other.[2] Domestication is likely to include processes of 're- and de-domestication' (Berker et al. 2006: 3) that may be the consequence of technological enhancements or biographical changes. The household has to be seen as an economic, social and cultural unit that is linked to the public economy by the consuming activities of its members. It represents the place where technological innovations, social relations and cultural identities meet and constitute the household's transformative relationship to the public sphere. Correspondingly, the domestic practices of everyday life are not taking place in the isolation of the home but tie in with economical, technological and cultural circumstances and conditions. In domestication theory, the home is thus considered a microcosm of mediatization – the cultural and social change that is associated with the use of media – and is closely connected to the macrocosm of society.

Even though the role of the household as the pivotal context of media use was particularly emphasized in the early accounts on domestication theory, this original point of significance seems to have become less relevant in more recent domestication studies (e.g. Vuojärvi, Isomäki and Hynes 2010). By hinting at the importance of social relationships in media use, Haddon (2001), for example, makes some instructive suggestions on how to extend domestication outside the home. Morley (2003) follows a different perspective when he argues for a reconsideration of the home as a dynamic space produced by interactions and negotiations that can be experienced through the use of mobile and other media (cf. Peil 2011; Röser 2007b). The shift away from the household as signifying context of media use is also partly due to the emergence of mobile phone research drawing on the domestication concept. Whereas some of these studies are concerned with mobile phone use in the specific context of home (e.g. Dobashi 2005), others underpin the need for a reconceptualization of the domestication concept or just refer to the more general perspectives of domestication theory (e.g. Hjorth 2009; Ling 2004).

The Contribution of the Domestication Approach to the Question of Diffusion

Whereas most of the domestication literature shares the above-mentioned assumptions of the social character of media technologies that do not develop to an inner logic but are related to negotiations, social interactions and changing discourse, there is another dimension of domestication theory that has rarely been made explicit. In addition to grasping media appropriation as part of everyday life, the domestication approach can be used as an analytical framework for describing and theorizing the diffusion process of new media. It provides a specific appropriation-oriented perspective of analysis which primarily focuses on the increase of participation as a consequence of domestication. This, until now, rather neglected perspective of domestication theory centres on the question of to what extent the diffusion of new media technologies is fostered by their integration into the domestic sphere.

Domestication and Participation: Historical Forerunners and Current Issues

This second perspective of the domestication concept analysing the diffusion of new media technologies across society can be underpinned by historical studies about early radio (Moores 1988, 1993; Morley 1992, 2000) and the telephone (Fischer 1994; Rakow 1988). These studies show some interesting analogies with the diffusion of computers and the Internet in the 1990s (Röser 2005, 2007b): the radio was at first, just like the PC and Internet, almost exclusively used by a minority of men with a strong interest in technology. Their engagement in radio listening was more about the quality of reception than about programme content. Radio back then was something profoundly technical, and it constructed a male sphere within the household from which women were mostly excluded. Within years, however, the signification of the technology underwent some major transformations. Starting with the implementation of loudspeakers, not only was the reception improved but the devices also became more user friendly and the programmes were fitted more and more to housewives' needs and schedules – all of which processes initiated the gradual domestication of the radio. As Morley and Silverstone put it, 'The domestication of the radio was a gradual process in which, from being initially a disturbance which separated men and women in the household, it came to be accommodated to the household's spatial and social relations' (1990: 38).

The important role of women in integrating new technologies into everyday life becomes evident in the domestication process of the telephone as well – even though, in this case, the coding as a professional tool was more significant than the technical framing. As Fischer (1994) explored in more detail, fixed-line telephones in the United States were at first strongly linked to the male domain as the devices were viewed as communication tools primarily for business. Not only were the phones not marketed as privately used technologies but their usage for chatting was also perceived as incorrect and distracting from their legitimate purpose (Rakow 1988). However, the social use of the telephone prevailed, and women's uses became a driving force behind the domestication of the telephone. Their new and escalating telephone habits led to a change in advertising strategies and eventually to a reinterpretation of the technology as a social communication tool for daily use (Fischer 1994; van Zoonen 2002).

In a similar way, these kinds of processes have taken place with computers and the Internet. Here we are dealing with media that were dominated in early years by professional users and tinkerers who were mostly male and strongly interested in technology. In the process of opening up to more diverse user groups, the technical framing of the Internet (Schönberger 1999) became less dominant while its cultural contextualization in everyday life had gained relevance. Internet technology, just like the radio, moved from the insiders and experts to the layperson, from specialized segments of the public to a wider audience. Social inequalities – concerning access and use – that usually come into play in the introduction phase of a new medium were levelled during this process. This 'outcome' of domestication, an increased participation of broader user groups, particularly becomes evident regarding women's uses of new media technologies. But disparity in terms of age, educational/ professional background and financial resources is reduced as well. Yet the broadening of the Internet is not only driven by its users. Their everyday-related practices interact with economic, technological and social conditions, for example, simplified handling, lower costs of hardware and cheaper rates (Röser 2007b). On the way to becoming a mass medium, new technologies must be incorporated into the daily activities of more and more people and need to prove their functionality in everyday life. If the users mistake the day-to-day value of the Internet, the diffusion process is interrupted. Only through the interplay of the users' appropriation practices and the potentials of the technology is the meaning of media technologies constructed (Morley 2000).

Given the close link between technology and gender discourse, the technical framing of a medium is accompanied by its coding and discursive gendering as male (van Zoonen 2002). When a medium as part of the domestication process is increasingly framed as an everyday object, it is usually subject to a de-gendering – to a relevance loss of the gender-related coding of the device (van Zoonen 2002). In the course of this process, it becomes appealing to more and more users – not only women but also older people and men who are less interested in technology. Accordingly, it can be shown that the integration of the Internet into domestic life has led to new dynamics within the diffusion process: it has come with an increased Internet participation by the broader public that amounts to a mitigation of inequalities regarding access and use of new media. Morley (2000: 95), referring to early radio, called this process 'democratisation', as it describes the broadening of user groups and the decline of social disparities regarding usage and ownership.[3]

This crucial aspect of domestication points at the capacity of the approach to include questions of diffusion and to expand the perspective from the micro- to the societal level. Although domestication, in its original conceptualization, already connects the micro-politics of the household to broader society, the macro-level has often been overlooked. By analysing the implications of domestic appropriation practices that bring about an increased participation in new media technologies, the domestication approach contributes to a deeper understanding of the diffusion process. Other than the term 'diffusion', which refers to the technology and its distribution across society, 'participation' includes the subjects and takes into account their everyday-related activities in the context of media use. Hence, by speaking of participation, we signify the diffusion of new media technologies from the perspective of the users. The term implies a decline of digital differences concerning access and use. This does not mean, however, that the broadening of user groups automatically neutralizes any hierarchies. In fact, it seems possible that Internet participation of rather reluctant households increases, but at the same time inequalities are being reproduced. This might be the case with households of different social status, or with couples, when the medium is used inside the home according to a gender-related division of labour (re-gendering). Participation can hence be analysed by considering both the domestic routines, arrangements and social interactions and the changing structure of users that is likely to exceed social boundaries in the course of domestication. Consumers' domestic everyday life plays an ambivalent role in this process, for it stimulates Internet participation, on the one hand, while reproducing inequalities, on the other.

Domestication as Counter Concept to Classical Diffusion and Digital Divide Theory

As should have become clear, the domestication approach differs from classical diffusion and digital divide theory. Diffusion theory by Rogers (2003) describes the diffusion of innovations mainly as a top-down process composed of five different phases. It grasps the adoption as a linear, rational process and often neglects what is happening after the purchase of a product. Richardson (2009: 600) calls diffusion theory 'a deficiency model of ICT adoption' because of its implicit and rather undifferentiated assumptions of users who appear to be privileged and non-users who are considered as disadvantaged. A similar criticism applies to the digital divide concept. It critically looks at the exclusion of certain population groups from the use of the Internet or other digital media and clearly lacks an interest in the emergence of participation. In this way, the digital divide concept loses sight of some crucial aspects and coherences in the diffusion process of new media.

The digital divide concept has its theoretical roots in the knowledge gap hypothesis first identified by Tichenor, Donohue and Olien (1970). It is based on the assumptions that the access to online technologies and the resources to use them is marked by social differences and that the differences between users and non-users increase over time. At first, digital divide research primarily centred on the question of whether people access digital technologies. The concept refers to the underlying idea that the access to information technologies is perceived as valuable because it provides social resources and translates into power (Bonfadelli 2002). Disregarding media appropriation as a complex social practice, the concept has been criticized for its notions of technological determinism and for the binary code online/offline characteristic of early studies in this vein. In recent years, digital divide research has been further elaborated (Hargittai 2004; van Dijk 2005). Newer studies that differentiate between access and ability, for example, are more concerned with qualitative differences in online usage and their implications for social inequality. These kinds of considerations are expressed in concepts like 'second-level digital divide' and 'digital inequalities' (Hargittai 2002; Hargittai and Hinnant 2008; Zillien and Hargittai 2009). A problematic issue remains, however, that the approach implicitly considers a lot of online use as generally positive. Only rarely is it further worked out and specified what kind of online uses are likely to close the digital gap (Krotz 2007). On the contrary, domestication theory is not primarily concerned with the proof of some kind of profitable Internet usage but with the well-founded analysis of the ambiguities, complexities and intricate dynamics of the diffusion and adoption process. Beyond that, the overemphasis of exclusion in digital divide theory appears problematic. Research in this tradition critically looks at the population groups that are 'lagging behind' or 'missing out' on Internet use. Here lies, in our opinion, one of the strengths of the domestication concept because it is capable both of analysing social inequality in the field of media consumption and of focusing on the dynamics that contribute to an increase in media participation.

The Domestication of the Internet in Germany (1997–2007)

In this section, we give a short outline of our research project on the domestication of the Internet in Germany. We reconstructed the diffusion process of the Internet in Germany over a period of 10 years (1997–2007) based on empirical data from quantitative research and qualitative household studies. We obtained evidence of the merits of domestication theory by tracing the entry of the technology into the domestic sphere and following its integration into everyday life. In particular, we were interested in how people accessed the Internet at different stages of its diffusion process. We assumed that the motives in 1997, when the Internet was an elite medium of only 7 per cent of the German population, were different from those in 2007, when more than 60 per cent was online and the Internet had become more and more embedded in everyday practices. The dynamic process of Internet domestication was examined from two different levels. At the macro-level, our objective was to outline the opening process of the Internet for large parts of the population. At the micro-level, the access to the Internet and its change over time was in the focus. We took into consideration differences in age and education and paid special attention to gender relationships within the domestic context. The micro-analysis of the households was meant to be linked back to general societal issues so as to analyse how power relationships are lived inside the home and how they are shifted over time (Röser 2007b).

Methodological Design

Given the aim of this study – to elaborate on the diffusion perspective of the domestication concept and provide proof of the crucial role of home Internet uses for the participation of broader user groups – we drew on qualitative interviews and representative data about online activities in Germany between 1997 and 2007. In this way, we avoided a mere concentration on the micro-analysis of the households and were able to reconstruct the domestication process at the societal level as well. In 25 ethnographically oriented household studies we retraced the access to the Internet from the perspective of its users and analysed the changes over time. For building the sample, we first conducted a written survey with 135 individuals who were recruited through snowball sampling. With respect to three different age groups (28–35, 36–50, 51–65) and two different educational groups (general/intermediate secondary school, high school graduation or vocational diploma), 25 people (including their partners) were selected for our qualitative household studies. Also considered were certain attributes, such as the date of Internet acquisition, professional affinity and non-affinity to the Internet as well as children, housewives, and retirees within the household (see Table 1).

To investigate domestic processes of inclusion and exclusion regarding Internet appropriation, we interviewed cohabiting (heterosexual) couples, thus 50 men and women in total. The household studies included a visit to the couple's household, where a detailed guided interview and a home inspection (including photographs of all computers in use) took place. Husband and wife were interviewed together since our primary interest was not in the individual but in the social situations, communication practices and gender-related arrangements which shape the daily lives of the couples. In addition, this setting proved to be very beneficial when it came to the reconstruction of the early days of Internet use because the couples mutually supported, supplemented and corrected their memories.[4]

We developed the genre of ethnographic household portraits for the data analysis: by drawing on interview transcripts and memos (with impressions from the interviews), as well as other empirical material such as questionnaires, lists and photographs, we created a detailed portrait of each household and supported it with interview quotes. In this way, we were able to perform a context-oriented analysis of all Internet activities. Instead of interpreting the data in an individual-based way, as it is done in most other studies, we had a special focus on social constellations and interrelations of various factors within the household. Based on these portraits, a comparative analysis was carried out followed by a grouping and typification of the households according to selected questions.

Access to the Internet in Transition

A central finding from the interpretation of the quantitative data was the significance of private and domestic uses that have given a major boost to Internet diffusion in Germany. In 1997, at the time of the first ARD/ZDF online study[5], only about 7 per cent of the German population was (occasionally) using the Internet. The socio-demographic composition of this minority clearly indicates that the Internet was an elite medium at that time: 41 per cent of all German Internet users had a university degree, and 62 per cent had a high school diploma equivalent to English A Levels. Male users (73 per cent) and 30- to 39-year-olds

Table 1: Composition of the sample by socio-demographic characteristics (age, education, sex, profession)

Sample (married) couple households		Education		Σ
		Simple (secondary general school or intermediate secondary school)	Upscale (high school graduation or vocational diploma)	
Age –classification refers to the age of the first recruited partner–	**Younger (28–35 years)**	**Maier** –all names are pseudonyms– electrician (33)/nurse (25) **Markuse** worker (33)/nurse (33) **Brandt** hairdresser (26)/hairdresser (29) **Schunk** waste worker (37)/housewife and kitchen helper in part-time (33)	**Sarholz** sport therapist (41)/PR consultant (32) **Trautwein** musician and service employee (41)/ teacher (35) **Olsen** clerk (33)/copywriter (29) **Bunk** doctor (29)/advertising consultant (29)	8
	Middle (36–50 years)	**Meckel** administrative officer (50)/ administrative officer (48) **Bindseil** waste worker (38)/clerk (42) **Weinert** self-employed carpenter (44)/school secretary in part-time (43) **Mück** administrative clerk (43)/housewife (55) **Wulf** postman (38)/educator (38)	**Flick** self-employed coach (42)/ physiotherapist (40) **Mahlmann** senior executive (48)/pharmaceutical representative and project manager (46) **Schneider** teacher (39)/clerk (37) **Brinkmann** teacher and vice-principal (49)/ senior executive in a national welfare association (48)	9
	Older (51–65 years)	**Steffen** software developer (56)/accountant (57) **Frey** insurance salesman in part-time due to retirement (60)/accountant (57) **Sommer** taxi employer (63)/accountant in part-time (61) **Ziegler** communal civil servant for data processing (59)/housewife (58)	**Wiegand** lawyer (63)/housewife and service employee (61) **Nagel** teacher (53)/clerk (51) **Bauer** retired banker (63)/retired teacher (62) **Frings** IT employer in part-time due to retirement (62)/teacher in part-time (58)	8
Σ		13	12	25

(35 per cent), as well as 20- to 29-year-olds (31 per cent), were over-represented. The typical user was a 34-year-old employed man with a higher education. This characterization was still effective in 1999 when 18 per cent of the population already had access to the Internet. It seems understandable given these data that digital divide concerns were raised at this time. This was expressed in the fear that parts of the population, such as women, the elderly and people with low income or education, would permanently stay offline and become the 'losers' of digitization (Kubicek and Welling 2000). In the further course of time, however, the diffusion of the Internet did not proceed according to digital divide predictions. In fact, there was a rapid increase in Internet participation and a growing socio-demographic diversity within the population of Internet users. In 2002, people with a lower educational background already represented two-thirds of all Internet users. Women and young people had significantly increased their share. In light of this development, it would be misleading though to assume that social differences no longer mattered. With regard to gender differences in Internet use, for example, the data hint at two different trends: first, a relatively constant advance by men can be noticed throughout the decade. In 2007, 69 per cent of men compared to 57 per cent of women were at least occasionally online. It hence becomes obvious that a gender gap has still remained. However, second, the overall number of users had considerably increased, and because women proportionally supported the diffusion process, the number of female users also rose, adding up to nearly 20 million in 2007. Based on these findings, it now seems inappropriate to claim an 'exclusion' of women from the Internet.

In a nutshell, the well-known socio-demographic differences regarding the composition of Internet users were still visible in 2007. At the same time, the Internet had diffused in all social groups. Other than predicted, there had been a dynamic development towards an opening of the Internet. The analysis of the representative data provides a further insight as to the background of this process: in large parts, the ascertained expansion of the user community had taken place via the domestic context. In 1997, places like the office and school were the preferred localities of Internet use: 73 per cent of all users accessed the Internet at work; only 14 per cent of them also had an Internet connection at home. The number of people using the Internet from home increased from 1.7 to 37 million in the following decade; their share of all Internet users more than doubled (from 42 to 91 per cent). These figures refer to a general domestication process of the new medium. In the decade after 2000, the share of people using the Internet exclusively at home had risen significantly: in 2007, they already added up to some 20 million people, which accounted for half of all the Internet users in Germany. This especially applied to population groups where professional inputs were likely to be lacking (due to maternity leaves, retirement or 'deskless' professions): women over the age of 30, the elderly (over the age of 60) and people with a lower educational background. To sum up, the data on Internet usage in Germany between 1997 and 2007 already point to the interplay of various factors that are characteristic of the domestication process: (a) the implementation of the Internet into the domestic sphere, (b) the broadening of the user community, (c) the integration into everyday life at home and (d) the emergence of specific contents that are linked to private interests and domestic life. Apparently, a participatory dynamic goes along with the domestication of the Internet, which is worth being examined more closely.

This is where qualitative data come into play. They go beyond the question whether people go online or not as they provide deeper understanding of Internet participation based on the consideration of the contexts, consequences and meanings of online use. One essential objective of the 25 household studies was to analyse the reasons for accessing the Internet at home. In terms of time, we identified two different phases that individually correspond to a specific set of motives and contexts for domestic Internet use and to certain person- and household-related attributes.

The first phase covers a total of 11 households that had already set up an Internet connection in the (late) 1990s and were characterized by the following features. Academic and/or professional careers were the dominant reasons for Internet purchase. In eight out of the 11 households, the initial contact to the new medium was established at the workplace or at university. Generally, this experience was crucial for setting up an Internet connection at home. In nine households, a keen interest in (media) technological innovations turned out to be either the decisive motive for the purchase of the Internet or one of the driving forces for Internet domestication. Content wise, (job-related) information enquiries and e-mail communications were central in this early phase of Internet implementation.

The second phase refers to a group of 14 households that started home Internet use from 2000 onwards. Predominantly, they found access to the online technology via the domestic context. Their motives for Internet acquisition were based on different factors, some of which were overlapping in some of the households. In half the households of this group, people had concrete, privately motivated interests and ideas that they wanted to accomplish with the Internet (e.g. requirements from a specific hobby or the desire to use appealing online applications gave cause for the purchase). The motive of keeping up with new developments and the fear of being left behind were mentioned in seven of the 14 households in this group, often initiated by conversations or online activities within the immediate social environment. Children's interests or anticipated needs played a role in some of the households. Sometimes, lower cost of Internet access and financial conditions of the household had an influence on the acquisition process.

One central context of Internet access at home was the availability of people with some technical know-how in the broader circle of friends and family members; some of our sample's respondents themselves served as such 'friendly helpers'. Bakardjieva (2005: 98) also found such helpers in her study and described them as 'warm experts'.

Thus, on the one hand, our study shows that to domesticate the Internet, technical expertise is still required. On the other hand, the increase of online services in the area of leisure, consumption, daily needs and private communication has gradually reduced the technical framing of the Internet. As a consequence, more people without technical interests began accessing the online world. This is one reason why the gender relations regarding

Internet use have progressed in the course of the decade. Most of the 'early households' were characterized by a gender gap as only the man used the Internet at home. Such bipolarity did not generally apply to the 'later households', where either both partners started using the Internet from the very beginning of its implementation into the household or there was just a short time delay between the two partners' beginning. All in all, the gender constellations have multiplied in recent years; in the 'later households', we also found a few couples where the woman plays the more active part in Internet involvement at home. However, the technical side of the medium is a major reason for the continuing male coding of computer and Internet at the hardware level. Overall, there is still a gap between men and women in terms of range, intensity and diversity of use. This difference is repeatedly constructed by both partners as part of a doing gender process at home.

Comparing Internet appropriation of the couples with regard to educational differences, it must be concluded that school education (as well as age and gender) cannot be causally linked to a competence gap, as is suggested by the digital divide concept. A strong technical interest, for example, or a certain (communicative) need resulting from a private concern or hobby would lead to a confident use of the Internet and to its dynamic integration into everyday life, regardless of the age, gender or educational background of the user.

Discussion and Outlook

Both parts of our empirical research underpin the potential of the domestication approach to adequately grasp the key aspects of social and cultural change expressed within the mediatized sphere of home. As opposed to the ideas of the digital divide concept, the integration of the Internet into the domestic sphere and into the politics of everyday life marked the initial point of a specific dynamic that opened up the technology for the broader population and promoted online participation of more diverse user groups. This process can be linked back to an increased importance of private interests, everyday-related concerns and social needs that have been decisive for going online. Thus, domestic Internet use, as well as Internet-related negotiations and arrangements in the home, have considerably contributed to the participation in online technologies. It is important to note, however, that participation is not to be mistaken for equality. After the opening of the Internet to more distant online population groups, inequalities and hierarchies have not been neutralized. Other than the radio or television set, the Internet in Germany remains a medium that is until now significantly framed by its technology. Consequently, it cannot yet be as easily integrated into the media menu.[6]

Although the mediatized home has been subject to major changes since the first emergence of the domestication idea only about 20 years ago, the concept has not lost its analytical power. In fact, domestication theory proves particularly fruitful in the light of the ongoing processes of mediatization, digitization and mobilization. Mediatization (Krotz 2007; Lundby 2009) refers to the saturation of media communications in all sociocultural spheres of our everyday life (of which the domestic sphere is an essential one) and is currently being intensified by the process of digitization. Despite other recent developments such as the mobilization of media communications, the home is still a significant context and meaningful locality of media appropriation because it is the place where everyday life is actually lived and shaped. Other spheres outside the home may have gained relevance regarding the adoption, use and implications of media, but this tendency is not accompanied by a concurrent significance loss of the home. Rather than turning away from the consideration of household interactions, domestic constellations and social arrangements in media reception analysis, we therefore advocate a more sophisticated examination of the home that takes into account the evermore complex communicative connections between the household and the outer world, and pays attention to different kinds of manifestations of societal change within the domestic sphere.

References

Ang, I., 1996. *Living room wars. Rethinking media audiences for a postmodern world.* London and New York: Routledge.

Bakardjieva, M., 2005. *Internet society. The Internet in everyday life.* London: Sage.

Bausinger, H., 1984. Media, technology and everyday life. *Media, Culture & Society*, 6(4), pp. 343–351.

Berker, T., Hartmann, M., Punie, Y. and Ward, K.J., eds, 2006. *Domestication of media and technology.* Berkshire, UK: Open University Press.

Bonfadelli, H., 2002. The Internet and knowledge gaps. A theoretical and empirical investigation. *European Journal of Communication*, 17(1), pp. 65–84.

Dobashi, S., 2005. The gendered use of *keitai* in domestic contexts. In M. Ito, M. Matsuda and D. Okabe, eds, *Personal, portable, pedestrian: Mobile phones in Japanese life.* Cambridge, MA: MIT Press. pp. 219–236.

Fischer, C.S., 1994. *America calling. A social history of the telephone to 1940.* Berkeley, CA: University of California Press.

Haddon, L., 2001. Domestication and mobile telephony. In *'Machines that Become Us' Conference*, 18–19 April, Rutgers University, New Jersey [online]. Available at: http://www2. lse.ac.uk/media@lse/whosWho/AcademicStaff/LeslieHaddon/Domestication and mobile.pdf [Accessed 2 January 2011].

—— 2006. The contribution of domestication research to in-home computing and media consumption. *The Information Society*, 22(4), pp. 195–203.

Hargittai, E., 2002. Second-level digital divide: Differences in people's online skills. *First Monday*, 7(4) [online]. Available at: http://firstmonday.org/htbin/cgiwrap/bin/ojs/index.php/fm/ article/view/942/864 [Accessed 30 May 2006].

—— 2004. Internet access and use in context. *New Media & Society*, 6(1), pp. 137–143.

Hargittai, E. and Hinnant, A., 2008. Digital inequality. Differences in young adults' use of the Internet. *Communication Research*, 35(5), pp. 602–621.

Hartmann, M., 2006. The triple articulation of ICTs. Media as technological objects, symbolic environment and individual texts. In T. Berker, M. Hartmann, Y. Punie and K.J. Ward, eds, *Domestication of media and technology.* Berkshire, UK: Open University Press. pp. 80–102.

Hepp, A., Hjarvard, S. and Lundby, K., 2010. Mediatization – empirical perspectives: An introduction to a special issue. *Communications,* 35(3), pp. 223–228.

Hjorth, L., 2009. Domesticating new media. A discussion on locating mobile media. In G. Goggin and L. Hjorth, eds, *Mobile technologies. From telecommunications to media.* New York: Routledge. pp. 143–157.

Hynes, D. and Richardson, H., 2009. What use is domestication theory to information systems research? In Y.K. Dwivedi, B. Lal, M.D. Williams, S.L. Schneberger and M.R. Wade, eds, *Handbook of research on contemporary theoretical models in information systems.* Hershey, PA: Ideas Publishing Group. pp. 482–494.

Krotz, F., 2007. *Mediatisierung: Fallstudien zum Wandel von Kommunikation.* Wiesbaden, Germany: VS.

Kubicek, H. and Welling, S., 2000. Vor einer digitalen Spaltung in Deutschland? *Medien & Kommunikationswissenschaft,* 48(4), pp. 497–517.

Ling, R., 2004. *The mobile connection: The cell phone's impact on society. The Morgan Kaufmann series in interactive technologies.* Amsterdam, The Netherlands: Morgan Kaufmann.

Livingstone, S., 1992. The meaning of domestic technologies: A personal construct analysis of familial gender relations. In R. Silverstone and E. Hirsch, eds, *Consuming technologies. Media and information in domestic spaces.* London and New York: Routledge. pp. 113–130.

———— 2007. On the material and the symbolic: Silverstone's double articulation of research traditions in new media studies. *New Media & Society,* 9(1), pp. 16–24.

Lundby, K., ed., 2009. *Mediatization: Concept, changes, consequences.* New York: Peter Lang.

Moores, S., 1988. 'The box on the dresser': Memories of early radio and everyday life. *Media, Culture & Society,* 10(1), pp. 23–40.

———— 1993. *Interpreting audiences. The ethnography of media consumption.* London: Sage.

Morley, D., 1992. *Television, audiences and cultural studies.* London: Routledge.

———— 2000. *Home territories. Media, mobility and identity.* London: Routledge.

———— 2003. What's 'home' got to do with it? Contradictory dynamics in the domestication of technology and the dislocation of domesticity. *European Journal of Cultural Studies,* 6(4), pp. 435–458.

Morley, D. and Silverstone, R., 1990. Domestic communication: Technologies and meanings. *Media, Culture & Society,* 12(1), pp. 31–55.

Peil, C., 2011. *Mobilkommunikation in Japan. Zur kulturellen Infrastruktur der Handy-Aneignung.* Bielefeld, Germany: Transcript.

Rakow, L.F., 1988. Women and the telephone: The gendering of a communication technology. In C. Kramarae, ed., *Technology and women's voices. Keeping in touch.* New York: Routledge & Kegan Paul. pp. 207–228.

Richardson, H.J., 2009. A 'smart house' is not a home: The domestication of ICTs. *Information Systems Frontiers,* 11(5) [online]. Available at: http://www.springerlink.com/content/5442142361376h87/fulltext.pdf [Accessed 6 January 2011].

Rogers, E.M., 2003. *Diffusion of innovations.* 5th ed. New York: Free Press.

Röser, J., 2005. Das Zuhause als Ort der Aneignung digitaler Medien: Domestizierungsprozesse und ihre Folgen. *Merz Wissenschaft*, 49(5), pp. 86–96.

Röser, J., ed., 2007a. *MedienAlltag. Domestizierungsprozesse alter und neuer Medien*. Wiesbaden, Germany: VS.

—— 2007b. Der Domestizierungsansatz und seine Potenziale zur Analyse alltäglichen Medienhandelns. In J. Röser, ed., *MedienAlltag. Domestizierungsprozesse alter und neuer Medien*. Wiesbaden, Germany: VS. pp. 15–30.

—— 2007c. Wenn das Internet das Zuhause erobert: Dimensionen der Veränderung aus ethnografischer Perspektive. In J. Röser, ed., *MedienAlltag. Domestizierungsprozesse alter und neuer Medien*. Wiesbaden, Germany: VS. pp. 157–171.

Röser, J. and Peil, C., 2010a. Diffusion und Teilhabe durch Domestizierung. Zugänge zum Internet im Wandel 1997–2007. *Medien & Kommunikationswissenschaft*, 58(4), pp. 481–502.

—— 2010b. Räumliche Arrangements zwischen Fragmentierung und Gemeinschaft: Internetnutzung im häuslichen Alltag. In J. Röser, T. Thomas and C. Peil, eds, *Alltag in den Medien – Medien im Alltag*. Wiesbaden, Germany: VS. pp. 220–241.

Schönberger, K., 1999. Internet zwischen Spielwiese und Familienpost. Doing Gender in der Netznutzung. In E. Hebecker, F. Kleemann, H. Neymanns and M. Stauff, eds, *Neue Medienwelten. Zwischen Regulierungsprozessen und alltäglicher Aneignung*. Frankfurt, Germany: Campus. pp. 259–281.

Silverstone, R., 2006. Domesticating domestication. Reflections on the life of a concept. In T. Berker, M. Hartmann, Y. Punie and K. J. Ward, eds, *Domestication of media and technology*. Berkshire, UK: Open University Press. pp. 229–248.

Silverstone, R. and Haddon, L., 1996. Design and the domestication of information and communication technologies. Technical change and everyday life. In R. Silverstone and R. Mansell, eds, *Communication by design. The politics of information and communication technologies*. Oxford, UK: Oxford University Press. pp. 44–74.

Silverstone, R. and Hirsch, E., eds, 1992. *Consuming technologies. Media and information in domestic spaces*. London and New York: Routledge.

Silverstone, R., Hirsch, E. and Morley, D., 1992. Information and communication technologies and the moral economy of the household. In R. Silverstone and E. Hirsch, eds, *Consuming technologies: Media and information in domestic spaces*. London and New York: Routledge. pp. 15–31.

Tichenor, P.J., Donohue, G.A. and Olien, C.N., 1970. Mass media and the differential growth in knowledge. *Public Opinion Quarterly*, 34(2), pp. 159–170.

van Dijk, J.A.G.M., 2005. *The deepening divide*. London: Sage.

van Eimeren, B. and Frees, B., 2010. Fast 50 Millionen Deutsche online – Multimedia für alle? Ergebnisse der ARD/ZDF-Onlinestudie 2010. *Media Perspektiven*, 7–8, pp. 334–349.

van Zoonen, L., 2002. Gendering the Internet. Claims, controversies and cultures. *European Journal of Communication*, 17(1), pp. 5–24 [online]. Available at: http://ejc.sagepub.com/cgi/reprint/17/1/5.pdf [Accessed 27 January 2009].

Vuojärvi, H., Isomäki, H. and Hynes, D., 2010. Domestication of a laptop on a wireless campus. Case study. *Australasian Journal of Educational Technology*, 26(2), pp. 250–267.

Zillien, N. and Hargittai, E., 2009. Digital distinction: Status-specific types of Internet usages. *Social Science Quarterly*, 90(2), pp. 274–291.

Notes

1   Strictly speaking, we prefer the expression 'ethnographically oriented research' to 'media ethnography' because most of the ethnographic media studies are not based on long-term observations or cohabitation of researchers and participants. However, their focus on everyday practices, social constellations and meaning attribution is clearly in the tradition of ethnography.

2   Although the original concept of domestication already included these thoughts on the non-linearity of the domestication process, it can be argued that the four phases are mainly theoretical in nature. So far, we are not aware of any study that systematically analyses the domestication process of a new media technology on the basis of this distinction. Accordingly, we suggest one considers that the conversion phase is only vaguely described by Silverstone, Hirsch and Morley (1992), whereas incorporation seems to be the most important phase as it refers to a whole set of changes within the household that come with the integration of the technology into the domestic sphere.

3   Democratization is part of domestication and it is associated with a process that Morley labelled as 'feminisation', by which he specifically targeted the increased involvement of female users: 'the whole point about the domestication of such a technology is that in this process of "democratisation" (beyond the hands of the technical specialist) it becomes effectively "feminised" as it is made more consumer friendly' (Morley 2000: 95). However, the expression seems to be misleading because only a minority of highly 'tech-savvy' men belong to the group of early users, whereas the majority of users – both male and female – approach the technology in the ongoing process of domestication.

4   Other data collection instruments, such as questionnaires, a timeline and a list with online applications that were used by each respondent, were applied during the interviews. On the one hand, these instruments activated the couple's memories. On the other hand, they served as a comprehensive documentation of the contents that were used online.

5   The quantitative data were originally collected by the ARD/ZDF online studies that annually survey the Internet usage of the German population over the age of 14. Since 1997, the studies are commissioned by the media board of the two main public service broadcasters in Germany, ARD (Arbeitsgemeinschaft der öffentlich-rechtlichen Rundfunkanstalten der Bundesrepublik Deutschland) and ZDF (Zweites Deutsches Fernsehen), that made the data available to us for secondary analysis. Some, but not all, of the data are regularly published in the journal *Media Perspektiven* (e.g. van Eimeren and Frees 2010).

6   Our new research project on the mediatized home in which our sample of 25 couple households was transferred into a panel is likely to reveal whether this technical framing will become less dominant in the near future.

Chapter 13

Creating, Sharing, Interacting: Fandom in the Age of Digital
Convergence and Globalized Television

Mélanie Bourdaa and Seok-Kyeong Hong-Mercier

Introduction

Traditionally, fans were considered frighteningly out of control, undisciplined and unrepentant rogue readers who devoted their love to a cult TV show. But early cultural studies researchers were the first to think that fans were the 'ultimate example of active, productive audiences, exercising their capacity for resistance in relation to the cultural industries' (Gripsrud 2002: 114). This chapter focuses on how fans relate to TV shows in the age of media convergence and globalized television consumption, and how they create new viewing experiences and new interactions. We observed TV series fandom considering the specific sociocultural processes that series motivate in societies.

The national audience has been the most important frame of interpretation up to 1990, and it continues to be an important reference for national TV series producers by evidence of numerous studies on national identity and TV fictions (Castello 2007). It has been observed that successful TV series become national media events and generate dynamic social interactions where different social values and representations are *mis-en-scène* in a competitive way (Macé 2006). The dominance of US TV series in the international programme market contrasts this national character of TV series and has been the object of cultural imperialism critics since the 1970s. Meanwhile, globalization and digitalization have been changing this situation of unilateral dominance, as global TV markets have been witnessing the rise of Latin American telenovela, East Asian drama and Indian Bollywood series. Moreover, in terms of offer and demand, the Internet gives new possibilities in the way fans consume their favourite TV series, which are no longer the sole domain of national networks. All cultural contents are virtually available for global audiences with access to a high-speed Internet connection and a computer.

Growing fan interactivity and expressiveness on the Internet needs a new set of qualitative methods for a more comprehensive audience research. This research applies a cyber-ethnography methodology to selected TV series' websites and forums. This is an audience study method, adapted to changing media environments and audience activities, which go beyond the act of reading. The analysis is based on participant observations in TV series website forums. We created a user profile to analyse social interactions of fans, the content of discussion themes and ways of creating a hierarchy between fans and moderators. This method respects the conditions of an ethnographical research where observation is based on naturally formed fan communities rather than on artificially created viewing groups, as it was the case in many reception studies since the 1980s (Chalvon-Demersay 1999; Morley 1980). Allard (2005) argues that cyber-ethnography has advantages in reducing the danger of 'presentation of the self' of participants. The most significant advantage of cyber-ethnography is that this will help to investigate the fans' practices in the age of media convergence and globalization, an area where traditional reception studies have some limits. Cultural industries are developing cross-media strategies, which widen fans' engagement and favour the creation of communities and activities. All this is observable in a concentrated way in websites, where digital culture becomes generalized for industries and fans. Now huge amounts of content from different cultural and geographical areas are virtually available for anyone. These websites create a timely moment of trans-cultural communication where the official mediation of corporate media intersects with the creative, alternative and sometimes subversive practices of fans. We have chosen, in this chapter, to observe both the sci-fi Internet website for *Battlestar Galactica*, a US series, and a French fan forum of East Asian TV drama. These are examples that we think illustrate new dimensions of fandom in digital convergence and globalization era as well as question important communicative and cultural issues which are central in current fan studies.

Active Audiences and Fandom: Main Paths of Research in the English-Speaking World and in France

In English-speaking countries, research on active audiences and fans has been flourishing since the late 1970s. Scholars argued that reception of television is not limited to the very moment of the programme airing on a channel but goes beyond this thanks to several activities that fans express and practice within a community. These can include writing fan fictions and cultural reviews, creating fan-arts, videos, websites and finding other fans with which to talk and share passions (Bielby, Harrington and Bielby 1999; Jenkins 1992, 2006). The concept of polysemy has indeed opened paths to understand

> how fans interpret their chosen television texts, how they relate them to their personal experiences, how they produce subsidiary texts of their own (fan fiction, fan art, fan videos, etc.), and how they form interpretative communities predicated on a common interest in a particular text. (Jones 2000: 405)

Fans usually belong to a community in which the same passion, language, media practices and the will to participate are expressed. This sense of belonging is strong among fans. The Internet provides immediacy, even a sense of urgency, for viewers who go online, erasing the frontiers of time and space, creating something that is familiar: fandom.

According to Jenkins (1992, 2006), fans are active receivers, who use new technologies to adapt to a new sociocultural environment to create and redefine language, practices, identities and values. He sums up the core of new television practices in three points:

re-circulation, participation and virtual communities. 'Re-circulation' symbolizes the transmission of (fan) materials and texts to a larger audience. The participative dimension is where fans engage actively and widely in the creation and circulation of cultural materials. The cultural logic of fans draws a blurred border between consumption versus production, and between reading versus writing. Finally, virtual communities are places of Internet-mediated social relations. Many viewers take pleasure in the fact that they are part of a 'special and specialized social audience' (Ross 2008) while also working to defend their texts as worthy of a broader social audience. Today, virtual communities are spreading, drilling and colonizing websites. They allow fans to re-circulate their tastes from one community to another. Social networks such as Facebook and Twitter, where producers and fans meet and interact, tend to amplify this phenomenon and spread the social links formed in these communities.

Digital media allow a new relationship with media and television contents. TV series are now developing into 'transmedia storytelling' (Jenkins 2003) that fans consume in different media, on different personal and mobile devices such as a cell phone, a computer, a game box or a TV receiver. Mittel (2009) coined the term 'forensic fandom' to explain that fans in the digital age tend to dig deeper in the reception of their favourite show because they have the technical tools and skills. Pearson, in an article entitled 'Fandom in the Digital Age', observes that 'the digital revolution has had a profound impact upon fandom, both empowering and disempowering, blurring the lines between producers and consumers, creating symbiotic relationships between powerful corporations and individual fans, and giving rise to new forms of cultural production' (Pearson 2010: 84).

In France, studies on active audience and fans came quite late to academia. In the 1980s, audiences were only discussed as a market and viewed as a ratings number. Television viewing was not considered seriously by the sociology of culture, which developed an influential theory on cultural legitimacy under the imposing work of Bourdieu (1965, 1979). According to his theory, a social hierarchy structures cultural practices; a homological difference exists between high culture (elite taste) and low culture (popular taste). This theoretical position made it epistemologically impossible to conceive (mass) audiences as creative and participative or to admit that they are composed of people from all over the social strata, without significant social hierarchy.

It is only since the late 1980s that French theorists and media scholars began to take interest in audience activities and started analysing how audiences perceive and interpret media messages (Boullier 1987; Dayan 1992, 1993; Proulx 1998). 'À la recherche du public', a special issue of the journal *Hermès* edited by Dayan (1993), was one of the first French collective publications on audiences and reception studies. In this issue, it is argued that any audience theory implies a television theory and is therefore a representation of the society. In this inaugural issue, the social link between audiences was also underlined. For example, in his article 'La télévision du pauvre', Macé (1993) wrote that far from being imposed from 'the high', the format of TV game shows actually fulfils the participatory needs of popular audiences and that in doing so it raises the question of whether television might act as a substitute for other social or political forms of participation.

Later, in her analysis of the teen show *Hélène et les Garçons*, sociologist Pasquier (1999) looked at how teen girls watched the show and understood its importance in their socialization. She used a three-point methodology: an analysis of the letters sent by fans to the production or the actors of the show, an open questionnaire and participant observation in family viewing environment. Thanks to this combined ethnographic methodology, evidently influenced by British cultural studies, she managed to highlight the interactions between fans themselves and between fans and the show. She argued that cultural practices could be understood in terms of social activities, underlining the importance of communities (Pasquier 2005). Mehl (1996), another French sociologist, defined the concept of 'television of compassion' through a new genre: reality-based shows. She stated that ordinary people's voice in these shows is a form of audience participation as well as catharsis. In 2000, *Loft Story*, the French version of *Big Brother*, became the media event of the year. It marked a new television era, which was symbolized by the blurred borders between fiction and reality, between privacy and public life, and by the use of new technologies for real-time audience participation.

In early 2000, a cultural turn occurred in France because of the introduction of British and American cultural studies and a revision of the French cultural legitimacy theory. Scholars generated syncretistic publications on audiences covering all sociological approaches (e.g. Esquenazi 2003; Le Grignou 2003). Other scholars engaged in translation of ideas in a more radical way and established the new age of audience studies in France. Whereas *Penser les Médiacultures*, a collective work edited by Maigret and Macé (2005), opened up new ways of thinking about the sociology of cultural practices, the anthology *Cultural Studies*, edited by Glevarec, Macé and Maigret (2008), proposed the first French translations of some important classic texts on active audiences and fans, such as those of Jenkins, Fiske and Radway, among others.

Lahire (2004) criticized the cultural legitimacy theory of cultural consumption in one of the most important French sociological works of the decade. He underlined cultural dissonances of individuals, observing that cultural consumption is not only dependent on class differences but also on individual practices and preferences. Similarly, in his article entitled 'La fin du modèle classique de la légitimité culturelle', Glevarec (2005) argued that the sociocultural heterogeneity of superior groups was expanding as well as their tastes and that social control of cultural practices was decreasing. Empirical evidence has been supporting this revision of the cultural legitimacy model. Generational factors as well as technical skills and digital literacy have a growing importance in the evolution of cultural practices in France (Donnat 2009b).

Recently, fan studies have been gaining importance in France. For example, François (2007) and Martin (2007) both analysed fan fictions as presentations of the self and proposed a typology of the various fan fictions they studied. One of the most influential French journals in communication studies, *Réseaux*, tackled the issue of fans versus amateurs in one of its recent issues (Donnat 2009a). Moreover, Flichy (2010) explained the part played by the Internet in legitimating fans' practices.

French scholars continue the analytical tradition of the French sociology of culture when conducting audience and fans studies. These works are increasing the understanding of the social dimension of cultural practices – an issue which is at the centre of the revisionist movement of the Bourdieusian cultural legitimacy legacy – by taking structural forces into consideration, such as gender, generation, social groups, subcultures and countercultures. The notion of 'mediaculture', which implicates the consubstantial nature of media in every cultural formation, is of major importance in the current development of audience studies in France (Maigret and Macé 2005).

Battlestar Galactica and the Community-Centred Fans

Our research focused on the American sci-fi show *Battlestar Galactica* and on the use of the official website and forum by its fans. *Battlestar Galactica* was selected because this show is part of the 'quality television' movement,[1] which has been resurgent in western television since the early 2000s. This series reinvents the space-opera genre. It also deals with provocative contemporary issues and has a solid fan base. Even if mainstream, this TV show represents what Hills (2002) calls 'cult TV', a must-see series which is widely dissected and analysed on the official forum. Besides proposing a forum, the *Battlestar Galactica* website introduces some transmedia strategies by the producers, such as the presentation of an interactive game ('Join the Fight') which is popular among fans. The forum contributes to the extension of the show to a mainstream audience as it is hosted by the official sci-fi website.

In our cyber-ethnography, we first watched all the episodes of the show to become familiar with the mythology and narrative before entering the website forum community. Then, we created a user profile, mentioning that we were media scholars. During 6 months we read all the posts and comments, watched the various interactions and participated in debates and discussions regarding plots or theories to act as a full member of the community. When we sensed the community accepted us, we posted an open questionnaire online, for every member to see and comment. The fact that we were doing research on their fandom was not a problem for two main reasons: we were accepted as a member of the community and other members of the forum included media scholars. The aim of the questionnaire was to ask fans about their television practices, their reception in the digital age and to know how the Internet has changed fans' activities. We obtained 48 answers that were analysed thematically. We scanned the posts titles and discussions and identified the main themes concerning how fans watched and perceived the show. We found four broad topics of discussion among the members of the community: television practices, social relationships, creative activities as fans and authorship.

Television Practices of the Fans

All the fans who responded to the questionnaire agree that the Internet has modified their consumption of TV programmes, providing new technologies and allowing new temporalities that help them in enjoying the show according to their desires. The forum is a virtual place where they gather to discuss the show, and the website is the best and official source of information they can find on the Internet. Many fans favour the streaming of episodes, buy past seasons on DVD, record the episodes on TiVo or download them illegally via peer-to-peer software. New interactive technologies and the convergence of television and the Internet have offered possibilities to create a new private media temporality, allowing fans to enjoy their favourite show whenever they want, with whom they want, on any digital devices, such as television, personal laptop, iPod or cell phone. TV programmes can now be defined as mobile and time-flexible. But because fans can now watch their episodes anytime and several times, it allows them to experience *Battlestar Galactica* on a different level during each viewing. As a result, fans better understand the programme and speculate about future plots and character relationships. Fans in forums even call these 'theories'.

Social Relationships in the Forum

Fans of the show appreciate this flexible media temporality and the multiple ways to watch their show, but the Internet represents above all a way to be a member of a virtual and creative community. It is obvious that there are no critics among the fans. To be part of the community of the *Battlestar Galactica* devotees, fans have to be respectful and have to know the show by heart and be aware of its mythology. Fans of the show who are members of the official forum are passionate and like the fact that they are part of a virtual community in which they can be themselves and where they can meet fellow lovers of the show. In their definition of connectivity, Russell, Norman and Heckler (2004) qualify these relationships between fans as 'horizontal relationships', as opposed to 'vertical relationships' (between fans and the show) and 'vertizontal relationships' (between fans and the cast). The social links created by the fans within the forum are important for them because they symbolize and respect virtual friendship. The Internet and possibilities of interactivity have abolished time and space distances between fans, who can now log on instantly to the forum and discuss the episode they have just watched with virtual friends. In the beginning of fandom, fans had to wait for the annual convention to meet other fans and had to subscribe to a fanzine to get the 'latest' information on the show, the cast, the plots and the future episodes. Now, fans are experiencing what Hills (2002) calls 'just-in time' fandom: a fast, global and resourceful fandom.

All the answers from the questionnaire we posted underscore the social bond that binds all the fans in this virtual discussion board. They also appreciate the fact that nobody is going to laugh at them, and that the debates are clever, the comments are food for thought, which can lead to endless dialogue between the fans, showing their understanding of the plots of the series. In all the answers we received, we note how each fan engaged the forum to meet other devotees of the show, to discuss and elaborate on so-called theories with them, to be with people like them who are not ashamed to be part of a virtual community, and who engage in some virtual debates to help each other unravel the mysteries of *Battlestar Galactica*.

Fan Fictions and Poaching

For the most active fans, the Internet is also a way to share their writing talents with the community, by posting fan fictions. In his now famous book *L'invention du quotidien: Arts de faire*, de Certeau (1990) coined the concept of 'cultural poaching'. He explained how the audience, with their tactics, poaching and reemployments, could do something else with the technocratic structures than what is dictated to them. He opposed the strategies of the cultural industries to the tactics of the receivers who take what interests them in the initial media text to recreate their own texts. Jenkins, reemploying de Certeau's notion of 'poaching', explains how and why fans are active and creative 'textual poachers': 'Fan speculations may, on the surface, seem to be simply a deciphering of the aired material but increasingly, speculation involves fans in the production of new fantasies, broadening the field of meanings that circulate around the primary text' (Jenkins 1992: 12).

Textual polysemy allows the elaboration of hypothesis or multiple interpretations of the text. Moreover, polysemy involves both a notion of fascination and frustration for fans, which are the foundations for the creation of fan fictions. The complexity of *Battlestar Galactica* as well as the relationships between Cylons and humans make fans create their own stories. Fan fictions are a way for fans to make the show evolve in a new direction they would have loved see the show go. Fan fictions can be described as a collaborative work in progress. Indeed, authors of fan fictions wait for other fans' reactions, approbations and comments to change their creation or to go ahead and write new ones. Belonging to a virtual community is as important in this process of creation as in the posting of messages on the forum boards. Fans create fan fictions to share with the other devotees and to create debates.

Interactivity and Authorship

Based on questionnaire data, only two fans think that their interactions on the forum or on the website can influence how producers conceive and write the show. The producers of the show often log on to the forum to see fans' reactions, and fans are very aware of this practice. That is why they sense that their discussions in a way inspire the producers who scrutinize and analyse what fans post on the forum. However, fans are realistic concerning their supposed co-producing and creative power. Fans know they do not have any decision-making power when it comes to the writing of the show. For example, one of them criticizes openly the voting process of *American Idol* and rejects the idea that fans could influence in any way the end of the show or the decisions made by the producers. Furthermore, fans are even totally opposed to the idea of being given the opportunity to have authorial power in the creation process. Although fans of science fiction shows such as *Battlestar Galactica* are eloquent and always willing to post their so-called theories for the other fans to discuss, they acknowledge that if producers wanted to take every comment into consideration, the show would be a mess and lose its appeal and originality. *Battlestar Galactica* is a show that stays faithful to its mythology and fans must not change this. For forum members, it is unthinkable to have a show in which fans could vote for the best plot conclusion or for the best on-screen couple's relationship, typical of *American Idol*.

Fans appreciate and respect the producers for giving them opportunities for interaction (forum, online games, podcasts etc.), but they do not think they have – or should have – a real impact on the decision making concerning the show's evolution. They use the official website to seek important information, to keep in touch with the mythology and plots, and to communicate with their fellow members to elaborate so-called theories and then discuss them in the forum. The Internet, above all, has increased the speed with which fans communicate and consume the show. The Internet is a real-time communication tool, allowing virtual relationships and debate within a virtual community of devotees. This is the most important aspect for *Battlestar Galactica*'s fans, the possibility to be in constant touch with their friends, with the show and with the producers and cast.

East Asian TV Drama, Worldwide Fan Community and Global Cultural Public Sphere

In our second study, we chose an East Asian television drama and conducted research on its French fandom. The choice of drama for our observation requires more profound understanding of the actual French media environment. As mentioned earlier, imported US series have gained a cultural legitimacy in Europe, especially in France where they are massively programmed during prime time. Actually, a certain hierarchy of TV series can be observed in France between high-quality US series, French series viewed by a national audience and other imported European and non-European series. Comparatively, watching East Asian drama exclusively on the Internet is an activity which requires a great level of involvement as well as digital and linguistic literacy on the part of fans. Because of the low status of East Asian drama in the French cultural hierarchy, fans feel compelled to justify their viewing both to themselves and to their families and friends.

Current East Asian TV drama fandom in France is not an isolated and accidental cultural consumption but a logical consequence of a cultural formation whose origin goes back to the intensive diffusion of anime on television during the 1980s. This 'Goldorak generation' is the seed population who transformed into manga fans, forming the second largest manga market in the world after Japan (Bouissou 2010). Active manga fans use the Internet, doing scanlations and creating fan fictions, without waiting for the legal release in France of Japanese manga. Developing cross-media adaptations in East Asian cultural industries between manga, anime and TV drama prepared the exposure of French manga fans to TV drama on the Internet. Once fans are 'contaminated', as the hardcore fans describe their experience of 'the first contact' with East Asian drama, they enter a passionate and addictive viewing experience overcoming diverse technical and cultural difficulties to be able to continue to nurture their passion. This fandom formation needs a set of material conditions. These include a high-speed Internet connection, rapid uploading possibilities which make a pseudo live streaming possible and Internet protocol HD videos. The last element is an important condition to digital scopophilia during intensive viewing.

We have chosen *Dorama-World*, one of the most active forums on drama in France, for the cyber-ethnography. How have French fans discovered East Asian drama, which has never aired in France or Western Europe? Why do they continue to watch episodes? What are the social, cultural and aesthetic reasons of this 'illegitimate' but passionate cultural practice? From the beginning of 2009 to the end of 2010, we conducted participant observation on the forum as well as a Web observation on the drama consumption circuit composed of Youtube, a videos sharing network, and of information and fansub sites. We read posts of *Dorama-World* following established discussion groups, participated in discussions and, if necessary, interviewed participants. We also carried out a diachronic analysis of posts, which made possible the reconstitution of the sociocultural identity of some active members. This knowledge was cross-checked by sending personal messages to forum members.

Dorama-World is a middle-sized French discussion group (2000 subscribers in December 2010), specializing in East Asian drama. Created in 2005, it is a space dedicated to passionate followers of drama: bloggers, fansubbers, critics, cover makers and ordinary viewers. The majority of fans are French with European origins, except some members with Asian and African roots. Some members have a multiethnic history and multicultural family trajectories. The most active members are educated, working women, between 25 and 40 years of age, and generally without children. They are multi-genre consumers and devourers of popular cult content in general, including films, pop music, manga, US TV series and dramas, and in some cases, novels.

Drama Viewing and New Temporality Experience

Without official media broadcasting in France,[2] the most important everyday work for fans is to search available uploaded videos of the drama. To do so, fans surf the Web regularly, reading the background stories on stars, productions and related cultural industries news. This enriches the drama viewing experience, creates expectations, reinforces the passion and maintains programme desire.

The question of temporality has crucial importance. Fans are recreating their own timetable thanks to the global drama fans' community. Fans living in East Asian countries upload the day's prime-time episodes, which are therefore available for the French fans. But fans in general do not like to view episodes via the Internet because of general poor quality. They prefer to download them in HD format and to watch them as soon as the fansub is available. Curiously, some fans recreate a pseudo live condition, watching the show together at the same time, chatting about the drama via Internet connections.

The drama format preferred by fans is the miniseries, with 11 to 20 episodes packed in a single season. This seriality is considered a big difference compared to dominant US episodic series broadcast as separate seasons over years. Drama is a serial with a dramatic narrative structure and efficient cliffhangers. It proposes a reasonable ending. This difference is one of the reasons why fans prefer drama to US series, which often have no logical and plausible ending. It is also the major element that makes drama fans addicted and passionate. Fans have a list of the must-see dramas, try to promote them, watch them several times and are used to listen regularly to the original programme soundtrack on their MP3 player. Self-control of viewing habit and the time budget are important issues on the forum. The most frustrating addiction is felt when they follow ongoing dramas. They even feel frustrated when their beloved dramas are finished. Some of them spoil it, without waiting for the fansub, even though they will not understand the dialogue. They consider it a big loss because the best viewing condition is, according to them, viewing all the episodes and fansubs when available. In this case, they can watch them all at once without suffering the delay for the next episode.

Social Relationships Online and Offline

The active members of *Dorama-World* are dominantly female. They react in a passionate way to the East Asian male actors. The founding members of the forum, dominantly male, continue to post about actresses but in a less passionate way. Female fans are reflexive about their late 'fan girl attitude', in a kind of *adulescent* phenomenon they assume. They are commenting on the acting skills, scenarios, cult scenes and dialogues, and cultural mysteries that they do not understand. They do this during lunchtime and after work. Even though they are well informed about East Asian countries, drama remains a mysterious cultural object. Discussions can go beyond the world of drama, covering political, social and cultural issues related to East Asian countries. Some post and download during work hours doing 'masquerade' (de Certeau 1990). Fans also organize offline activities. They buy drama and Asian pop culture goodies, visit Japan Expo, go together to Korean restaurants, attend language classes and organize viewing camp meetings if they can afford it. They are consciously sustaining each other in their collective but not yet legitimate passion, animating the forum and 'contaminating' others.

Global Internet Community of Drama Fans

For fan activities to be possible, an organized global work division is necessary, including voluntary uploading and globally recruited fansub teams governance. In this vast space of collaboration, fansubbers are endowed figures of experts, intellectuals who mediate and make possible the understanding of the East Asian other.

Drama fandom is a dynamic intercultural communication process in which individuals are interpolated as citizens of the world. It is an open space, where multiple origins of members and interbreeding are idealized. It is a virtual community based on individuals' donation of self, in which primo uploaders and fansubbers are playing a pivotal role. As the members of *Dorama-World* illustrate, they gently receive newcomers in the forum without judging their level of knowledge, share information on novelty and rumours, give technical tips on how to access episodes and extol cultural expertise for understanding the East Asian everyday life represented in drama. In doing so, members of *Dorama-World* enact their capacity of expression in tastes and aesthetic judgement as well as perform a critical reflection towards their own culture. We could make sense of this community formation as that of a 'cultural public sphere' (McGuigan 2005) in the global era.

Social and Cultural Citizenship of the Fans

In this chapter, we have chosen two different observation fields, applying different kinds of cyber-ethnography, addressing different questions, mobilizing different sets of theoretical frames. Notwithstanding the variety in size of sites, forums' infrastructures, community governance and range of fans activities, we can find an important concordance: fans place great importance on the social dimension of their activities. Fans who post on the official site of *Battlestar Galactica* are active in creating fan fictions and producing so-called theories. But they are doing them above all to be in contact with other fans, having pleasure to be read and discussed by the community members.

Fans of the East Asian drama, observed in *Dorama-World*, take part in the global community of fans who organize themselves in mobilizing volunteer cultural workers. They are sharing and sustaining their 'illegitimate' passion – by stealing time away from other activities and in the illegal nature of video loading and fansubbing. Their interest in Asia goes beyond the fantasized world of drama. Discussions of larger cultural, social and political issues are not rare. Actually, fans carry out a wide range of activities, like social bonding (communities, offline activities, propagation of passion, virtual friendship), collaborative creation (wikis, games, fan fictions, theories) and sharing (uploading, fansubbing, knowledge).

Recent discourses on cultural citizenship have emphasized the importance of collective connection through media including alternative forms, even though they exhibit no effective link to public issues (Couldry 2006). Some researchers underline the contemporary importance of the cultural dimension of the public sphere, revisiting Habermas' founding notion as literary forum (McGuigan 2005). What can be observed on the fan activities of US *Battlestar Galactica* and of East Asian drama indeed claims the cultural citizenship of fans in the digital and global era.

References

Allard, L., 2005. Express yourself 2.0! In É. Maigret and É. Macé, eds, *Penser les médiacultures. Nouvelles pratiques et nouvelles approches de la représentation du monde*. Paris: INA/Armand Colin. pp. 145–169.

Bielby, D.D., Harrington, C.L. and Bielby, W., 1999. Whose stories are they? Fan engagement with soap opera narratives in three sites of fan activity. *Journal of Broadcasting & Electronic Media*, 43(1), pp. 35–51.

Bouissou, J.M., 2010. *Manga. Histoire et univers de la BD japonaise*. Paris: Philippe Picquier.

Boullier, D., 1987. *La conversation télé*. Rennes, France: Lares.

Bourdieu, P., 1965. *Un art moyen. Essai sur les usages sociaux de la photographie*. Paris: Minuit.

———— 1979. *La distinction. Critique sociale du jugement*. Paris: Minuit.

Castello, E., 2007. The production of television fiction and nation building. The Catalan case. *European Journal of Communication*, 22(1), pp. 22–49.

Chalvon-Demersay, S., 1999. La confusion des conditions: Une enquête sur la série télévisée Urgences. *Réseaux*, 95, pp. 235–283.

Couldry, N., 2006. Culture and citizenship. The missing link? *European Journal of Cultural Studies*, 9(3), pp. 321–339.

Dayan, D., 1992. Les mystères de la réception. *Le Débat*, 71, pp. 146–162.

———— 1993. Avant-propos. Raconter le public. *Hermès*, 11–12, pp. 15–21.

de Certeau, M., 1990. *L'invention du quotidien, tome 1: Arts de faire*. Paris: Gallimard.

Donnat, O., 2009a. Présentation. *Réseaux*, 153, pp. 9–16.

———— 2009b. *Les pratiques culturelles des Français à l'ère numérique. Enquête 2008*. Paris: La Découverte.

Esquenazi, J.-P., 2003. *Sociologies des publics*. Paris: La Découverte.

Flichy, P., 2010. *Le sacre de l'amateur*. Paris: Seuil.

François, S., 2007. Les *fanfictions*, nouveau lieu d'expression de soi pour la jeunesse. *Agora. Débats et Jeunesses*, 46, pp. 58–68.

Glevarec, H., 2005. La fin du modèle classique de la légitimité culturelle. Hétérogénéisation des ordres de légitimité et régime contemporain de justice culturelle. L'exemple du champ musical. In É. Maigret and É. Macé, eds, *Penser les médiacultures. Nouvelles pratiques et nouvelles approches de la représentation du monde*. Paris: INA/Armand Colin. pp. 69–102.

Glevarec, H., Macé, É. and Maigret, É., eds, 2008. *Cultural studies. Anthologie*. Paris: Armand Colin.

Gripsrud, J., 2002. Fans, viewers and television theory. In P. Le Guern, ed., *Les cultes médiatiques. Culture fan et oeuvres cultes*. Rennes: PUR. pp. 113–131.

Hills, M., 2002. *Fan cultures*. London: Routledge.

Jenkins, H., 1992. *Textual poachers: Television fans and participatory culture*. London: Routledge.

———— 2003. Transmedia storytelling. *Technological Review* [online]. Available at: http://www.technologyreview.com/biomedicine/13052/page1/ [Accessed 19 June 2011].

———— 2006. *Convergence culture. Where old and new media collide*. New York: NYU Press.

Jones, S.G., 2000. Histories, fictions, and Xena: Warrior princess. *Television and New Media*, 1(4), pp. 403–418.

Lahire, B., 2004. *La culture des individus. Dissonances culturelles et distinction de soi.* Paris: La Découverte.

Le Grignou, B., 2003. *Du côté du public. Usages et réceptions de la télévision.* Paris: Economica.

Macé, É., 1993. La télévision du pauvre. *Hermès,* 11–12, pp. 159–176.

——— 2006. *Les imaginaires médiatiques: Une sociologie postcritique des médias.* Paris: Amsterdam.

Maigret, É. and Macé, É., eds, 2005. *Penser les médiacultures. Nouvelles pratiques et nouvelles approches de la représentation du monde.* Paris: INA/Armand Colin.

Martin, M., 2007. Les 'fanfictions' sur internet. *Médiamorphoses. Hors série: Les raisons d'aimer les séries télévisées.* Paris: INA/Armand Colin. pp. 186–189.

McGuigan, J., 2005. The cultural public sphere. *European Journal of Cultural Studies,* 8(4), pp. 427–443.

Mehl, D., 1996. *La télévision de l'intimité.* Paris: Seuil.

Mittel, J., 2009. Sites of participation: Wiki fandom and the case of Lostpedia. *Transformative works and cultures,* 3 [online]. Available at: http://journal.transformativeworks.org/index.php/twc/article/view/118/117 [Accessed 19 June 2011].

Morley, D., 1980. *The 'nationwide' audience. Structure and decoding.* London: British Film Institute.

Pasquier, D., 1999. *La culture des sentiments. L'expérience télévisuelle des adolescents.* Paris: MSH.

——— 2005. La culture comme activité sociale? In É. Maigret and É. Macé, eds, *Penser les médiacultures. Nouvelles pratiques et nouvelles approches de la représentation du monde.* Paris: INA/Armand Colin. pp. 103–120.

Pearson, R., 2010. Fandom in the digital era. *Popular Communication,* 8(1), pp. 84–95.

Proulx, S., ed., 1998. *Accusé de réception. Le téléspectateur construit par les sciences sociales.* Québec/Paris: Presse de l'Université Laval/L'Harmattan.

Ross, S.M., 2008. *Beyond the box. Television and the Internet.* Oxford, UK: Blackwell.

Russell, C.A., Norman, A.T. and Heckler, S.E., 2004. People and 'their' television show. An overview of television connectedness. In L.J. Schrum, ed., *The psychology of entertainment media. Blurring the lines between entertainment and persuasion.* Mahwah, NJ: Lawrence Erlbaum. pp. 275–290.

Notes

1 'Quality television' is a term used by some scholars, critics and industry professionals in reference to a re-emergence (from US television in the 1950s) or mix of several genres, an engagement by viewers, a complex seriality and narrative, and multiple story arcs (among other characteristics). HBO, the American pay-per-view channel, is generally understood to have reinitiated this movement with shows like *The Sopranos* and *The Wire.*

2 The only exception is *Dramapassion*, an Internet VOD site of South Korean TV drama, launched in 2010.

Conclusion

Exciting Moments in Audience Research: Past, Present and Future

Sonia Livingstone

Introduction

To understand the commonalities and diversity in the contributions to this volume, this final chapter traces two interlocking histories. Hall's (1980) 'exciting moment' in audience research gave birth to reception studies and, as part of the advent of British cultural studies, much intellectual energy has been expended in debating the unfolding narrative of audience research. At the same time, society is witnessing more and more transformations in the now digital, convergent, networked landscape, resulting in more diverse modes of audiencing and a fascination with the narrative of audiences. Audiences no longer are predictable; they no longer inhabit only the living room sofa. Instead, they are everywhere and nowhere, which is demanding that audience researchers follow the latest trends to be where the action is. This chapter argues that these two narratives are converging in the phenomenon of participation, arguably one of the key social uses of media (as addressed by this volume more broadly), with more or less 'participatory audiences' displacing the 'active audience' as a consequence of the onward march of mediatization processes. Participation in society increasingly means participation in and through the uses of media, while, in a parallel shift, the complex media landscape offers increasing, though heavily qualified and contingent, opportunities for participation.

> A new and exciting phase in so-called audience research ... may be opening up.
> (Hall 1980: 131)

Fifteen years ago, following a careful look at our field, two sociologists offered a doubly articulated account that attracted considerable attention (Abercrombie and Longhurst 1998). First, they told the story of changing audiences, from the simple, physically co-located yet carefully managed theatre and concert hall audiences and the mass audiences of first print media and then broadcasting, to the diffused audience in the modern complex and globalized media landscape. This history can be deepened by drawing on the work of others. It constitutes a kind of fusion of Butsch's (2000) fascinating account of the perennially contested nature of active versus passive audiences across the centuries and Thompson's (1995) sociological analysis of the shift in modernity from interpersonal through mass to quasi-mediated communication. Noting that the phases (simple, mass, diffused) are conceived as cumulative rather than substitutive (e.g. today we have live comedy club, prime-time comedy shows and peer exchange of comic clips on YouTube), Abercrombie and Longhurst's sketch provided a promising starting point, which has been taken forward in various ways by the rich and diverse contributions to this volume.

Abercrombie and Longhurst's second account attracted more attention in audience studies. Overlaying their history of how audiences have changed, they articulated a history of how audience research throughout the twentieth century can be periodized. They identified the initially dominant 'behavioural paradigm' of media effects and uses and gratifications research, moving through what they called the 'incorporation-resistance paradigm' of British cultural studies to their own assessment of contemporary research, which they described as the 'spectacle-performance paradigm' of late or even postmodern society. This history has also been told by many others. For some, the driving force was a fruitful if sometimes conflicting diversification from few to many intellectual traditions (Jensen and Rosengren 1990); others emphasize how audience research has served as a fertile bridging point between divergent perspectives (Livingstone 1998). For Curran (1990), there was no significant increase in understanding; active audience studies offered merely a revision of what was already known but often overlooked. Most often, however, the story of audience research is retold as having been pivotally transformed by the then exciting merger of ideology critique, reception-aesthetics and ethnographic work developed by the Birmingham Centre for Contemporary Cultural Studies (Alasuutari 1999; Nightingale 1996; see also Meers and Biltereyst, and Schrøder, this volume); although other canonical texts than Hall's (1980) 'Encoding/Decoding' paper, originally written and distributed in 1973, have also attracted attention (Katz et al. 2003).

Similar to other phases of audiencehood, these patterns of audience research have proved cumulative rather than substitutive. Specifically, the behavioural approach has survived its many critics (notably Barker and Petley 2001; Rowland 1983; see Ruddock's updating of Gerbner's cultivation theory in this volume, along with Soto-Sanfiel's application of uses and gratifications theory to the playing of first-person shooter games). Similarly, the influence of reception and cultural studies remains strong (see several of the chapters in this volume), continuing to stand alongside the insights of the spectacle-performance paradigm and postmodern accounts of a culture of narcissism on which it draws. The result is multiple theories and concepts, although hope for a single, consensual theory of audiences persists (Michelle 2007).

Transforming Societies, Transforming Audiences

When national media predominated over transnational forms (Scannell 1988), when social hierarchies were more salient than the horizontal flows of people or ideas (Appadurai 1996), and when generic forms (news, soap opera, documentary) were only beginning to be challenged by emerging hybrid forms, for many in our field, it seems that the theory, methods and politics of audience research were more absorbing than investigating changing audiences. During Hall's exciting period in audience research, reflexive self-examination and internal debate dominated conferences and journals (Barker and Beezer 1992; Livingstone 1998; Morley 1981), while the empirical effort to show how audiences variously responded to yet another text or genre was 'business as usual'. However, although researchers were debating their internal differences, audiences were changing.

Audiences no longer sit in family groups, enjoying leisure time in their living rooms and being available for broadcasters or researchers (Livingstone 2009a). The long-standing and formative fascination with mass audiences absorbed in national broadcast television (Scannell 1988), viewed on family television sets (Morley 1986) in domestic living rooms, with audiences that were lively (Palmer 1986) or conflictual (Ang 1996), was, it seems, historically (and culturally) contingent. So too were the associated assumptions about neatly scheduled lifestyles, parental regulation of children's viewing and the reproduction of gendered power relations through viewing practices. Much of this is consigned to history. The questions now are where are audiences to be found, what are they now part of and why does this matter?

In retrospect, it may seem curious that developments in the nature of media *qua* objects or technologies, for example, the advent of satellite and multichannel broadcasting, video recording and electronic games machines, initially attracted such little interest from researchers absorbed by probing the semiotic play among audiences of media *qua* texts (Livingstone 2007). Similarly, work on the social uses of computers and telephones seemed to be the preserve of a parallel world unrelated to the all-absorbing focus of (mainly) television studies on the interdependencies of mass media and mass society (e.g. Alasuutari 1999; Curran and Gurevitch 1991; Nightingale 1996). Works on audiences published in the 1980s and 1990s often refer only to television, with other social uses of media marginalized with what, in hindsight, is an extraordinary blindness to the convergent media landscape around the corner.

What broke the mould? Most obviously, changes in the media landscape eventually forced themselves onto the academic agenda. Also, experienced much more as a threat than an opportunity, scholars in other fields (information systems, education, political science, sociology, anthropology and more) became interested in the social shaping and social consequences of technologies – in ways that seemed sometimes to trample on or, more positively, to intersect with the traditional domain of audience research. Different kinds of projects sprang up, motivated by the excitement of bridging interdisciplinary domains in new and creative ways rather than carving out a new, more finely distinguished paradigm. I recall, in particular, the excitement at the 1990 International Communication Association conference in Dublin over the Brunel project on Household Uses of Information and Communication Technologies (Silverstone et al. 1989). This fused semiotics and consumption studies located audience members in real families and encompassed all media goods, not just television but also the home computer, the telephone, magazines and music – wherever they were engaged – in the living room, but also in the bedroom, the kitchen, cars or in the street (see Peil and Röser, this volume).

As media changed, new questions were being asked about changing audiences. They included deceptively banal questions, such as how is television like the washing machine, as well as familiar but still taxing ones, such as whether everyday audience activities play a constitutive role in the changes. As Pavlíčková argues in this volume, renewed attention was paid to the related question of whether agency belonged more to the technology (now more inclusively defined) or the user, notwithstanding that this often under-theorized concept tends to underestimate the power of social structure to determine individual user practices (Morley 1981; see also Dhoest, and Döveling and Sommer, this volume). As audiencing becomes evermore embedded in the complex and diverse structures of modernity, understanding the social context extends out from the living room to embrace – in Habermas's terms – all aspects of both the lifeworld and the system world, including the ways in which their interrelations increasingly are mediatized (Hepp 2011). Today, multimethod projects that embrace the ordinary person's whole way of life (Radway 1988) have become common (e.g. Bakardjieva 2005; Couldry, Livingstone and Markham 2010; Hoover and Clark 2008; and argued by Dover in this volume), although the analysis of the social uses of media in all their diversity remains methodologically demanding.

The 'audience' is everywhere and nowhere. (Bird 2003: 3)

Also, the rethinking that digital networked communication demands is well underway, replacing separate attention to television, radio, computer or film audiences (Meers and Biltereyst, this volume) with audiences embedded variously in a complex media ecology (Ito et al. 2010), 'media culture' (Maigret and Macé 2005, cited in Bourdaa and Hong-Mercier, this volume) or 'convergence culture' (Jenkins 2006), and engaging with particular 'constellations of media' (Couldry, Livingstone and Markham 2010), cross-media (Schrøder, Pavlíčková, this volume) or media convergence (across network, mass and interpersonal communication; Jensen 2009). In a similar vein, Evans (2011) argues that transmedia combines narrative, technology, mobility, space and engagement in new ways, enabling particular audience paths or trajectories. Relatedly, Hasebrink and Hölig (2011) examine communication modes emerging between mass and interpersonal communication, arguing that the traditional focus on genres (and the contract of mutual expectations they establish with their readers or audiences) would be better reconceived as modes of communication, albeit still enabled by a co-evolved, human-technological interface.

How can we study everything, now that everything is mediated, and retain some coherence as audience researchers (Livingstone 2004)? This is especially demanding when it is not just the media landscape, however conceptualized, that is changing. Crucially, in a world where everything is mediated (Livingstone 2009b), the implications for audiences, as Thompson (1995) early identified, are bound up with fundamental changes in modernity. Observing the notable diversity in the approaches and topics explored in this volume might seem to question what we have been doing in the past few decades after escaping from the history/culture-blind agenda of the behavioural paradigm and overcoming the equally universalistic 'spectator' or 'subject' dominant in film, screen and literary studies (see Meers and Biltereyst in this volume). What was so all absorbing in television studies that we recognized other important technological changes only rather late in the day?

Have we, as sometimes suggested by outsiders looking in, merely been chasing the latest fads and fashions in the changing media – perhaps in an effort not to be wrong-footed again by technological developments? When audience research broke away from adherence to the encoding/decoding (or incorporation/resistance) model, with its emphasis on Corner's (1991) 'public knowledge' rather than 'popular culture' project, there was an initial boom in studies of soap operas in the 1980s, which inverted established value systems that denigrated housewife viewers (Geraghty 1990). This was followed quickly by studies of talk shows, which brought a new recognition that audiences talk meaningfully, not only in front of the screen but also sometimes on the screen (Carpignano et al. 1990; Livingstone and Lunt 1994). Attention then turned to the new phenomenon of reality television (Hill 2002), which seemingly ridiculed – and certainly demanded a rethinking of – our carefully built advocacy of audiences as serious players in the cultural public sphere. As genres multiplied and hybridized faster than we could investigate the emerging contract of mutual expectations that underpinned audience researchers' analysis of more established genres, the kaleidoscope was given another shake, and suddenly, it seemed, the audience was dead (Jermyn and Holmes 2006).

The simultaneous diversification and convergence of many media technologies, television being just one, was suddenly made evident. Katz and Scannell (2009) proposed that this, in fact, meant the end of television and, therefore, the (television) audience. For others, once media technologies enabled audiences to talk back, and to talk to each other in public, this transformed them into 'the people formerly known as the audience' (Rosen 2006; see also Gillmor 2004; for a critique, see Ridell, this volume). Both media genres and social spheres were regarded as being so hybridized as to produce new kinds of individuals – the 'produser' (Bruns 2008), the 'citizen-consumer' (Murdock 1992; see also Schrøder, this volume) or, more prosaically, the 'user' – which were replacing audiences. The last term of 'user' is especially problematic, though the particular semantic infelicity of applying the term 'audience' to computer-based media has produced an inexorable rise in its popularity (e.g. Peil and Röser, this volume; see also Bakardjieva 2005). But 'user' lacks any necessary relation to the processes of communication, and also it is difficult to conceive of users collectively (compare, audience, public), both of which are defining features of audiences (Livingstone 2005).

However, it would be wrong to conclude that while audience research may have chased the latest fashion in the television industry, it has missed the bigger picture – the fundamental shift from mass to networked media, which, supposedly, has killed off the audience. In fact, the opposite is true: audience researchers, in this flurry of activity, have been making sure that they are in the right place at the right time; they have been putting themselves 'where the action is' regarding the changing conditions of communication. For it is the conditions of communication that shape the conditions for what really fascinates many audience researchers, which is not so much media, technologies or texts, as identities and social relations, the practices that engender common understandings and sources of difference, and the determinants of acquiescence, collusion with or resistance to power (Silverstone 2002).

Tracking the Changing Conditions of Communication

It is pertinent, then, rather than a mere historical peculiarity that Goffman's master's thesis was on housewives' responses to the radio soap opera (Manning 2005). In the same way, several decades earlier, it was indicative rather than exceptional in the history of audience research that on the day after H.G. Wells's *War of the Worlds* was broadcast, Cantril's (1940) research team was in the streets of America to gather the varieties of audience response to the apparently cataclysmic end of the world. This tradition of 'just-in-time' research has persisted, evidenced by the tracking of immediate global reception to the release of the third part of the *Lord of the Rings* trilogy (Barker and Mathijs 2008). In the 1980s, when the world was asking 'Who shot J.R.?', surely it was admirable, not faddish, that audience researchers dropped everything to enquire, in all seriousness, why the world cared about the answer to this question (Ang 1985; Liebes and Katz 1990; see also Dayan and Katz (1992) on other heavily mediated moments which, however briefly, stopped the world in its tracks – a political summit, a royal wedding, the death of a celebrity, a natural disaster).

These, and many other instances spanning mass and networked media, have enabled a subtle rearrangement of people and media, adjusting the possibilities for identity, relationships, commonality and resistance. For this reason, and rightly, they have attracted the attention of audience researchers because they capture the changes afoot in the conditions of 'audiencing', to use Fiske's (1994) term. Even nearly 20 years ago, Fiske was urging us not to reify the audience as a thing distinct from other things such as publics, markets or families (Livingstone 2005) but rather to consider audiencing. The verb demands analysis of the contextualized processes whereby people and media become mutually defining in a dynamic intertwining of agency and structure, which Giddens (1984) termed 'structuration'. Ridell (this volume) describes it as follows: 'people act as an audience every time they assume the position in which they receive and interpret a cultural performance or media representation.' This definition encompasses both mass and networked media, raising (rather than foreclosing) the key question of what roles or modes of participation are afforded to people by the particular cultural performance or media representation with which they engage? People *qua* audiences not only take up multiple roles in relation to (usually) screen media (whether in front of the screen, on it, creating for it or reusing its contents elsewhere) but they also explore and invent new ways of connecting with each other, through and around screen media.

In this sense, analysis of the rearrangements among people afforded by the mediation of mobile phones or social networking or blogging is a continuation of rather than a radical break from earlier analyses of the rearrangements among people afforded by soap operas, talk shows or reality television. So it is a continual process of reshaping the communicative possibilities for ordinary people that links, say, the astonishing first series of *Big Brother* (Hill 2002), the curiously unexpected adoption by youth of text messaging (Ling and Haddon 2008), the moment when personal stereos enabled private music listening in public (Bull 2000), the under-the-radar explosion in fanzines, remixed music and other forms of user-generated content (Jenkins 2006), and the apparent 'take over' of private communication by one company, Facebook (boyd and Hargittai 2010). Capturing moments of change before they become past – in this case, all these assorted instances of shifting interrelations and remediated modes of participation or disconnection – is vital if we are to understand the present.

Frameworks of Participation

How should we analyse these changing conditions for communication, these shifting arrangements of practices, technologies and institutions that enable people to act in relation to each other in particular ways? One theme emerges strongly from many of the chapters in this volume, that of the move from active audiences (characteristic of late twentieth-century research) to participatory audiences in the twenty-first century. Although avoiding the common but mistaken claim that audiences of networked media are more active than audiences of mass media (Livingstone 2010), several chapters in this volume (e.g. Schrøder) pursue the idea that these audiences are more participatory. It is not so much that people have changed, but more that the mediated 'opportunity structures' (Cammaerts, 2012) or, as Spitulnik (2010) calls them, the 'participant structures', in certain respects, that have become more open and enabling of participation. In short, the nature of mediation changes as mediatization advances. Renewed interest in participation is changing the research focus because – as in the case of Abercrombie and Longhurst's spectator/performance paradigm (though not, I would suggest, their two previous paradigms) – it is motivated by recognition of an underlying change in the conditions of audiencehood. Indeed, the focus on participation appears to be taking precedence over earlier fascination with spectatorship in a narcissistic culture, demonstrated by the close examination in several of the foregoing chapters of the motivations for and the modes and consequences of mediated participation.

A complex media ecology requires careful analysis of the specific conditions for communication. Interestingly, several contributors to this volume propose new terms to conceptualize the interlinking of people and media in context. Pavlíčková draws on hermeneutic theory to reveal the protocols for the social uses of media, these being conventionalized practices anchored in cultural and value-laden horizons of expectations. Ruddock opens up the communication event to reveal the social and material coding of relationships being constituted in and through such an event (see also Giles's account of parasocial relationships). Ridell refers to 'modes of action' and Nyre and O'Neill examine the dialogic, social and ethical parameters of 'mediated situations' to understand varying levels of individual media uses. However, these situations or protocols are not well understood, and it is noteworthy that for researchers of new media contexts considerable effort is required to explain the particular conditions, relations and conventions they are concerned with (e.g. in this volume, see Bourdaa and Hong-Mercier on a fan forum, and Soto-Sanfiel on an electronic game), before the possibilities for audience participation can be grasped.

In a parallel effort, initially to understand the significance of audience participation programmes (Livingstone and Lunt 1994, in press), I found Goffman's (1981) analysis of the participation framework helpful. Goffman unpacks the fundamental dualism – between speaker and hearer – on which subsequent dualisms (text and reader, encoder and decoder, affordances and user; Livingstone and Das, in press) rely. Goffman argues that the folk category of speaker can be decomposed into author (of the message), animator (of the sounds and images) and principal (the social identity constituted through the communication). The hearer, meanwhile, may be listening or not, ratified (sanctioned by social norms) participant or not, bystander or overhearer. For example, in talk shows the expert animates ('research shows that …') authoritative knowledge of science (the principal) but is revealed as inauthentic because he or she is not the 'author' of that knowledge. By contrast, the ordinary person ('in my experience …') better fits the expectations of the folk category of speaker (with author and animator aligned) and so is received empathetically – though he or she can only establish the ordinary person as principal, and this is easily disregarded by the often sceptical overhearers (the viewers).

Reality television goes a step further as participants both represent and generate their personal experience, then and there, during the show (via a competition, a challenge, a group task), making the home audience witness to the studio audience's struggle to sustain a credible identity. As Hill (2002) observes, the fascination of this form of audiencing lies in detecting who is participating and on what terms, and deserving of what judgements of trust and authenticity, involving the home audience shifting constantly between ratified observer (of the intended action) and unratified observer of the telling 'slip' that makes sense of all the rest. Using and extending Goffman's wider repertoire of concepts, researchers of new media audiences and users in private, public and semi-public places can throw light on emerging modes of communication in the new media landscape (reviewed in Livingstone and Lunt, in press). Consider the way that Facebook, for example, builds circles of semi-ratified participants ('friends') who contribute or overhear with impunity, while privacy settings allow people control over the social roles ('family members', 'friends of friends') that enable belonging to the participation framework.

Although participation frameworks are as numerous as the situations in which people communicate, these, in turn, can be categorized according to the emergent conventions that typify certain common situations. For Gershon (2010), Spitulnik (2010) and other media ethnographers, the participation framework can be encompassed at a higher order level by the notion of media ideologies, which 'focus on how people understand both the communicative possibilities and the material limitations of a specific channel' (Gershon 2010: 284) and, in turn, 'will shape, although not determine, their communicative practices' (Gershon 2010: 285). Although the notion of communication ideology usefully focuses analysis on questions of power, the alternative notion of participatory genres focuses analysis on the interlocking of structural affordances (on the part of social or civic structures) and lived understandings (on the part of people, the audiences who engage with these structures).

Applying the notion of 'genre' to conventionalized practices of participation may seem infelicitous, but it is useful for continuing the tradition in reception studies of conceptualizing genre not as a property of the text per se but rather as emerging from the conventionalized or contractual interaction between text and audience. Thus, it concerns, as Livingstone and Das (in press) argue in relation to this and other core concepts in audience research, the interface between audience and text, user and technology, agency and structure. In this vein, Dufrasne and Patriarche (2011) examine how stakeholders' conceptions of participatory genres, enacted by creating or closing down particular organizational structures for citizen engagement, shape public policy-making. Ito et al. (2010) take a more bottom-up approach, revealing the participation genres by which youth organizes its life-stages and lifestyle-specific modes of communication and participation (e.g. the genres of 'hanging out', 'messing around' and 'geeking out'). The terms 'participant structures', 'opportunity structures' or 'participatory genres' (the last being the only one that encompasses both audience agency and structural affordances) invite audience researchers to move beyond the binaries of speaker/hearer, encoder/decoder or user/technology, and to identify the genres of participation (i.e. the types of participation frameworks emerging from people's engagement with diverse media) that are significant in the unfolding media landscape. This may enable the development of a paradigm of participation, which would appear increasingly important for both audiences and audience research.

Taking the Longer View

As will be apparent, I am proposing that we recognize participation as a fourth paradigm, extending Abercrombie and Longhurst's original sequence of three. It recognizes continuities with previous concern over performance, while displacing (or at least supplementing) earlier fascination with self by renewed normative commitment (again from both audiences and audience research) to participation in the wider world (Couldry, Livingstone and Markham 2010; Nyre 2009). It would seem that audience researchers want to understand how media enable or impede the possibilities for audiences *qua* mediated publics to participate in society (Carpentier 2009; Dahlgren 2009), concern of which is apparently overtaking earlier concerns first with resistance and then with identities, and supplementing long-standing interest in interpretation by growing interest in media practices (Drotner 2008; Spitulnik 2010). More importantly, audiences often are keen to engage with media as a means of connecting with (though sometimes disconnecting from) the wider public realm (Couldry, Livingstone and Markham 2010).

Standing back from the particularities of shifting modes of participation, the question then becomes participation in what (Livingstone 2011)? Is the goal (as advocated by audience researchers or as understood by audiences) to participate in media per se or to participate in society through media? Although much previous research on this point is unclear, it seems (conveniently) that in an increasingly mediatized society, these goals are converging. To participate in media increasingly means participating in society, with media no longer sequestered in the disconnected domain of private leisure, as Schrøder insightfully points out in his chapter on mediated citizenship. Moreover, participation requires the structured activities of a collectivity: one cannot participate alone. Here the notion of participation improves on the sometimes decontextualized notions of activity in earlier audience reception studies and on the sometimes (though not necessarily) individualized notions of use and user in new media research.

Colombo and Vittadini (2011) propose that audience research should – and often does – recognize the contingent interrelations between three forms of social collectivities, each partially or wholly constituted through the interpretative practices of audience engagement with social structures. They point, first, to audiences (understood in terms of identity, interpretative repertoires and imagined community; oriented towards common or distinctive cultural products); second, to publics (understood in terms of practices of consumption, reflection and participation; oriented towards common goals); and, third, to social groups or networks (understood in terms of relationships and belonging, social and civic uses; oriented towards community). In some sense, we can consider audiences, publics and networks as reflecting more abstract genres of participation, each specifying a somewhat different 'contract' between (media/social/civic) structures and (ordinary people's) agency in the lifeworld.

As media, political and social landscapes change, audiences become more pervasive (diffusing and extending, with 'audiencing' everywhere), creating and rematerializing cultural products, relocating their practices in new network paths, enabling reflexive, self-generated publics. Colombo and Vittadini (2011) go on to argue that the first collectivity positions people in relation to cultural performances and media products, the second in relation to civic and democratic (or antidemocratic) structures and institutions, and the third in relation to the communities (of work, locale, ethnicity and heritage) in which they live. Historically, audience research has devoted most attention to the first of these, examining the importance of audiencing the power of re-presentation, the contribution of interpretation and practice to the circuit of culture and political economy, and the fluctuating trends in acquiescence to appropriation of or resistance to the inexorable rise in commercialized communications. But, increasingly, we are interested in the contribution of audiences to understanding other civic and social collectivities, with the emphasis on participation in these wider domains rather than to (just) to participation in media.

Earlier in this chapter, I considered the shifts in particular participation frameworks and the wider genres of participation that mark the exciting moments of recent decades. However, viewed over a longer time scale, this period can be characterized in terms of a single paradigmatic shift (from mass broadcasting to networked communication), shaped by more fundamental changes in modernity, which Krotz (2007) identifies as 'globalization', 'mediatization', 'commercialization' and 'individualization'. This shift may be positioned within the longer periodization of audience history with which I began this chapter to understand how changing communication infrastructures connect media forms (texts, artefacts, devices) with the activities and practices through which people communicate and the social arrangements by which they are organized and institutionalized (Lievrouw and Livingstone 2006).

If we take a longer view, we can recognize that the domestic family television audience of the 1950s and 1960s was a rather particular and, in key ways, limited model of the wider cultural and historical phenomenon of audiencing; so too did the associated model of encoding and decoding prove a rather limited (though still valuable) guide to analysing audiencing. For a wider conceptual repertoire, we need to look further back to the history of forms of communication and participation, to oral cultures, writing and the emergence of print. From this perspective, Livingstone and Das (in press) distinguish oral communication cultures (multimodal, situated, co-located communication with low literacy requirements), print cultures (monomodal, linear, dispersed communication requiring high literacy), broadcast cultures (audio/visual, linear mass communication requiring low literacy) and networked cultures (multimodal, hypertextual, niche/mass communication placing high literacy requirements on its users).

Conclusion

Audiences are dead yet audiences are everywhere. Audiences are global yet audiences are evermore niche. Audiences are consumers of ever more media and yet – in a manner almost without precedent – they are also creators of content. Audiences have become irrevocably plural, notwithstanding marketers' efforts to homogenize and commodify 'the audience' (Ang 1991). The media landscape is more globalized, although national framing persists especially for broadcasting and print. This landscape is increasingly diversified, with both homogeneity and fragmentation in audience response occasioning critical concern. It offers evermore participatory opportunities, yet sustained public engagement is evermore in doubt. And it is more convergent, rendering the very notion of 'audience' or 'user' problematic. In trying to make sense of their object of study, audience researchers may seem always to be chasing the latest fad. But I argue that a better interpretation is that they are tracking audiencing as a shifting practice embedded in specific historical, cultural and technological contexts.

This interpretation led me to reconsider what audience researchers find interesting. How do they identify the moments when audiences participate in the reshaping of time/space/sociality? Two answers seem feasible. First, influenced by British cultural studies, feminist studies and media anthropology, audience researchers have sought to bring into view the phenomena that tend to be unnoticed, ignored or repressed by established institutions – examples include housewives reading romance novels or watching soap operas (Geraghty 1990), the spread of diasporic media under the national radar (Georgiou 2006), young people's transgressive sexual practices online or their quiet rejection (easily mistaken for apathy) of the generic address of 'news' (Spitulnik 2010); see also Dover's analysis (this volume) of the 'identities-in-interaction' mobilized through media-related chat during lessons in a British secondary school and Peil and Röser's account (this volume) of how Internet use is associated with greater gender equality at home than the desk-top computer that preceded it.

This approach typically motivates critique of the participant (or opportunity) structures that allow or often prevent people from participating fairly, critically and creatively in the media landscape in which their lives increasingly are embedded. Second, and especially recently, audience researchers have produced critical examinations of whatever was current, whatever was being heralded as new – whether the arrival of the iPhone, establishment of Al Jazeera, the multimedia phenomenon of Harry Potter, 'everyone' watching *X Factor* – because mass change enrols mass participation and is often mobilized by public controversy. Consider the frequent focus of audience research on moral panics: where there's the smoke of popular anxiety, there may really be a fire. In both cases, what is at stake are the opportunities to participate through diverse modes of mediated communication, whether they work to reproduce or to change existing power structures.

To mobilize our collective resources for tracking and critiquing these fast-evolving forms of audiencing within the evolving participatory paradigm, it seems that audience researchers are setting aside once-fraught clashes between theory, epistemology and political standpoints, and following the path of more peaceful efforts of bridge-building, eclecticism in methods and hybridization or convergence of theory that parallels our topic of investigation (the convergent media landscape). This is not to imply that all has been resolved. Abercrombie and Longhurst's concepts of spectacle and performance admirably capture today's apparently narcissistic audience experiences centred on media events. But whether, for example, phenomena such as reality television or celebrity fandom wholly replace the workings of ideology, resistance or media effects remains controversial. Debates over developments in audience research will continue and may produce new ideas. But clearly, many audience researchers' interest is in analysing developments in audiences, their object of study, which itself is transforming.

In this chapter, I have argued that audience research must be multidisciplinary, acting fast to capture insights and findings as they spring up. At the same time, it must be open minded in scope and integrative in focus. And, last, it must pursue the dual analysis of, on the one hand, ordinary people's social uses of and, especially, their participation in media and, on the other hand, the mediation of social and civic participation more widely. Although audience researchers work out their next steps, the frameworks for participation are themselves shifting and diversifying as digitally convergent and networked media become evermore tightly embedded in diverse spheres of life, resulting in new modes of audiencing. As the participant structures afforded to audiences *qua* publics, citizens and consumers, and the genres of participation that result, recalibrate the arrangements among people, media and social institutions, we must pay ever-closer attention to the changing conditions of communication in everyday life.

References

Abercrombie, N. and Longhurst, B., 1998. *Audiences: A sociological theory of performance and imagination*. London: Sage.

Alasuutari, P., 1999. *Rethinking the media audience*. London: Sage.

Ang, I., 1985. *Watching Dallas: Soap opera and the melodramatic imagination*. New York: Methuen.

—— 1991. *Desperately seeking the audience*. London: Routledge.

—— 1996. *Living room wars: Rethinking media audiences for a postmodern world*. London: Routledge.

Appadurai, A., 1996. *Modernity at large: Cultural dimensions of globalization*. Minneapolis, MN: University of Minnesota Press.

Bakardjieva, M., 2005. *Internet society: The Internet in everyday life*. London: Sage.

Barker, M. and Beezer, A., eds, 1992. *Reading into cultural studies*. London: Routledge.

Barker, M. and Mathijs, E., eds, 2008. *Watching the Lord of the Rings: Tolkien's world audiences*. New York: Peter Lang.

Barker, M. and Petley, J., 2001. *Ill effects: The media/violence debate*. New York: Routledge.

Bird, S.E., 2003. *The audience in everyday life: Living in a media world*. New York: Routledge.

boyd, D. and Hargittai, E., 2010. Facebook privacy settings: Who cares? *First Monday*, 15(8) [online]. Available at: http://firstmonday.org/htbin/cgiwrap/bin/ojs/index.php/fm/article/view/3086/2589 [Accessed 25 October 2011].

Bruns, A., 2008. *Blogs, Wikipedia, second life, and beyond: From production to produsage* (Digital Formations). New York: Peter Lang.

Bull, M., 2000. *Sounding out the city: Personal stereos and the management of everyday life*. Oxford, UK: Berg.

Butsch, R., 2000. *The making of American audiences: From stage to television 1750–1990*. Cambridge, UK: Cambridge University Press.

Cammaerts, B., 2012. Protest logics and the mediation opportunity structure. *European Journal of Communication*, 26(2).

Cantril, H., 1940. *The invasion from Mars: A study in the psychology of panic*. Princeton, NJ: Princeton University Press.

Carpentier, N., 2009. Participation is not enough: The conditions of possibility of mediated participatory practices. *European Journal of Communication*, 24(4), pp. 407–420.

Carpignano, P., Andersen, R., Aronowitz, S. and Difazio, W., 1990. Chatter in the age of electronic reproduction: Talk television and the 'public mind'. *Social Text*, 25/26, pp. 33–55.

Colombo, F. and Vittadini, N., 2011. What is an audience in a techno-social landscape? In: COST Action 'Transforming Audiences, Transforming Societies', Meeting of the Working Groups, 31 August, London, University of Westminster.

Corner, J., 1991. Meaning, genre and context: The problematics of 'public knowledge' in the new audience studies. In J. Curran and M. Gurevitch, eds, *Mass media and society*. London: Methuen. pp. 267–285.

Couldry, N., Livingstone, S. and Markham, T., 2010. *Media consumption and public engagement: Beyond the presumption of attention*. Basingstoke, UK: Palgrave Macmillan.

Curran, J., 1990. The new revisionism in mass communication research. *European Journal of Communication*, 5(2–3), pp. 135–164.

Curran, J. and Gurevitch, M., eds, 1991. *Mass media and society*. London: Edward Arnold.

Dahlgren, P., 2009. *Media and political engagement: Citizens, communication, and democracy*. Cambridge, UK: Cambridge University Press.

Dayan, D. and Katz, E., 1992. *Media events: The live broadcasting of history*. Cambridge, MA: Harvard University Press.

Drotner, K., 2008. Leisure is hard work: Digital practices and future competencies. In D. Buckingham, ed., *Youth, identity, and digital media*. Cambridge, MA: MIT Press. pp. 167–184.

Dufrasne, M. and Patriarche, G., 2011. Applying genre theory to citizen participation in public policy making: Theoretical perspectives on participatory genres. *Communication Management Quarterly*, 6(21), pp. 61–86.

Evans, E., 2011. *Transmedia television: Audiences, new media and daily life*. London: Routledge.

Fiske, J., 1994. Audiencing: Cultural practice and cultural studies. In N.K. Denzin and Y.S. Lincoln, eds, *Handbook of qualitative research*. London: Sage. pp. 189–198.

Georgiou, M., 2006. Cities of difference: Cultural juxtapositions and urban politics of representation. *International Journal of Cultural and Media Politics*, 2(3), pp. 283–298.

Geraghty, C., 1990. *Women in soap operas*. London: Polity Press.

Gershon, I., 2010. Media ideologies: An introduction. *Journal of Linguistic Anthropology*, 20(2), pp. 283–293.

Giddens, A., 1984. *The constitution of society: Outline of the theory of structuration*. Cambridge, UK: Polity.

Gillmor, D., 2004. *We the media: Grassroots journalism by the people, for the people*. Sebastopol, CA: O'Reilly Media, Inc.

Goffman, E., 1981. *Forms of talk*. Oxford, UK: Blackwell.

Hall, S., 1980. Encoding/decoding. In S. Hall, D. Hobson, A. Lowe and P. Willis, eds, *Culture, media, language*. London: Hutchinson. pp. 128–138.

Hasebrink, U. and Hölig, S., 2011. What is the TV audience? The audience's perspective. In: COST Action 'Transforming Audiences, Transforming Societies', Meeting of the Working Groups, 31 August, London, University of Westminster.

Hepp, A., 2011. Mediatization, media technologies and the 'moulding forces' of the media. 2011 Virtual Conference of the *International Communication Association*. 23 May–10 June 2011 [online]. Available at: http://www.mediatisiertewelten.de/fileadmin/mediapool/documents/Vortraege_ICA_Virtuelles_Panel/Hepp.pdf [Accessed 25 October 2011].

Hill, A., 2002. Big brother: The real audience. *Television and New Media*, 3(3), pp. 323–340.

Hoover, S. and Clark, S., 2008. Children and media in the context of the home and family. In K. Drotner and S. Livingstone, eds, *International handbook of children, media and culture*. London: Sage. pp. 105–120.

Ito, M. et al., 2010. *Hanging out, messing around, and geeking out: Kids living and learning with new media*. Cambridge, MA: The MIT Press.

Jenkins, H., 2006. *Convergence culture: Where old and new media collide*. New York: New York University Press.

Jensen, K.B., 2009. *Media convergence: The three degrees of network, mass, and interpersonal communication*. London: Routledge.

Jensen, K.J. and Rosengren, K.E., 1990. Five traditions in search of the audience. *European Journal of Communication*, 5(2–3), pp. 207–238.

Jermyn, D. and Holmes, S., 2006. The audience is dead; long live the audience! Interactivity, 'telephilia' and the contemporary television audience. *Critical Studies in Television*, 1(1), pp. 49–57.

Katz, E. and Scannell, P., eds 2009. The end of television? Its impact (so far). *The Annals of the American Academy of Political and Social Science*, 625(1).

Katz, E., Peters, J.D., Liebes, T. and Orloff, A., 2003. Editors' introduction. In E. Katz, J.D. Peters, T. Liebes and A. Orloff, eds, *Canonic texts in media research*. Cambridge, UK: Polity. pp. 1–8.

Krotz, F., 2007. The meta-process of 'mediatization' as a conceptual frame. *Global Media and Communication*, 3(3), pp. 256–260.

Liebes, T. and Katz, E., 1990. *The export of meaning: Cross-cultural readings of Dallas*. New York: Oxford University Press.

Lievrouw, L.A. and Livingstone, S., 2006. Introduction to the updated student edition. In L.A. Lievrouw and S. Livingstone, eds, *Handbook of new media: Social shaping and social consequences of ICTs*. London: Sage. pp. 1–14.

Ling, R. and Haddon, L., 2008. Children, youth and the mobile phone. In K. Drotner and S. Livingstone, eds, *International handbook of children, media and culture*. London: Sage. pp. 137–151.

Livingstone, S., 1998. Audience research at the crossroads: The 'implied audience' in media theory. *European Journal of Cultural Studies*, 1(2), pp. 193–217.

—— 2004. The challenge of changing audiences: Or, what is the audience researcher to do in the Internet age? *European Journal of Communication*, 19(1), pp. 75–86.

—— 2005. On the relation between audiences and publics. In S. Livingstone, ed., *Audiences and publics: When cultural engagement matters for the public sphere*. Bristol, UK: Intellect Press. pp. 17–41.

—— 2007. On the material and the symbolic: Silverstone's double articulation of research traditions in new media studies. *New Media and Society*, 9(1), pp. 16–24.

—— 2009a. Half a century of television in the lives of our children and families. *The Annals of the American Academy of Political and Social Science*, 625(1). pp. 151–163.

—— 2009b. On the mediation of everything. ICA presidential address. *Journal of Communication*, 59(1), pp. 1–18.

—— 2010. Giving people a voice: On the critical role of the interview in the history of audience research. *Communication, Culture & Critique*, 3(4), pp. 566–571.

—— 2011. Digital learning and participation among youth. *International Journal of Learning and Media*, 2(2–3), pp. 1–13.

Livingstone, S. and Das, R., in press. The end of audiences? Theoretical echoes of reception amidst the uncertainties of use. In J. Hartley, J. Burgess and A. Bruns, eds, *Blackwell companion to new media dynamics*. Oxford: Blackwell.

Livingstone, S. and Lunt, P., 1994. *Talk on television: Audience participation and public debate*. London: Routledge.

Livingstone, S. and Lunt, P., in press. Mediated frameworks for participation. In N. Pachler and M. Böck, eds, *Transformation of representation: Essays in honour of Gunther Kress*. New York: Routledge.

Manning, P., 2005. Erving Goffman. In G. Ritzer, ed., *Encyclopedia of social theory*. London: Sage. pp. 333–339.

Michelle, C., 2007. Modes of reception: A consolidated analytical framework. *Communication Review*, 10(3), pp. 181–222.

Morley, D., 1981. The 'nationwide' audience: A critical postscript. *Screen Education*, 39, pp. 3–14.

———— 1986. *Family television: Cultural power and domestic leisure*. London: Comedia.

Murdock, G., 1992. Citizens, consumers, and public culture. In M. Skovmand and K.C. Schrøder, eds, *Media cultures: Reappraising transnational media*. London: Routledge.

Nightingale, V., 1996. *Studying audiences: The shock of the real*. London: Routledge.

Nyre, L., 2009. Normative media research: Moving from the ivory tower to the control tower. *Nordicom Review*, 30(2), pp. 3–17.

Palmer, P., 1986. *The lively audience: A study of children around the TV set*. London: Allen & Unwin.

Radway, J., 1988. Reception study: Ethnography and the problems of dispersed audiences and nomadic subjects. *Cultural Studies*, 2(3), pp. 359–376.

Rosen, J., 2006. The people formerly known as the audience, *Pressthink*, weblog post, June. Available at: http://archive.pressthink.org/2006/06/27/ppl_frmr.html [Accessed 25 October 2011].

Rowland, W.R., 1983. *The politics of TV violence: Policy uses of communication research*. Beverly Hills, CA: Sage.

Scannell, P., 1988. Radio times: The temporal arrangements of broadcasting in the modern world. In P. Drummond, ed., *Television and its audience: International research perspectives*. London: British Film Institute. pp. 15–31.

Silverstone, R., 2002. Complicity and collusion in the mediation of everyday life. *New Literary History*, 33, pp. 761–780.

Silverstone, R., Morley, D., Dahlberg, A. and Livingstone, S., 1989. Families, technologies and consumption: The household and information and communication technologies. Centre for Research into Innovation, Culture and Technology CRICT Discussion Paper, London, Brunel University.

Spitulnik, D., 2010. Millennial encounters with mainstream television news: Excess, void, and points of engagement. *Journal of Linguistic Anthropology*, 20(2), pp. 372–388.

Thompson, J.B., 1995. *The media and modernity: A social theory of the media*. Cambridge, UK: Polity.

Notes on Contributors

Helena Bilandzic is a professor at the University of Augsburg, Germany, where she teaches media effects, media psychology and empirical methods. She earned her Ph.D. from the Ludwig-Maximilians-Universität in Munich in 2003 with a thesis on television programme selection and her habilitation degree from the University of Erfurt with work on the differential processes of media effects in 2009. Her current research interests include narrative experience and persuasion, cultivation, media use and methodology. She is chair of the Audience and Reception Studies Division of European Communication Research and Education Association (ECREA) and vice chair of the COST Action IS0906 'Transforming Audiences, Transforming Societies'.

Daniel Biltereyst is a professor in film and media studies at Ghent University, where he is head of the Department of Communication Studies and director of the Centre for Cinema and Media Studies. His work on film and screen culture as sites of public debate and censorship has been published in journals like *European Journal of Communication, European Journal of Cultural Studies, Media, Culture & Society, New Media and Television* and *Screen* as well as in collections including recent articles in *Je t'aime, moi non plus: Franco-British Cinematic Relations* (Berghan Books 2010), *Billy Wilder, Moviemaker* (McFarland 2011) and *The Handbook of Political Economy of Communication* (Wiley-Blackwell 2011). He is an editor of *Explorations in New Cinema History* (Wiley-Blackwell, 2011) and *Cinema, Audiences and Modernity* (Routledge, 2012), both with Richard Maltby and Philippe Meers. He is now editing a volume on film censorship around the world (*Silencing Cinema*, for Palgrave-Macmillan).

Mélanie Bourdaa is an associate professor in media studies at the University of Bordeaux 3. She is a member of the research team MICA (Médiation, Information, Communication, Art). She teaches and lectures on transmedia storytelling, Alternate Reality Game (ARG) and digital devices, TV culture and American TV series. Her current research interests include fan studies, transmedia strategies and seriality. She is part of the COST Action 'Transforming Audiences, Transforming Societies' and leader of the task force on 'cross-media production and audience involvement'. She is also a member of the research network S.E.R.I.E.S and of the Société Française des Sciences de l'Information et de la Communication (SFSIC).

Alexander Dhoest is associate professor in media studies at the University of Antwerp. In 2002, he got his Ph.D. in social sciences at the KU Leuven, working on the construction of national identity in Flemish television drama. Since then, he has specialized in qualitative audience research, looking in particular at the relationship between TV viewing and social (in particular national, ethnic and sexual) identities. The role of media use in social integration is a key theme in his recent work, also as leader of the task force 'Media, Citizenship and Social Diversity' of the working group 'Audience Transformations and Social Integration' in the COST Action 'Transforming Audiences, Transforming Societies'.

Katrin Döveling is currently a professor at the University Dresden, Germany, where she teaches media use, effects and structures, and organization of mass media. She earned her Ph.D. from the University of Erfurt in 2004 with a thesis on emotions, media and group cohesion. Recently, she published the *Routledge Handbook of Emotions and Mass Media* (Routledge, Taylor & Francis), together with C. von Scheve and E.A. Konijn. Her research interests include emotions and mass media, visual communication, gender studies and online media. She has been a visiting professor at the Université XII, Paris; Westminster University, London; University of Innsbruck, Austria; and Centre for Cultural & General Studies Karlsruhe, Germany.

Caroline Dover completed a Ph.D. in the Department of Media & Communications, Goldsmiths College, University of London in 2001. She is an adjunct professor at Annenberg School for Communication and Journalism, University of Southern California London Program and also works as a research consultant in audience and user studies. Her current research interests include the use of ethnography to investigate media use in everyday life, media and popular culture consumption, and identity. She was editor of the journal *Westminster Papers in Communication & Culture* published by the Communications and Media Research Institute, University of Westminster from 2009–2011.

David Giles is a reader in media psychology at the University of Winchester in Southern England. He has been publishing on the psychology of the audience for more than a decade, and his books include *Illusions of Immortality: A Psychology of Fame and Celebrity* (Macmillan, 2000), *Media Psychology* (Lawrence Erlbaum, 2003) and *Psychology of the Media* (Palgrave, 2010). He is an editor and founder of the Taylor & Francis journal *Qualitative Research in Psychology*. His principal research interests are parasocial relationships between audiences and media figures, particularly celebrities, the social influence of news media and interaction in online communities, particularly in the field of mental health.

Seok-Kyeong Hong-Mercier completed a Ph.D. in communication at the University of Grenoble, France, in 1995. After having worked as a full-time researcher in Korean Broadcasting Commission (Seoul, Korea) for 3 years, she has been an associate professor at the University of Bordeaux since 2000, where she teaches media studies, television sociology, serial culture, theories in cultural studies and visual methods. She is a coordinator of Citizenship in Colours (2009–2014), a research project which addresses the relationship between media practices and citizenship in Europe. Her current research interests include the East Asian cultural industry and its intercultural circulation.

Sonia Livingstone is a professor in the Department of Media and Communications at the London School of Economics and Political Science. Her research examines children and the Internet, media and digital literacies, the mediated public sphere and public understanding of communications regulation. Her recent books include *Audiences and Publics* (edited, Intellect, 2005), *Media Consumption and Public Engagement: Beyond the Presumption of Attention* (with Nick Couldry and Tim Markham, Palgrave, 2010), *Children and the Internet* (Polity, 2009) and *Media Regulation* (with Peter Lunt, Sage, 2012). She was the president of the International Communication Association (2007–2008).

Philippe Meers is an associate professor in film and media studies at the University of Antwerp, Belgium, where he is deputy director of the Visual Studies and Media Culture research group. He has published on historical and contemporary cinema cultures in journals such as *Screen, Communications, Javnost* and *Journal of Popular Film and Television* as well as in collections such as *The Contemporary Hollywood Reader* (Routledge, 2009), *Film, Cinema, Spectator* (Schüren 2010) and *The Handbook of Political Economy of Communication* (Wiley-Blackwell, 2011). With Richard Maltby and Daniel Biltereyst, he edited *Explorations in New Cinema History* (Wiley-Blackwell, 2011) and *Cinema, Audiences and Modernity* (Routledge, 2012). He is chair of the ECREA film studies section.

Lars Nyre is a professor at the Department of Information Science and Media Studies, University of Bergen, Norway. He wrote his Ph.D. on the role of sound in the media and published it as *Sound Media* (Routledge, 2008). Nyre now works with medium design methods and qualitative research in new media, focusing primarily on the smartphone. His articles have appeared in *Journalism Studies* and *Javnost – the Public and Convergence*. He is the editor of the *Norwegian Journal of Media Studies* and a management committee member of the COST Action ISO906 'Transforming Audiences, Transforming Societies'.

Brian O'Neill, MA, Ph.D., is the head of the School of Media at Dublin Institute of Technology, Ireland and Government of Ireland Senior Research Fellow 2011/2012. His research interests include media literacy research, policy-making and public interest issues in media and communications. His research interests include media technologies and media literacy. He has contributed to journals such as *New Media and Society* and the *Journal of Children and Media*. He is a member of the management committee of COST Action ISO906 'Transforming Audiences, Transforming Societies' and the vice chair of the International Association for Media and Communication Research (IAMCR) Audience Section. He is also a member of EU Kids Online, funded by the European Commission Safer Internet Programme.

Geoffroy Patriarche completed a Ph.D. in communication at the Université libre de Bruxelles (ULB) in 2005. Since 2007, he has been a full-time lecturer at the Facultés universitaires Saint-Louis (FUSL, Brussels) where he teaches communication theories and social history of the media. He has been chair (2006–2010) and vice chair (2010–2012) of the Audience and Reception Studies section of ECREA. He also serves as chair of the COST Action IS0906 'Transforming Audiences, Transforming Societies' (2010–2014). His current research interests include (mobile) media uses in everyday life and mediated citizen participation.

Tereza Pavlíčková is a Ph.D. candidate at the Institute of Communication Studies and Journalism at the Charles University in Prague. She is interested in media users and their construction of understanding of media, building on hermeneutic philosophy. Her thesis examines how media users understand, construct and re-negotiate the identity of authors, and the role of perceived authors in users' understanding of texts. As part of her Ph.D. studies, she spent 2008 at Goldsmiths College, University of London where she carried out research on media users under the supervision of David Morley.

Corinna Peil is a postdoctoral researcher at the University of Salzburg's Center for Advanced Studies and Research in Information and Communication Technologies and Society (ICT&S). She completed a PhD about mobile media culture in Japan at the Leuphana University of Lüneburg in 2010. From 2004 to 2012, she was a member of the teaching and research staff at Leuphana University's Institute of Communications and Media Culture. Corinna Peil has been involved in the project "The Mediatized Home. Changes of Domestic Communication Cultures" which is part of the DFG priority program "Mediatized Worlds". Her research interests include innovations in media technologies, mobile communications, cultural studies, the history and future of television, and media uses in everyday life.

Seija Ridell works as a professor in the School of Communication, Media and Theatre at the University of Tampere, Finland, where she teaches courses in the theory and history of media and communication research. She received her Ph.D. from the University of Tampere in 1998 with a thesis that elaborated a critical social semiotic theory of genre and applied it to examining the reception of television news. Her most recent research focuses on people's media and information and communications technology (ICT)-related activities in the digitally shaped and spatially multilayered urban environment and other spatial contexts.

Jutta Röser is a professor in communications at the University of Münster (Germany). From 2003 to 2012, she was a professor at the Leuphana University of Lüneburg and head of the Institute of Communications and Media Culture. She earned her PhD from the University of Münster and her habilitation degree in 2000 from the University of Hamburg with a work on reading TV violence. Jutta Röser was a visiting professor at the Universities of Zurich (Switzerland) and Klagenfurt (Austria). Her current research interests include media and communication technologies in everyday life, audience and reception research, media sociology, cultural studies and gender media studies. Two of her latest research projects focus on the domestication of the Internet in Germany and – as part of the DFG priority program 'Mediatized Worlds' – on 'The Mediatized Home'.

Andy Ruddock is a senior lecturer in communications and media studies at Monash University, Australia, where he teaches classes on youth and the social influence of media. He is vice chair of the Popular Communication Division of International Communication Association and deputy director of the Research Unit in Media Studies at Monash. He has written two books on audience research and has also published a number of journal articles and book chapters on topics such as cultivation, media violence, reality television, fandom, media sport and political celebrity. He has taught at universities in the United States, the United Kingdom, New Zealand and the Republic of Korea.

Kim Christian Schrøder (http://www.ruc.dk/komm/Ansatte/vip/kimsc/) is a professor in Communication Studies at Roskilde University, Denmark. His authored and edited books in English include *The Language of Advertising* (Blackwell, 1985), *Media Cultures: Reappraising Transnational Media* (Routledge, 1992), *Researching Audiences* (Arnold, 2003) and *Digital Content Creation* (Peter Lang, 2010). His current research deals with cross-media news consumption in the media landscape of the digital age and with methodological issues about the quantitative/qualitative divide. He is chair of the working group on 'new media genres, media literacy and trust in the media' in the COST Action 'Transforming Audiences, Transforming Societies' (2010–2014).

Denise Sommer is a research associate at the University of Leipzig where she teaches theories of communication and reception studies. She studied psychology at the Humboldt-University Berlin and the University of Illinois at Urbana-Champaign and received her Diploma (M.Sc.) in 2002. She earned her Ph.D. in Communication Studies in 2007 from the Friedrich-Schiller-University, Jena with a dissertation on the characteristics and effects of interpersonal communication about TV news. Her research interests include interpersonal communication, attitudes and communication processes, media and migration and communication theories.

Maria T. Soto-Sanfiel is an associate professor at the Departament de Comunicació Audiovisual i Publicitat I at the Universitat Autónoma de Barcelona (Spain). She holds bachelors in Social Communication (Advertising and Public Relationships) and Information Sciences (Journalism). She holds masters in Interactive Communication (Telecommunications and Multimedia) and in New Audiovisual Technologies. She is doctor in Audiovisual Communication. Her research activity has focused on the study of the voice (synthetic and natural) in broadcast communication, audiovisual perception, media entertainment, multimedia content (production and reception) and interactive television and scientific communication. She is currently head of Contents of the Design, Accessibility and Reception Group at the Centre d'Accessibilitat i Intelligència Ambiental de Catalunya (CAIAC) and co-directs the scientific outreach IPTV, Insciencetv.org. She has worked as audiovisual producer and journalist.

Paul J. Traudt works in the area of social theory and audience reception studies. His most recent research examines the role of ethnic media in cultural assimilation and pluralism. He teaches courses in media theory and audience research, global media and video criticism in the Hank Greenspun School of Journalism and Media Studies at the University of Nevada, Las Vegas. He has been a guest professor at the Institut fur Angewandte Medienforschung (Institute for Applied Media Research) at Universität Lüneburg, Germany. He received his Ph.D. from the Department of Radio, Television, and Film at the University of Texas at Austin in 1981.